LYRIC TRAGEDY

By the same author

D. H. LAWRENCE
D. H. LAWRENCE: THE CRITICAL HERITAGE (*editor*)
HARDY: THE TRAGIC NOVELS (Casebook)(*editor*)
GEORGE ELIOT: *THE MILL ON THE FLOSS* AND
    SILAS MARNER (Casebook)(*editor*)
TRAGEDY DEVELOPMENTS IN CRITICISM (*editor*)

LYRIC TRAGEDY

R. P. Draper

St. Martin's Press   New York

Excerpts from *High Windows* © 1974
by Philip Larkin, reprinted by permission
of Faber & Faber Publishers, and Farrar, Straus & Giroux Inc.

Printed in Great Britain
Published in the United Kingdom by The Macmillan Press Ltd.
First published in the United States of America in 1985

ISBN 0-312-50053-X

Library of Congress Cataloging in Publication Data
Draper, Ronald P., 1928–
Lyric tragedy.
Bibliography: p.
Includes index.
1. English poetry – History and criticism.
2. Tragic, The, in literature.   I. Title.
PR508.T72L9 1985   821'.04'0916   85-2448ᴶ
ISBN 0-312-50053-X

Contents

Acknowledgements

The author and publishers wish to thank the following, who have kindly given permission to quote from copyright material:

excerpt from 'Musée des Beaux Arts' by W. H. Auden, in *W. H. Auden: Collected Poems*, ed. Edward Mendelson (1966), by permission of Faber & Faber Publishers and Random House Inc.;

excerpts from 'The Love Song of J. Alfred Prufrock' and *The Waste Land* by T. S. Eliot, in *Collected Poems 1909–1962*, copyright 1936 by Harcourt Brace Jovanovich Inc., copyright © 1963, reprinted by permission of Faber & Faber Publishers and Harcourt Brace Jovanovich Inc.;

excerpts from 'Aubade' by Philip Larkin, by permission of the author, and from 'Next, Please', 'Church Going' and 'Maiden Name' by Philip Larkin, in *The Less Deceived* (1955), by permission of The Marvell Press;

excerpts from 'The Old Fools', 'The Building' and 'The Explosion' by Philip Larkin, in *High Windows* (1974), by permission of Faber & Faber Publishers and Farrar, Straus & Giroux Inc.;

excerpts from 'Nothing To Be Said' by Philip Larkin, in *The Whitsun Weddings* (1964), and from *The North Ship* (1945, 1966) by Philip Larkin, by permission of Faber & Faber Publishers;

excerpts from *The Complete Poems of D. H. Lawrence*, ed. V. de S. Pinto and Warren Roberts (1964), *Phoenix II* (1968), *The Letters of D. H. Lawrence, 1901–13*, ed. James T. Boulton (1978) and *The Letters of D. H. Lawrence, 1913–16*, ed. George J. Zytaruck and James T. Boulton (1981), by permission of Laurence Pollinger Ltd, on behalf of the Estate of Mrs Frieda Lawrence Ravagli;

excerpts from *Wilfred Owen: War Poems and Others*, ed. with Notes and Commentary by Dominic Hibberd (1973), by permission of Chatto & Windus;

excerpts from *The Collected Poems of Sylvia Plath*, ed. Ted Hughes (1981), poems copyright © 1960, 1965, 1971, 1981 by the Estate of Sylvia Plath, editorial material copyright © 1981 by Ted Hughes, and excerpts from *Johnny Panic and the Bible of Dreams and Other Prose Writings*, copyright 1952, 1953, 1955, © 1956, 1957, 1960, 1961, 1962 by Sylvia Plath, copyright © 1977, 1979 by Ted Hughes, reprinted by permission of Olwyn Hughes, on behalf of Ted Hughes, and Harper & Row Publishers Inc.;

excerpt from 'Dead Man's Dump' by Isaac Rosenberg, in *The Collected Works of Isaac Rosenberg*, ed. Ian Parsons (1979), by permission of the author's Literary Estate and Chatto & Windus;

excerpt from 'The Rear Guard' by Siegfried Sassoon, in *Collected Poems*, copyright 1918, 1920 by E. P. Dutton & Co., copyright 1936, 1946, 1947, 1948 by Siegfried Sassoon, reprinted by permission of George Sassoon and Viking Penguin Inc.;

excerpts from *The Collected Poems of Edward Thomas*, ed. R. George Thomas (1978), by permission of Oxford University Press;

excerpts from 'Lapis Lazuli' by W. B. Yeats, in *The Collected Poems of W. B. Yeats* (1950), from 'Deirdre' by W. B. Yeats, in *The Variorum Edition of the Plays of W. B. Yeats*, ed. Russell K. Alspach and Catharine C. Alspach (1966), and from 'The Tragic Theatre' by W. B. Yeats, in *Essays and Introductions* (1961), by permission of A. P. Watt Ltd, on behalf of Michael B. Yeats and Miss Anne Yeats.

1 Introduction

In poetical drama there is, it is held, an antithesis between
character and lyric poetry, for lyric poetry – however much
it move you when you read out of a book – can, as these
critics think, but encumber the action. Yet when we go back
a few centuries and enter the great periods of drama,
character grows less and sometimes disappears, and there is
much lyric feeling, and at times a lyric measure will be
wrought into the dialogue, a flowing measure that had well
befitted music, or that more lumbering one of the sonnet.

W. B. Yeats, 'The Tragic Theatre' (1910)

Yeats quarrels with both of the assumptions which dominate
dramatic criticism prior to the twentieth century: that the all-
important end of drama is action, or alternatively character. The
supremacy of action goes back to Aristotle, who, in tragedy in
particular, regards the plot as the overriding consideration:
'Thus the incidents and the plot are the end aimed at in tragedy,
and as always, the end is everything. Furthermore, there could
not be a tragedy without action, but there could be without
character.'[1] The essence of the Aristotelian view is that man
defines himself by action. He is what he does rather than what he
feels. As John Jones expresses it: 'Aristotelian man cannot make
a portentous gesture of "I have that within which passes show"
because he is significantly himself only in what he says and
does.'[2] This leaves room for definition through speech as well as
action. Aristotle goes so far as to say that 'the plot should be so
ordered that even without seeing it performed anyone merely
hearing what is afoot will shudder with fear and pity as a result
of what is happening',[3] but he does not envisage a production
consisting only of mime or dumb-show. Character, thought,
diction, music and spectacle are all additional constituents, but
plot is the supremely important mode of revelation. The other
elements, including speech, are in effect means towards the

1

prime end of putting the *dramatis personae* into motion so that a certain pattern of events may be demonstrated.

The character-based critic, however, sees action as that which reveals character – in A. C. Bradley's phrase, 'characteristic deeds'.[4] In his exposition of the Aristotelian view John Jones takes issue with this attitude, which he regards as an unexamined assumption underlying much modern dramatic criticism. Aristotle's emphasis on action thus becomes an assault on

> the now settled habit in which we see action issuing from a solitary focus of consciousness – secret, inward, interesting – and in which the status of action must always be adjectival: action qualifies; it tells us things we want to know about the individual promoting it; the life of action is our ceaseless, animating consideration of the state of affairs 'inside' him who acts.[5]

Action loses its active quality and becomes adjectival rather than substantive. It points inward towards the originating state of mind rather than outward to the expression of mind in consequential performance.

The second assumption might seem more favourable to Yeats's interest in lyric poetry than the first, and it is, of course, more in keeping with the subjective emphasis of Romanticism and Symbolism which manifests itself in Yeats's own poetry. Yet he dislikes the relegation of poetry to a subordinate role that is implicit in either view; and to overcome it he appeals to the great drama of the past, which, he argues, tends towards moments of intensity and passion when lyricism rather than action or character seizes the audience's attention. Such moments belong to tragedy, however, not comedy. Comedy emphasises the qualities that distinguish one man from another – it is, in fact, essentially a 'character' medium, whereas tragedy, particularly in its moments of intensity, submerges those isolating distinctions: 'Tragic art, passionate art, the drowner of dykes, the confounder of understanding, moves us by setting us to reverie, by alluring us almost to the intensity of trance. The persons upon the stage, let us say, greaten till they are humanity itself.'[6]

For Yeats, then, there is no inherent incompatibility between poetry and tragic drama. On the contrary, poetry – even of the song-like intensity that belongs to lyric – is a necessary means to the universalising end of tragedy. What he envisages is well illustrated by the relationship between the lyric and the dramatic in his own writing for the theatre. In *Deirdre*, for example, the situation of Deirdre and Naoise's betrayal by the vengeful Conchubar becomes a dramatic context out of which a lyric is precipitated. When the lovers realise that there is no escape for them they sit down to play chess, as the hero, Lugaidh Restripe and his wife did before them, and Deirdre summons the Musicians to sing them an accompanying song:

> Make no sad music.
> What is it but a king and queen at chess?
> They need a music that can mix itself
> Into imagination, but not break
> The steady thinking that the hard game needs.[7]

What follows is, indeed, 'no sad song' in the sense of one that pathetically sentimentalises the situation, but a tragic song which singles out the essence of the moment as one in which the extravagance of love and the permanence of death meet:

> Love is an immoderate thing
>   And can never be content
> Till it dip an ageing wing
>   Where some laughing element
> Leaps and Time's old lanthorn dims.
>   What's the merit in love-play,
> In the tumult of the limbs
>   That dies out before 'tis day,
> Heart on heart, or mouth on mouth,
>   All that mingling of our breath,
> When love-longing is but drouth
>   For the things come after death?

The subsequent action of the play shows the love of Deirdre and Naoise triumphing even in their defeat over Conchubar's destructive jealousy: Naoise is executed and Deirdre (with an echo of Shakespeare's Cleopatra) fools Conchubar by her suicide, while in the closing moments an angry crowd gathers offstage shouting, 'Death to Conchubar!' Tragedy thus turns into an affirmation of the unworldly heroic eros which Deirdre and Naoise symbolise, and which the lyrical expression of the Musicians favours and supports. At its emotional centre, however, when the game of chess is being played and the song being sung, the play suspends action – even the sense of the triumph of love – to allow a deeper feeling of the perilous uncertainty of human values to emerge. The play is more tragic at this suspended point of lyrical intensity than at its subsequent climax of the death of Deirdre.

Deirdre, then, is lyric tragedy in the sense that its lyrical elements are neither encumbrance to action nor subordinate to the embodying of character in 'characteristic deeds'. The lyrical feeling at its centre is its own justification. From this it is not a far step, as Yeats implies in the passage already quoted from 'The Tragic Theatre', to lyric tragedy independent of specifically dramatic form. It might be argued that the dramatic form is indispensable to the release of the tragic moment – that without the situation created by plot and the tension generated by characters in conflict the lyric cry lacks not only meaningful provocation, but also emotional validity. The tragic protagonist in drama gains his tragic status from the resistance he offers to the powers that destroy him. However futile his contest with them may be, the fact of his resistance ennobles him, and through the suffering it generates he gains an emotional resonance which is quite different from that of the merely passive victim. Some such feeling of resistance is certainly necessary. Without it suffering becomes pathos rather than tragedy – an appeal for pity and compassion rather than a confronting of suffering. But for this to be achieved the explicit forms of stage drama are not inevitably required. Narrative poetry offers an alternative means of providing the appropriate context, and reflective poetry, though receding still further from the immediacy of drama as such, may offer juxtaposition of attitudes against which lyrical feeling can be tested. In the lyric proper, however, the means are both more subtle and more elusive. A dramatic voice may take the place of a specific dramatic structure, and the tension may be provided by inner conflict. The form of the poem, by creating a pressure against which language exerts itself, also contributes, and all the modifications of tone and attitude that are effected by diction, rhythm, syntax and rhetorical and figurative devices are likewise the means by which an equivalent of the tragic protagonist's resistance rather than capitulation to suffering may be created within the lyric. Lyric tragedy is, in fact, that form of tragic expression in which the protagonist is the poet himself, and the means by which he presents and controls his awareness of pain and suffering are the touchstone of his tragic status.

A useful point of departure is Robert Henryson's *The Testament of Cresseid* since it represents a half-way house between the Aristotelian and lyric forms of tragedy. This is a narrative poem which has its obvious action, but which approaches tragedy through its poetic organisation. And it is especially useful from the present point of view that Henryson opens with a statement about the relationship between tragic subject and tragic atmosphere:

> Ane doolie sessoun to ane cairfull dyte
> Suld correspond and be equiualent:
> Richt sa it wes quhen I began to wryte
> This tragedie; the wedder richt feruent,
> Quhen Aries, in middis of the Lent,
> Schouris of haill gart fra the north discend,
> That scantlie fra the cauld I micht defend.[8]

The *Testament* has sufficient of an Aristotelian structure for the tragic sense to be seen as manifesting itself in action. Indeed, its climactic moment is a highly original semi-'recognition' scene: the encounter of Troylus with the leprosy-afflicted Cresseid. Though 'not witting quhat scho was', he is nevertheless reminded of

> The sweit visage and amorous blenking
> Of fair Cresseid, sumtyme his awin darling.
>
> (503–4)

Prompted by this sight he makes an unusually generous donation of alms, and when Cresseid afterwards realises who the donor is (hers, too, is a slightly unorthodox 'recognition'), she is pierced with remorse. She at last understands how little she has hitherto appreciated the real worth of Troylus, and, at the same time, to what extent she is herself to blame for her own downfall:

> All faith and lufe I promissit to the
> Was in the self fickill and friuolous:
> O fals Cresseid and trew knicht Troilus!
>   (551–3)

As a result, she ceases to complain against the gods and rail on
Fortune. Like Shakespeare's Richard II, who in Pomfret castle
comes to the realisation that 'I wasted time and now doth time
waste me', Cresseid turns her attention inward upon her own
self: 'Nane but my self as now I will accuse' (574).

It is at this point that Cresseid becomes a truly tragic character; but this moment is a precipitation of the tragic feeling which
is present throughout the poem. The opening does more than
provide a suitable setting for the story which is to follow. The
dismal season of contradictory heat and cold which composes
the bitter–sweet spring of this poem (whether it is a true reflection of the Scottish season, or, as Denton Fox suggests, 'traditional meteorology'[9]) fittingly relates both to the theme of
youthful love and its tragic aftermath. Moreover, the poet's own
age adds a chillier perspective of experience:

> Thocht lufe be hait, ȝit in ane man of age
> It kendillis nocht sa sone as in ȝoutheid
> Of quhome the blude is flowing in ane rage.
>   (29–31)

Though previously dedicated to Venus and trusting that his
'faidit hart of lufe scho wald mak grene' (24), he finds that he is
frustrated by the 'greit cald' and is forced to retreat to his
chamber – where he will study the tale of Cresseid, with actual
fire as an ironic substitute for passion.

The implications of this contradiction between spring and winter, youth and age, are continued in Cresseid's protest against
Cupid and his mother:

> O fals Cupide, is nane to wyte bot thow
> And thy mother, of lufe the blind goddess!
> Ȝe causit me alwayis vunderstand and trow
> The seid of lufe was sawin in my face,
> And ay grew grene throw ȝour supplie and grace.

Bot now, allace, that seid with froist is slane,
And I fra luifferis left, and all forlane.

(134–40)

The juxtaposition of 'grene' and 'froist' deepens the meaning of
this protest for the reader, who connects it with what has gone
before; but for Cresseid herself this deeper meaning is something
of which she is as yet unaware. It is a seed planted in her
consciousness, but not yet growing. That growth can, however,
be sensed in the dream of the seven planetary deities which
comes to her after she faints. These gods are the embodiment of
forces, some evil, some beneficent, which control the life of man;
collectively they present an allegorical pageant of the human
condition. But individually they are also touched with the col-
ours of Cresseid's still dormant tragic awareness and feeling of
guilt. This is most apparent in the description of Saturne, a
wintry figure who can be related to the cold at the beginning of
the poem:

> His face fronsit, his lyre was lyke the leid,
> His teith chatterit and cheuerit with the chin,
> His ene drowpit, how sonkin in his heid,
> Out of his nois the meldrop fast can rin,
> With lippis bla and cheikis leine and thin;
> The ice schoklis that fra his hair doun hang
> Was wonder greit, and an ane speir als lang.

(155–61)

Mars, 'Wrything his face with mony angrie word' (189), reflects
something of the anger which led Cresseid to her protest; and,
more pertinently, Venus, characterised in terms of dissimulation
and inconstancy, reflects Cresseid's own faithlessness – the
quality for which she is destined to become a byword. Finally,
the portrait of Cynthia, most junior of the planetary deities, but
joined with Saturne in pronouncing doom on Cresseid, is a
melancholy study in leaden colouring, or absence of colour, and
'full of spottis blak' (260) – a touch which seems to hint at the
disease which will be visited on Cresseid as punishment for her
offence. And it is indeed Cynthia, following and reinforcing the
judgement of Saturne depriving Cresseid of her youthful 'wan-
tones', who reads the bill blighting her with leprosy:

> Thy cristall ene mingit with blude I mak,
> Thy voice sa cleir vnplesand hoir and hace,
> Thy lustie lyre ouirspred with spottis blak,
> And lumpis haw appeirand in thy face.
>
> (337–40)

In the conventional language of compliment Cresseid is earlier
called 'the flour and A per se / of Troy and Grece' (78–9). Now
the 'frostie wand' (311) of Saturne is laid on that flower, and its
beauty is turned by Cynthia into ugliness. In the 'Complaint'
which expresses her woe as a leper, Cresseid employs the *ubi sunt*
formula of medieval poetry to stress this theme once more
('Quhair is thy chalmer wantounlie besene. . . . Quhair is thy
garding with thir greissis gay / And fresche flowris', 416 and
425–6); and she warns the ladies of Troy and Greece that 'Nocht
is ʒour fairnes bot ane faiding flour' (461). This is part of a great
commonplace about the instability of earthly life, but it also
reveals a gathering sense of the destructive force inherent in
nature – especially in the insistent alliteration of 'ʒour roising
reid to rotting sall retour' (464). The commonplace, aided by its
context in the poem's recurrent seasonal imagery, is in process of
becoming a feelingly experienced tragic reality.

As already indicated, it is in the climactic meeting with
Troylus that this gathering sense bursts into Cresseid's consciousness as an immediate personal truth. It is there that the
pervasive lyric feeling and the specifically narrative and dramatic structure fuse into one. The subsequent action is brief and
sparely expressed, but, because of this fusion, made powerfully
symbolic. There are two simple episodes: Cresseid makes her
testament; and Troylus erects a tomb to her memory. The
testament sums up the theme of decay:

> Heir I beteiche my corps and carioun
> With wormis and with taidis to be rent
>
> (577–8),

and the ring which is to be returned to Troylus is the means by
which his 'recognition' is to be completed. Yet, as if to emphasise
that what has been done cannot be undone, the broach and belt
which he gave her remain irretrievably with Diomeid; Cresseid
touchingly dies in admitting this, her testament broken off in
mid-line with words that refer to Troylus's love:

'O Diomeid, thou hes baith broche and belt
Quhilk Troylus gaue me in takning
Of his trew lufe', and with that word scho swelt.
(589–91)

The tomb erected by Troylus, appropriately 'of merbell gray' (603), carries an inscription, in contrasting 'golden letteris' (606), which sums up the fading flower theme:

'Lo, fair ladyis, Cresseid of Troy the toun,
Sumtyme countit the flour of womanheid,
Vnder this stane, lait lipper, lyis deid.'
(607–9)

In itself this is cliché, but – as the gold of the letters betokens – it is cliché redeemed by the context which the complete poem provides.

The narrative and dramatic poetry of the ballads likewise provides a structure of action and conflict issuing in moments of tragic intensity. As texts they are incomplete without the accompaniment of the music to which they were traditionally sung, and their ambiguous history of oral transmission and more sophisticated revision at the hands of 'collectors' makes close examination of their verbal elements a necessarily uncertain business. However, Child's *English and Scottish Popular Ballads*[10] establishes something like an agreed canon on the basis of which two broad generalisations may be made: (1) that 'the ballad is a folk-song that tells a story' embracing a series of events which 'is seized at its culminating point and is envisaged in terms of the action which then takes place';[11] and (2) that, despite this concentration and focus on action, the forward movement is slowed down by repetition, redundancy of phrasing and the use of refrains to produce what has been called the typically 'lingering and leaping' progress of the ballads. The effect is not unlike that of a children's chanting game such as 'Oranges and Lemons'. The climax is 'Here comes a chopper to chop off your head'; all the players know this, and anticipate it with a nervously delighted terror, but its attainment is prolonged and deferred by the ritual chant which gives its own satisfaction, and in which the children exist for a time in a state of suspended excitement.

Thus in a ballad like the 'B' version of 'Edward' (from Percy's *Reliques*) the progress towards the climax when the son curses his mother is delayed through the extended series of questions and answers and the repeated refrains, while the unfolding of the dramatic situation is deliberately retarded to heighten the tension:

Why dois your brand sae drap wi bluid,
Edward, Edward,
Why dois your brand sae drap wi bluid,
And why sae sad gang yee O?'
'O I hae killed my hauke sae guid,
Mither, mither,
O I hae killed my hauke sae guid,
And I had nae mair bot hee O.'

'Your haukis bluid was nevir sae reid,
Edward, Edward,
Your haukis bluid was nevir sae reid,
My deir son I tell thee O.'
'O I hae killed my reid-roan steid,
Mither, mither,
O I hae killed my reid-roan steid,
That erst was sae fair and frie O.'

'Your steid was auld, and ye hae gat mair,
Edward, Edward,
Your steid was auld, and ye hae gat mair,
Sum other dule ye drie O.'
'O I hae killed my fadir deir,
Mither, mither,
O I hae killed my fadir deir,
Alas, and wae is mee O!'

'And whatten penance wul ye drie for that,
Edward, Edward?
And whatten penance will ye drie for that?
My deir son, now tell me O.'
'Ile set my feit in yonder boat,
Mither, mither,

Ile set my feit in yonder boat,
    And Ile fare ovir the sea O.'

'And what wul ye doe wi your towirs and your ha,
    Edward, Edward?
And what wul ye doe wi your towirs and your ha,
    That were sae fair to see O?'
'Ile let thame stand tul they doun fa,
    Mither, mither,
Ile let thame stand tul they doun fa,
    For here nevir mair maun I bee O.'

'And what wul ye leive to your bairns and your wife,
    Edward, Edward?
And what wul ye leive to your bairns and your wife,
    Whan ye gang ovir the sea O?'
'The warldis room, late them beg thrae life,
    Mither, mither,
The warldis room, late them beg thrae life,
    For thame nevir mair wul I see O.'

'And what wul ye leive to your ain mither deir,
    Edward, Edward?
And what wul ye leive to your ain mither deir?
    My deir son, now tell me O.'
'The curse of hell frae me sall ye beir,
    Mither, mither,
The curse of hell frae me sall ye beir,
    Sic counseils ye gave to me O.'

As a piece of narrative this builds up to the final stanza extremely well. Yet the function of the ballad is not so much to bring out the son's curse on his mother with the maximum effect as to dwell on the quality of their relationship. In this respect it is akin to the ballad of 'Lord Randal', which also proceeds by question and answer in repetitive, parallel forms and involves a close relationship between mother and son. In 'Lord Randal', however, the mother is not implicated, as the mother of 'Edward' is, in the act of violence; her relationship with her son, reflected in the refrains, 'Lord Randal, my son' and 'my handsome young man', is one of simple and touching pathos, the son himself being a victim of murder (by his sweetheart) rather than a murderer. The more complex situation of 'Edward' gives rise to a more tragic tension, and this shows itself in the handling of the repetitive elements. The mother's use of her son's name and his addressing her as 'Mither, mither' create a moving sense of intimacy between them, but the word of endearment, 'deir', is used only by the mother to the son, not by the son to the mother. When he does use it, it is in connection with his father, in the almost self-contradictory line, 'O I hae killed my fadir deir'; and it is used in connection with the mother only by the mother herself: 'And what wul ye leive to your ain mither deir?' Without being explicit about it this highlights the change brought about in their relationship by the deed that has been committed. Love remains on her side, on his side it has been turned to hatred; but a bond as close as that of lovers still holds them together, and is reflected in the lyrical incantation of the repetitive elements (the more so if the ballad is sung). The action is, of course, important. It is that which brings the relationship to its climax and reversal (though most of the action is already in the past); but what gives the ritualised exchange between mother and son its permanent hold is the sinister quality of the altered feeling on which it hypnotically dwells.

In ballads of this kind there is an almost Aristotelian concentration on violence within the family: 'when the sufferings involve those who are near and dear to one another, when for example brother kills brother, son father, mother son, or son mother . . . then we have a situation of the kind to be aimed at'.[12] What is lacking, however, in all the ballads is the meditative dimension that places suffering in a meaningful context. The action is sudden, irrational, arbitrary. The repetitive technique induces a 'lingering' on emotion – and this perhaps provides a primitive counterpart to the Aristotelian catharsis; but there is little sense of the human condition, except that it is uncertain and tossed by tempestuous forces of unpredictable passion. The nearest one comes to a sense of action placed in a distancing perspective such as that of more consciously tragic art is when the ballad has a dirge-like tailpiece, as in the concluding stanzas of 'Sir Patrick Spens':

> O lang, lang may their ladies sit,
>   Wi thair fans into their hand,
> Or eir they se Sir Patrick Spence
>   Cum sailing to the land.

> O lang, lang may the ladies stand,
>   Wi thair gold kems in their hair,
> Waiting for thair ain deir lords,
>   For they'll se thame na mair.
>
> Haf owre, haf owre to Aberdour,
>   It's fiftie fadom deip,
> And thair lies guid Sir Patrick Spence,
>   Wi the Scots lords at his feit.
>   (Child 'A' text, from Percy's *Reliques*)

The abrupt action of ill-chosen voyage and drowning storm recedes in these stanzas to a ritualised, funerary posture, weirdly transformed by being placed fifty fathoms beneath the surface of the sea. Here repetition does not dwell on a relationship (though that of husband and wife is alluded to), but emphasises, almost satirically, the world of distance that now separates the sophisticated ladies (the parallel phrasing of 'Wi thair fans into their hand' and 'Wi thair gold kems in their hair' points up the futility of their sophistication) from the permanent, undersea posture of Sir Patrick 'Wi the Scots lords at his feit'. No comment is made, but it is a chilling epiphany of life and death.

It is here that the ballads and the main tradition of English lyric tragedy come closest together. At the point where action ceases and suffering takes over the lyrical sense of something inherently tragic in the conditions of human life is born. Wordsworth (as it happens in his only tragic drama rather than in a lyric poem) expresses it as a reverberation from action:

> Action is transitory – a step, a blow,
> The motion of a muscle – this way or that –
> 'Tis done, and in the after-vacancy
> We wonder at ourselves like men betrayed:
> Suffering is permanent, obscure and dark,
> And shares the nature of infinity.[13]

In tragic drama action is the begetter of suffering; in the ballad action and suffering seem fused in a passionately prolonged state; in lyric tragedy it is the consciousness disturbed by suffering in 'the after-vacancy' of action that becomes the focus of the poetry. In certain of his own 'lyrical ballads' Wordsworth suggests how the mind is brought to the edge of such awareness. 'Strange fits of passion', for example, takes the simplest kind of action: a lover riding to his beloved's cottage 'Beneath an evening moon', and shows it on the point of being converted into anxiety and an intuition of mortality. The narrative is deceptively naive; indeed, the narrator is conscious that its simplicity might easily be misread as simplemindedness, and suggests therefore that it requires a sympathetic attention:

> And I will dare to tell,
> But in the Lover's ear alone,
> What once to me befell.

He begins his tale with an image of his beloved's beauty which seems part of this unthinking simplicity:

> When she I loved looked every day
> Fresh as a rose in June.

The freshness of every day is, however, set against the unobtrusive past tense of the verbs, 'loved' and 'looked'. The evening moon seems part of a similarly unconscious romantic beauty, and becomes the focus of the narrator's attention: 'Upon the moon I fixed my eye'. With this comes a slight sense of heightened response, echoed in the same stanza by the horse's 'quickening pace' as it approaches the beloved's home; and in the following stanza tension is increased by the ballad-like repetition:

> And now we reached the orchard-plot;
> And, as we climbed the hill,
> The sinking moon to Lucy's cot
> Came near, and nearer still.

The horse's climbing of the hill and the sinking moon which seems to creep up on Lucy's cottage are involved as a still unobtrusive opposition in these lines, but the next stanza shows the narrator lulled into 'sweet dreams', even while his eyes kept on 'the descending moon'. Action itself becomes trance-like:

> My horse moved on; hoof after hoof
> He raised, and never stopped:

but (the colon is telling) there is a sudden, and slightly absurd, change:

> When down behind the cottage roof,
> At once, the bright moon dropped.

In the final stanza 'thoughts' and dialogue are for the first time introduced. The 'thoughts', however, are apologised for – they belong to the 'fond and wayward' kind which 'slide / Into a Lover's head'; and this one is elementally simple in its formulation in speech:

> 'O mercy!' to myself I cried,
> 'If Lucy should be dead!'

If the poem works, and does not strike one as merely banal, it is because these words crystallise the hints provided by tense, falling moon and dream-complacency within the apparent naivety of the preceding narrative, and answer to the tension which has been gathering momentum. Other Lucy poems are elegies for the dead beloved, and this one may be interpreted as an intuition of her loss which has since proved true. But it does not matter if one imagines Lucy as still alive at the time of the narration; the 'lyrical' essence (as against the 'ballad' form) of the poem is the consciousness of mortality implicit in stanzas 2–6, but not articulated till the final brief speech. Security is destroyed, and the narrator is left (with the reader who has sympathetically followed the process) wondering not so much at Lucy as at himself like a man 'betrayed'.

In a famous letter Keats puts down what he calls 'a simile of human life' which might be related to Wordsworth's lyricising of the ballad in 'Strange fits of passion':

I compare human life to a large Mansion of Many Apartments, two of which I can only describe, the doors of the rest being as yet shut upon me. The first we step into we call the infant or thoughtless Chamber, in which we remain as long as we do not think . . . we no sooner get into the second Chamber, which I shall call the Chamber of Maiden-Thought, than we become intoxicated with the light and the atmosphere. . . . However among the effects this breathing is father of is that tremendous one of sharpening one's vision into the heart and nature of Man – of convincing one's nerves that the world is full of Misery and Heartbreak, Pain, Sickness and oppression – whereby this Chamber of Maiden Thought becomes gradually darken'd and at the same time on all sides of it many doors are set open – but all dark – all leading to dark passages – We see not the balance of good and evil. We are in a Mist. *We* are now in that state – We feel the 'burden of the Mystery', To this Point was Wordsworth come, as far as I can conceive when he wrote 'Tintern Abbey' and it seems to me that his Genius is explorative of those dark Passages.   (letter to John Hamilton Reynolds, 3 May 1818)

'Strange fits of passion' does not penetrate far into the dark passages to which Keats here refers. As he indicates, it is in 'Tintern Abbey' that Wordsworth's 'Genius' becomes 'explorative of those dark Passages'. But the sense of movement from Innocence to Experience is effectively created by his use of the narrative element in the ballad to figure mental through physical action, and the change in consciousness ends the poem with a lyrical reverberation which seems about to open one of Keats's doors.

This sense of being on the brink of dark discoveries is one of the great themes of Romantic poetry, from Blake through to Shelley and Keats himself; but it is perhaps Keats, even more than Wordsworth, who feels the 'burden of the Mystery' as a tragic burden. Blake and Shelley are fundamentally optimistic about the power of the imagination to transform the darkness into light (though there is a degree of unacknowledged uncertainty in Shelley which allows the tragic in as an undertone); Wordsworth finds consolation

> In the soothing thoughts that spring
> Out of human suffering;
> In the faith that looks through death,
> In years that bring the philosophic mind.
> ('Ode: Intimations of Immortality', 184– 7)

And – a point to be returned to later – his concern is with the education of emotional response; the placing of tragedy in relation to other possible attitudes. It is Keats who most unreservedly commits himself to the darkness in which 'We see not the balance of good and evil. We are in a Mist.' Willingness to look tragedy in the face is for him the mark of poetic authenticity.

'On Sitting Down to Read *King Lear* Once Again' states this position quite openly. To read Shakespeare's tragedy is to shut the book of smooth, seductive 'golden-tongued Romance' and commit oneself to a searing imaginative experience:

> Adieu! for, once again, the fierce dispute
>> Betwixt damnation and impassioned clay
>> Must I burn through, once more humbly assay
> The bitter-sweet of this Shakespearian fruit.

For Keats, moreover, this is to be no merely aesthetic satisfaction, but a direct stimulus to tragic writing of his own: 'Give me new Phoenix wings to fly at my desire.' A similar manifesto to himself is issued in the 1819 revised version of *Hyperion* through the admonition of the goddess Moneta to the dreamer-poet who speaks in the first person:

> 'High Prophetess,' said I, 'purge off,
> Benign, if so it please thee, my mind's film.'
> 'None can usurp this height,' returned that shade,
> 'But those to whom the miseries of the world
> Are misery, and will not let them rest.'
> ('The Fall of Hyperion: A Dream', 145–9)

Engagement with the fact of human suffering is thus a condition of serious poetic achievement; but in spite of attempts to create tragedy in the Shakespearean mould with plays like *Otho the Great* and the unfinished *King Stephen*, and two unfinished attempts at the Miltonic epic, Keats comes nearest to successfully 'flying at his desire' in the lyrical form of 'La Belle Dame Sans Merci' (more precisely a Keatsian lyrical ballad) and the Odes, where escape and commitment, luxuriating in the musical harmony of verse and severe attention to 'the miseries of the world', combine in equal proportions to create the 'bitter-sweet' of Keats's own peculiar fruit.

The seasonal imagery of *The Testament of Cresseid* and the Wordsworthian adaptation of the ballad to express the awakening to a world of Experience are fused together in 'La Belle Dame'. The time is late autumn, on the verge of winter ('The squirrel's granary is full, / And the harvest's done'), yet the dominant feeling is of chilled, withering loss, with the sedge 'withered from the lake' and, correspondingly, a feverish paleness on the brow of the knight-at-arms,

> And on thy cheeks a fading rose
> Fast withereth too.

His tale, however, is one that carries the poem back into the 'sweet dreams' of Wordsworth's lover marvellously amplified to include the whole exotic world of faery and medieval romance as seen through the metamorphosing imagination of the Romantic poet. It dwells lovingly on its own poetic diction, which removes things to a beautifully seductive 'language strange' and culminates in the knight's insistently repetitive dreaming of 'The latest dream I ever dreamt / On the cold hill side'. But what he dreams has the pallidness of death that the 'I' of the poem has already noted in the knight himself, and lies dormant in the unreal remoteness of his tale and in the curious sense of desolation caught by the truncated last line of each stanza: 'And no birds sing'. The belle dame's dream-world is one that starves, not nourishes (perhaps destroying as Moneta warns that those are self-destroyed 'who find a haven in the world, / Where they may thoughtless sleep away their days' – 'The Fall of Hyperion: A Dream', 150–3). Its tragic tone derives from its very attempt to evade the reality of tragic truth. The ballad ends, however, with the knight's waking and finding himself in what is the poem's present 'On the cold hill's side', and a coming full circle with a repetition of the opening lines. The knight is destroyed as his forebears have been, but the ballad itself expresses and contains his experience in its own tragic perspective.

The singular strength of 'La Belle Dame' lies in its simultaneous creation and criticism of the dream-world. As David Hume notes, there is a paradox inherent in the literary form of tragedy in that it creates an aesthetic object from material associated with sorrow and distress, what is painful becomes a source of pleasure; and the explanation he offers is that:

This extraordinary effect proceeds from that very eloquence, with which the melancholy scene is represented. . . . By this means, the uneasiness of the melancholy passions is not only overpowered and effaced by something stronger of an opposite kind; but the whole impulse of those passions is converted into pleasure, and swells the delight which the eloquence raises in us.[14]

The effect of Keats's poetry is more complex than this, for he offers a self-consciousness that goes beyond the seemingly unself-conscious paradox which Hume observes (in relation to dramatic tragedy). His theme is the necessity of the tragic vision and the barrenness of attempting to evade it, but presented in a melancholy eloquence which pleases even as it is rejected. In the 'Ode on Melancholy' there is thus a double satisfaction: that provided by the seductive music of melancholy, and that provided by the process of discrimination by which the false is separated from the true. Tension is generated from the opening words of emphatic negation: 'No, no, go not to Lethe, neither twist.' But the lines which express the negated means of oblivion are themselves a source of pleasure and contribute to the poem's total orchestration of melancholy harmonies. It is because they are so sensuously apprehended that the pressure of the negatives upon them can be so strongly felt, and the climax of the stanza – a statement that such narcotic forms of melancholy will 'drown the wakeful anguish of the soul' – can become a positive exhortation to sharper conscious awareness.

Consciousness, 'the wakeful anguish of the soul', is, for Keats, the essential condition for that 'bitter–sweet' experience which converts the 'melancholy fit' into tragic awareness. The imagination must dwell intensely on the simultaneous presence of beauty and decay in order to produce, like the 'weeping cloud' which brings both gloom and refreshment (contradictorily hiding 'the green hill in an April shroud'), the keen creative–destructive melancholy of reality fully encountered. It is then that Melancholy acquires her divine status:

> She dwells with Beauty – Beauty that must die;
>   And Joy, whose hand is ever at his lips
>   Bidding adieu; and aching Pleasure nigh,
>   Turning to poison while the bee-mouth sips:
>   Ay, in the very temple of Delight

> Veiled Melancholy has her sovran shrine,
>   Though seen of none save him whose strenuous
>   tongue
> Can burst Joy's grape against his palate fine;
> His soul shall taste the sadness of her might,
>   And be among her cloudy trophies hung.

This Melancholy springs from awareness of mutability and mortality. Its antitheses are not simple ones: 'Pleasure' is set against 'poison'; but Pleasure itself is 'aching', and though turning to poison, it does so 'while the bee-mouth sips'. And, with typically Keatsian synaesthesia, seeing and tasting (even to the tasting of impalpable 'sadness') are fused into an active, energetic consciousness ('strenuous' and 'burst') which is directly opposed to the sluggish, Lethean associations of the first stanza. Melancholy's true shrine, like Moneta's height, is to be achieved only by an almost heroic effort of complete imaginative immersion in the destructive element.

In the 'Ode to a Nightingale' Keats again addresses the problem of escape. Here, however, the 'bitter-sweet' movement is one of alternation between the nightingale image of imaginative creation aloof from human suffering and the tragic knowledge compelled by 'the wakeful anguish of the soul'. Numbing of consciousness is actually invoked, rather than rejected, in the first two stanzas; but in the third the very naming of what the unconscious nightingale has never known, aided by the insistently repeated parallel constructions, gives that negative an unavoidably positive emphasis:

> Fade far away, dissolve, and quite forget
>   What thou among the leaves hast never known,
> The weariness, the fever, and the fret
>   Here, where men sit and hear each other groan;
> Where palsy shakes a few, sad, last grey hairs,
>   Where youth grows pale, and spectre-thin, and dies;
>   Where but to think is to be full of sorrow
>   And leaden-eyed despairs;
>   Where Beauty cannot keep her lustrous eyes,
>   Or new Love pine at them beyond to-morrow.

Stanza IV renews the movement away from this world though now 'on the viewless wings of Poesy', in terms redolent of the 'golden tongued Romance' of the *Lear* sonnet, and continues it into the imaginatively recreated sensuousness of stanza V. But what is moon-lit in stanza IV now becomes 'embalmèd darkness', with a funereal overtone that leads, in stanza VI, to the wish for 'easeful Death' and, in stanza VII, to the transformation of the nightingale into an 'immortal Bird!' – an apotheosis of the earth-freed poet, who is, if not unconscious of, then immune from, human suffering. However, the line with which stanza VI concludes ('To thy high requiem become a sod') is an ominous development of the preceding darkness and death. It exalts the song of the nightingale to the splendour of a great musical ritual, but one which itself is tragical in its associations; and only to change its resonance to the contrastingly prosaic 'sod' which the poet's death would have made of him. In fact, it is a transition, once more, to the world of tragic reality; and, despite the deathlessness attributed to the Bird in stanza VII, 'No hungry generations tread thee down' is a reminder of human suffering, as is the reference to 'the sad heart of Ruth'. The nightingale's song lifts again in the last lines of the stanza towards the 'Romance' world of 'magic casements, opening on the foam / Of perilous seas, in faery lands forlorn'; but it is the tragic human perspective which is yet again asserted in that ultimate, post-positioned adjective, 'forlorn'. 'Forlorn' also bridges the gap to the final stanza of the Ode, and leads directly into the almost completely monosyllabic register of self-consciousness in:

> the very word is like a bell
> To toll me back from thee to my sole self!

Like the word 'sod' this brings the poet, and the reader, firmly back to reality. Even so, the song is not simply silenced: the 'plaintive anthem' (a word whose associations still echo those of 'requiem') grows less and less as, in poignant recessional, it

> fades
> Past the near meadows, over the still stream,
> Up the hill-side; and now 'tis buried deep
> In the next valley-glades;

and its ultimate status as 'vision' or 'waking dream', like the condition of the poet himself ('Do I wake or sleep?'), is left in undetermined poise.

The open-endedness of 'Ode to a Nightingale' appropriately reflects its poetic nature. To speak of it in terms of escape and reality, though true as far as it goes, is to oversimplify a poem which is as much a synthesis as a dialectic. The poem is written as it is – with alternating, but also interconnecting, movements – because its dual concern with mortality and immortality is always relative to the human mind. The immortality of the nightingale is an imaginative creation; and if 'the fancy cannot cheat so well / As she is famed to do, deceiving elf', it is because the imagination, though capable of envisaging a transcendent state, is conditioned by human experience and the transience of human life. It must humanise even what it creates by way of an extra-human world; hence the colouring of the nightingale's song with funereal tones of 'requiem' and 'plaintive anthem' and its reaching Ruth 'in tears amid the alien corn'.

'Ode to a Nightingale' imagines an extra-human world only to become more keenly aware of the tragic condition of the human. 'Ode on a Grecian Urn' may seem to resolve that problem by translating the human to the permanent, unchanging world of art and offering friendship to man in the form of an image of his life that can speak with unimpaired beauty from one woeful generation to the next. But, apart from the ambiguity of what the urn says (or if it speaks at all[15]), the image of humanity on the urn is one of arrested vitality: the 'Bold Lover' can never kiss; though the scene of the sacrifice is richly crowded with life, the imagined town is emptied of its folk 'and not a soul to tell / Why thou art desolate, can e'er return'; and the ironic 'brede' of the urn consists of 'marble men and maidens'. It is a teasingly 'Cold Pastoral!', exalting unheard melodies above the heard, and exciting imagination to scenes of Dionysiac revelry and fervent happiness (the six times repeated 'happy' of stanza III cannot be accidental) which are exempt from the fevered aftermath of 'breathing human passion', but frustrating the process of change and decay which is also the process of fruition and fulfilment. The curiously detached pun: 'O Attic shape! Fair attitude!' is appropriate to the ambiguous emotion which this urn arouses. The artistically frozen world it contains, and the stimulus it offers the imagination to create (in stanza IV) even beyond what is represented on it, demand wonder and admiration; but its stillness, quietness and silence isolate it – as the 'high requiem' of the nightingale is not isolated – from the deepest needs of man.

For this more real satisfaction we must turn to the Ode 'To Autumn'. The rich verbal texture which characterises all the Odes is at its maximum in this poem. A drenched fertility exudes from every line of the opening stanza; and the alliteration and assonance, focussing especially on full, rounded vowels and a harmonious interplay of 'm' and 'l', together with the phrasally extensive syntax, set in motion a tide of sound that gradually fills the entire stanza till an appropriate sense of fullness – to the point of overspilling – is reached in the last line: 'For Summer has o'er-brimmed their clammy cells.' Autumn, however, is the season of mists as well as 'mellow fruitfulness'; its fertility is carried almost to an excess verging on sickly sweetness and rottenness. In the second stanza the beauty of the personifi- cations is qualified by an impression of drooping carelessness and neglect, with 'the fume of poppies' recalling the narcotic suggestions included in the Melancholy and the Nightingale Odes, and the final line, 'Thou watchest the last oozings hours by hours', achieves a glutinous richness that emphasises still more the ambiguous balance between ripeness and rottenness in the first stanza. All of which is a minor-keyed music of fulfilment such as the arrested figures on the Grecian urn inevitably lack, but fused with the painful transience to which those figures are also placed in teasing opposition.

As if looking back to the lost state of pastoral perfection which is embodied with mocking coldness on the urn, the third stanza opens with a variation on the traditional questioning of time past: 'Where are the songs of Spring?' – only to have the question put by with an affirmation of the euphoniously broken music of Autumn:

> Think not of them, thou hast thy music too –
> While barrèd clouds bloom the soft-dying day,
>   And touch the stubble-plains with rosy hue:
> Then in a wailful choir the small gnats mourn
>   Among the river sallows, borne aloft
>   Or sinking as the light wind lives or dies;
> And full-grown lambs loud bleat from hilly bourn;
>   Hedge-crickets sing; and now with treble soft
>   The red-breast whistles from a garden-croft;
>   And gathering swallows twitter in the skies.

The progressive nature of this Ode has often been noted: 'the stanzas can be seen as moving through the season, beginning with pre-harvest ripeness, moving to the repletion of harvest itself, and concluding with the emptiness following the harvest, but preceding winter. It also progresses from the tactile senses, to the visual, culminating in the auditory senses. . . . It has also been read as a movement from morning to evening.'[16] All of this suggests a process of fructifying and harvest which is satisfyingly complete, though, as already suggested, the taint of excess is mingled with it even in the earlier stages. By the time the third stanza is reached excess merges with decay, and the verse becomes elegiac. Unlike the Grecian urn's 'ditties of no tone', the music of autumn, even though it arises exclusively from the natural world, is tinged with a suggestion of human mourning ('Then in a wailful choir the small gnats mourn'); and each of the creatures mentioned in the last four lines as contributing to this music has associations, if delicately muted, with mutability: the lambs of spring ('Where are the songs of Spring?') are now 'full-grown', hedge-crickets and robins hint at winter, and the 'gathering swallows' suggest migration. Dying is implicit also in the fading of the day ('barrèd clouds bloom the soft-dying day'), the lifting and falling of the gnats ('as the light wind lives or dies'), and the beautifully judged decrescendo of sounds from 'loud bleat', through 'sing' and 'with treble soft . . . whistles', to the final 'twitter in the skies'.

There may be implications of cyclic renewal in 'To Autumn', but, if so, these are left in abeyance. Its images and cadences are predominantly those of ripeness passing into rottenness and death. But, equally, it is never morbid or self-indulgent. In so far as the tragic sense involves 'the wakeful anguish of the soul' acutely conscious of 'the miseries of the world', 'To Autumn' is less tragic than 'Ode to a Nightingale'; but it builds a surer foundation by its mature acceptance of transience. The 'I' of 'Ode to a Nightingale' has apparently disappeared, replaced by personification of the season, addressed as 'thou', and this may seem to deprive the poem of a consciousness in which to focus tragic awareness. But what has happened is that the 'I' has transcended itself (though its more personal voice can just be heard in the first line and a half of the third stanza), losing its pity for its own, and human, mortality in a more objective contemplation of the natural condition to which both human and non-human life is subject. Yet the result is not objectivity as such. The poem is still an intensely personal lyric in which Keats's own feeling for transience attaches to the sensuous details. His very submission to their reality involves his recognition of their transitory nature, and the process of creating them with such loving care brings out the essence of their bittersweetness. This likewise generates the 'music' of autumn, which, as Hume observes, is an eloquence by which 'the whole impulse' of 'the melancholy passions' is 'converted into pleasure'. Delight in the fruition of autumn thus merges with the pain which comes from acknowledgement of its simultaneous existence as the season of decay to produce a calm tragic awareness of the indivisibility of life and death, and the guarantor of the authenticity of this synthesis is the profoundly pleasing eloquence through which it is expressed.

In the chapters which follow Keats's achievement in the Odes, though not intended as a precise standard of comparison, offers something like a criterion by which other writers of lyric tragedy may be judged. The Nightingale and Autumn Odes, in particular, suggest a poetry which sustains even while it disturbs. It stirs those anxieties which are inevitable in a living contact with reality, but also converts such anxieties into a tragic pleasure exempt from falsifying sweetness. It creates tragedy out of the pathos of transiency by avoiding the self-pity which consciousness of transience so easily produces. Pathos is an important element in lyric tragedy; but only when there is a sense of tension and resistance to it does it issue in true tragedy. It is the absence of this tension which makes Arnold's pathos, in poems like 'Requiescat' and 'Dover Beach', unsatisfactory. The sense of a trapped, frustrated spirit in 'Requiescat' is dissipated in sentiment; and though 'Dover Beach' involves the larger issue of man's isolation in a world of intellectual doubt, the retreat into personal consolation offers only a debilitating pathos:

> Ah, love, let us be true
> To one another! for the world, which seems
> To lie before us like a land of dreams,
> So various, so beautiful, so new,

Hath really neither joy, nor love, nor light,
Nor certitude, nor peace, nor help for pain;
And we are here as on a darkling plain
Swept with confused alarms of struggle and flight,
Where ignorant armies clash by night.

The statement of bleak disillusionment, culminating in a resonant image of intellectual confusion, ought to represent an
authentic recognition of tragic circumstances; but the string of
negatives is too generalised to carry conviction, and the image of
battle serves only to emphasise the babes-in-the-wood helplessness of the lovers and the futility of resistance in a situation
where it is impossible to discern what should be resisted. The
poem is a beautifully prolonged sigh, for which the sound of the
sea rising and falling on Dover beach is an apt symbol, but
which, even when transformed into a 'melancholy, long, with-
drawing roar', cannot escape the yielding plangency (despite the
allusion to Sophocles) of the 'eternal note of sadness' rather than
tragedy.

Arnold's 'Sea of Faith' is a Victorian concept – something to
be nostalgically regretted as part of a vanished past which
offered a maternal comfort denied to the intellectual orphans of
the modern world. It suggests that religion is a consolatory
illusion, protecting man from the desolating knowledge of his
true state. In 'The Scholar-Gipsy' and 'Thyrsis' this sense of a
lost spiritual haven joins with the tradition of the pastoral elegy.
A vaguely religious mystery suffuses the Cumnor Hills, and the
fugitive scholar who wanders among them, associated with the
youth of Arnold and Clough and the vigour of a now eroded
idealism. Yet the tradition to which both poems, but 'Thyrsis'
more specifically, are attached is one that has been modified by
Christianity and moulded, in Milton's *Lycidas*, into an ultimately
anti-tragic form. Arnold dwells on the modern implications of a
fallen world and a lost paradise; Milton contains his sense of loss
within a frame which his essentially heroic faith provides. Crisis
tests Milton's faith and stimulates a power of resistance that
gives more tragic force to his work than is to be found in
Arnold's; but the outcome is a vindication of his faith – despite
the suggestion made by some critics that *Lycidas* has a tragic
structure – which is beyond tragedy.[17]

Within the same tradition, but coming between Milton and

Arnold, are Shelley's *Adonais* and Tennyson's *In Memoriam*. Shelley rejects Milton's theology, but, for all his Platonism, still inhabits the emotional world of Christianised pastoral elegy; and Tennyson, while subscribing more conventionally to the theology, is pulled emotionally into the world of doubt. Both enter an area of uncertainty where anxieties about the human condition breed tragic feeling which, however, verges on uncontrolled pathos. They are uneven, but moving by virtue of their unevenness; while their attachment to, but uneasiness with, the tradition (Tennyson at a greater distance than Shelley, though still within it) becomes a telling commentary on the relationship between tragic and religious feeling.

The development and change of the pastoral elegy tradition from Milton, through Shelley and Tennyson, to Arnold reveals an increasing uncertainty of attitude towards the idea of tragedy itself. In Tennyson this affects the very form of his poem: *In Memoriam* (the title was suggested by his wife – Tennyson referred only to his 'elegies') is a constellation of lyrics rather than a Miltonically integrated whole. Many 'voices' assail his ears, each offering its own advice on how he should react to Hallam's death. As he exploits the advantage of lyric in being able to follow the subjectivity of feeling, and suspend commitment to theory or doctrine, the poetry becomes an exploration of possible responses, both tragic and non-tragic. This process had already begun with Wordsworth, who, with a stronger didactic purpose, had directed it towards the education of feeling. In 'Tintern Abbey', for example, he distinguishes what is appropriate to youth from the more tragic awareness of later years, and in 'The Ruined Cottage' attitudes towards Margaret's tale of sorrow are balanced against each other. The result is a tragic response which is self-conscious and self-critical.

The doubting of tragedy which this implies is none the less more typical of post- rather than pre-Arnoldian poetry. Yeats, in keeping with his argument in the 'The Tragic Theatre', finds a 'terrible beauty', which puts 'casual comedy' aside, born out of the violence of Easter 1916; and, in 'Lapis Lazuli', he asserts the time-honoured tragic view that suffering ennobles and that the true tragic protagonist meets his fate triumphantly:

> All perform their tragic play,
> There struts Hamlet, there is Lear,

> That's Ophelia, that Cordelia;
> Yet they, should the last scene be there,
> The great stage curtain about to drop,
> If worthy their prominent part in the play,
> Do not break up their lines to weep.
> They know that Hamlet and Lear are gay;
> Gaiety transfiguring all that dread.
> All men have aimed at, found and lost;
> Black out; Heaven blazing into the head:
> Tragedy wrought to its uttermost.

But there is already something anachronistic in this view, and Yeats's rhetoric is the rhetoric of defiance. He is, in effect, protesting against the diffidence and uncertainty which in the modern mind raise only two cheers for tragedy, represented by the timidity of Prufrock:

> No! I am not Prince Hamlet, nor was meant to be;
> Am an attendant lord, one that will do
> To swell a progress, start a scene or two,
> Advise the prince;

and the defeated heroism of *The Waste Land* where the quester cannot speak, though 'Looking into the heart of light, the silence', and

> Only at nightfall, aethereal rumours
> Revive for a moment a broken Coriolanus.[18]

The partial, narrowing focus of tragedy is distrusted; a wider view is preferred. Thus for W. H. Auden, although

> About suffering they were never wrong,
> The Old Masters,

what he admires is their understanding of its 'human position':

> how it takes place
> While someone else is eating or opening a window
> or just walking dully along.

The birth of Christ and the Massacre of the Innocents have their context of ordinariness; and the traditionally hubristic Fall of Icarus is scaled down to a pair of slightly ridiculous legs disappearing into the sea in a beautiful, but largely indifferent world:

> In Brueghel's *Icarus*, for instance: how everything turns away
> Quite leisurely from the disaster; the ploughman may
> Have heard the splash, the forsaken cry,
> But for him it was not an important failure; the sun shone
> As it had to on the white legs disappearing into the green
> Water; and the expensive delicate ship that must have seen
> Something amazing, a boy falling out of the sky,
> Had somewhere to get to and sailed calmly on.
>
> ('Musée des Beaux Arts')

Yet lyric tragedy persists. Its less heroic clamour allows a muted form of tragedy that the drama cannot so easily provide. D. H. Lawrence, for example, may brusquely dismiss tragedy as 'a loud noise / louder than is seemly',[19] but he is deeply interested in the tragic vision. His quarrel with tragedy is a quarrel with what he regards as its debasement, and even a quarrel with himself and his own need to come to terms with the same condition of mortality as Keats recognises in the Odes. In place of a falsely tragic defeatism he insists on the tragedy of 'creative crisis', but if he convinces it is through the evolution of an unhysterical attitude to the reality of death – a process which he both defines and embodies in the patient shaping of 'The Ship of Death'.

Edward Thomas and Sylvia Plath are also involved in a struggle to disentangle true from false attitudes to death. Thomas cautiously and tentatively searches for the clue to his hidden self in natural phenomena that speak most potently to him when they adopt an elusively tragic voice. He is acutely aware of the danger of self-pity and of the falsely isolating melancholia that may cause his preoccupation with tragic feeling to seem merely unreasonable to other men:

> Over all sorts of weather, men, and times,
> Aspens must shake their leaves and men may hear
> But need not listen, more than to my rhymes.

> Whatever wind blows, while they and I have leaves
> We cannot other than an aspen be
> That ceaselessly, unreasonably grieves,
> Or so men think who like a different tree.[20]

And with Sylvia Plath the risk of being in love with one's own defeat, though taken less cautiously, is likewise the uncertain centre of her consciousness. As a myth-maker she tries, often too deliberately, to give a public and universal significance to her private obsession with death; but she is sophisticatedly aware that the whole thing might be a shocking game:

> Dying
> Is an art, like everything else.
> I do it exceptionally well.
>
> I do it so it feels like hell.
> I do it so it feels real.
> I guess you could say I've a call.[21]

Her feminism, too, is involved with her exploration of death, and provides a tragic tension which is equally uncertain and potentially histrionic.

The need to express aggression may account for the self-dramatising violence in Sylvia Plath's poetry. She also, however, has the justification that violence – man's ability to inflict and receive pain – is a central concern of traditional tragedy. The outrage man does to man challenges his image of himself as a rational being, causing him to ask if there is 'any cause in nature that make these hard hearts'.[22] To this end she incorporates material from the atrocities of the Nazis as a way of making her poetry engage with the issues that arouse her own, and her contemporaries', deepest feelings of horror. It is not a trivialising of such issues, but an attempt to understand the tragic link between the violence within and the violence without. What presents the greatest problem is control over the emotions thus excited: 'Daddy' and 'Lady Lazarus' are powerful and disturbing poems, but it may be that her greatest achievement is in the less immediately tragic bee-keeping sequence.

In this respect her work echoes that of the First World War poets who break with the quietness of Georgian poetry to become brutally realistic about the slaughter on the Western Front.

A similar problem of control arises. It may be argued that violence too exclusively in the foreground distorts the tragic picture, which requires suffering to be placed in perspective; and the poetry of Wilfred Owen would seem to support this view. Much of his poetry disturbs, as it was meant to do: 'Yet these elegies are to this generation in no sense consolatory. They may be to the next. All a poet can do today is warn. That is why the true Poets must be truthful.'[23] But his finest poems tend to have their settings removed from the front line, or, as in the case of 'Strange Meeting', they dwell on 'The pity of war, the pity war distilled' rather than the physical violence and suffering. The effects of shock and horror remain important, but a distance is gained which neither drowns 'the wakeful anguish of the soul', nor blocks the deeper resonance of tragedy.

It is this sense of immediacy modified by distance that makes Hardy the most tragic of modern writers, in verse as well as in the novel. 'Modern' may not be the right word: his career spans both the nineteenth and twentieth centuries; he belongs with Shelley and Arnold more than with Yeats or Eliot; and he does not share the modern distrust of tragedy. For all that, he is distinctively modern in his focus on tragedy, not as something fundamentally reassuring to the human spirit, but as the expression of a reluctantly disillusioned coming to terms with reality. His highly personal poetry (though not 'confessional' like that of Robert Lowell or Sylvia Plath) often looks backward to a nostalgically regretted past, like that of Arnold or Tennyson, but it is a past coloured and tragically conditioned by knowledge peculiar to the present. The characteristically human tendency to idealise the past reacts with the equally characteristic tendency to disenchantment, and, especially in the poems of 1912–13 written after the death of his first wife, a more tragically complicating factor is his obliquely recognised sense of guilt in their relationship, 'past amend, / Unchangeable'.[24] In other poems his loss of faith is also part of the groundwork of disenchantment. The result is a poetry doggedly truthful about the bleakness of man's condition, but charged with the poignancy of sympathy and regret – a world like that of 'Dover Beach', but viewed with a tragic astringency that Arnold lacks.

Hardy's successor in contemporary English poetry is Philip Larkin. In the Introduction to *The North Ship* Larkin records how he began to read a selection of Hardy's poems early in 1946:

Hardy I knew as a novelist, but as regards his verse I shared Lytton Strachey's verdict that 'the gloom is not even relieved by a little elegance of diction'. This opinion did not last long; if I were asked to date its disappearance, I should guess it was the morning I first read 'Thoughts of Phena at News of Her Death'.[25]

The entire poem is relevant, but the stanza which seems to link most clearly with Larkin's own poetry is the second:

> What scenes spread around her last days,
>   Sad, shining, or dim?
> Did her gifts and compassions enray and enarch her sweet ways
>   With an aureate nimb?
> Or did life-light decline from her years,
>   And mischances control
> Her full day-star; unease, or regret, or forebodings, or fears
>   Disennoble her soul?

The crucial word is 'Disennoble'. It encapsulates the tragic feeling that spreads throughout the stanza – that the inevitable deterioration culminating in death would eradicate the illusion of a noble Tryphena. In the first stanza Hardy regrets that he has no memento of the dead woman, but, after the perception of the second stanza, he withdraws that regret in the third: it is better to retain only the 'phantom' maiden. Similarly, Larkin, in 'Maiden Name', seems to regret the unspecified married woman's maiden name as now 'a phrase applicable to no one' and therefore meaningless. But on reflection he changes his opinion; since the unmarried woman is 'past and gone':

> It means what we feel now about you then:
> How beautiful you were, and near, and young,
> So vivid, you might still be there among
> Those first few days, unfingermarked again.
> So your old name shelters our faithfulness,
> Instead of losing shape and meaning less
> With your depreciating luggage laden.

The unusual negative, 'unfingermarked', like Hardy's slightly odd 'Disennoble', carries a strange weight of moving sentiment. It suggests that life is a process of sullying what is originally bright and attractive; and though the 'name' is immune from this process, the whimsical fragility of such a shelter for 'our faithfulness' makes its own wry comment on the inescapable condition of depreciation.

Larkin's major theme is the fact of this fingermarking process underlying all human life, and its inevitable conclusion in death. He presents it stripped of protective illusions, and without the consolation of religious belief – though the widespread human need for that consolation, and the seriousness of mind with which it is traditionally associated, receive their full due. Death, however, is the insufferable bugbear that frightens in the night, and will not be blinked away in the day. It makes cowards of us all, not by 'the dread of something after death', but by remaining stubbornly unamenable to reason or imagination. If the ultimate justification of tragedy is that it affirms life by coming to terms with death, Larkin's poetry would seem to represent a final step in the modern dissatisfaction with tragedy. The most recent of his poems on death, 'Aubade', not only rejects all attempts at comfort, but also denies the value of courage in facing the truth on which it insists. The poem virtually mocks itself. But if, as Keats suggests, and the tradition of lyric tragedy seems to confirm, man has an innate need for conscious formulation and poetic shaping of his pain, even 'Aubade' makes its contribution. It satisfies the demand that even the unspeakable should be spoken.

In an often-quoted line from 'In Tenebris II' Hardy hesitantly affirms that 'if way to the Better there be, it exacts a full look at the Worst'. The business of lyric tragedy is to take this full look, and to exact it from its readers also. But the possibility of 'way to the Better' lies outside its territory, with faith rather than tragic vision. The two often exist in close proximity – as can be seen in the work of almost all of the writers discussed in the following chapters, not excluding Larkin; but the only kind of consolation that lyric tragedy as such can legitimately offer is in the facing of what appals, and, as Hume suggests, expressing it in a poetic form which is a source, however strange, of a deeply serious pleasure. Donne understandably mocks the notion that

> Griefe brought to numbers cannot be so fierce,
> For, he tames it, that fetters it in verse.[26]

The bringing of grief to numbers is more likely to intensify than tame it; and if the effect is too obviously one of fettering and reduction, then the value of the versifying process is undone for the reader. Nevertheless, in the shaped poem – no matter how much the shaping is indivisible from the exploration and sharp realisation of the grief – there is at least evidence of the imagination's capacity to create even out of what destroys.

2 Milton: *Lycidas* and the Christianised Pastoral Elegy

It is a critical commonplace to say that the death of Edward King is less the subject of *Lycidas* than the possible death 'ere his prime' of Milton himself, or, more broadly, the death of the young poet before he has accomplished what his gifts suggest he is capable of achieving. These three subjects are not, however, incompatible. Milton has so composed the poem that they may be seen as different facets of the one central preoccupation with talent versus the fact of mortality. Moreover, the pastoral elegy is chosen, not because it is 'easy, vulgar, and therefore disgusting',[1] but because it provides a traditional context in which personal grief may be expressed and transcended. Theocritus, Bion, Moschus, Vergil, Petrarch, Boccaccio, Sannazaro, Ronsard, Spenser, and many others, provide ample precedent for taking the occasion of a particular death, especially that of a promising young poet, and finding in it a type of something precious which is lost, but more than compensated for through universal sympathy and exaltation to the heavens.[2]

The most famous literary precedent is that provided by Vergil's Eclogue V. Here the sympathetic mourning and divine exaltation are divided between the two speakers, Mopsus and Menalcas. Their common theme is the death of Daphnis (a shepherd, though not in this instance one who is identified as a poet; the Vergilian shepherd–poet is Gallus in Eclogue X). Mopsus laments an idealised Daphnis. All nature, in the form of 'the Nymphs', weeps for him, and even the oxen and the lions of Africa sympathise. He is seen, retrospectively, as the source of life itself, and his death becomes a cause of universal sterility. In the epitaph for his tomb, however, his fame, reaching from the woods to the stars, gives his pastoral status a touch of more than earthly significance:

Daphnis ego in siluis, hinc usque ad sidera notus,
formosi pecoris custos, formosior ipse. (43–4)

[I am Daphnis. From these woods my fame spread to the very
stars. / Fair was the flock I shepherded, myself more fair than
they.[3]]

Menalcas takes up this hint and develops it into a song of
transfiguration, in which Daphnis, not only raised to the stars,
but wondering at his new surroundings in heaven, gazes at the
clouds and stars beneath his feet. Nature again sympathises,
though with joy now, and proclaims him a god. Both wolves and
men give up their predatory hunting, for *amat bonus otia Daphnis*
['peace is dear to kindly Daphnis']; and he is begged, as Milton's
Lycidas will later be, *sis bonus o felixque tuis* ['Oh be thou kind and
gracious to thine own']. Finally, Menalcas promises to make
sacrifice to the deified Daphnis, and proclaims that his glory will
last as long as nature itself:

> dum iuga montis aper, fluuios dum piscis amabit,
> dumque thymo pascentur apes, dum rore cicadae,
> semper honos nomenque tuum laudesque manebunt.
>
> (76–8)

> ['While the boar loves the mountain ridge, while
>   the fish loves the stream,
> While bees shall feed on thyme, and the cicadas
>   drink the dew,
> For so long shall thine honour, thy name and
>   praise endure.']

Grief is thus transformed into joy; and the transition from
earth to some kind of heaven points the way – which pastoralists
of the Renaissance were quick to follow – towards a religious
perspective which totally alters the secular view of mortality.
The pastoral becomes Christianised, and the shepherd figure,
already both ordinary countryman and idealised poet–god, acquires New Testament connotations as a spiritual guardian of
his flock.[4] This in its turn leads to attacks on the abuse of the
shepherd–priest's role – in, for example, Petrarch, Mantuan and
Spenser's *The Shepheardes Calender* (specifically in 'Maye', 'Julye'

and 'September') – which, though not incorporated with elegy as they are in *Lycidas*, greatly widen the scope of pastoral to include much that is outside the mellifluous unreality usually associated with this form.

As it came down to Milton, therefore, the pastoral was capable of both simple and complex meanings. It bore the character of a naively sensuous, but also stylised, poem of country life, and it also carried with it a long tradition endowing its shepherd figures with the aura of poet and priest. Its topics might be conventionally rural, but also of the gravest and most impressive kind. The very artificiality of the form made it capable of a high degree of flexibility, and a variation in intensity and seriousness that could be controlled at will.

The extent of Milton's departure from simple pastoral does, however, remain a difficulty for many readers. Clay Hunt, for example, one of the most intelligent commentators on *Lycidas*, endorses G. Wilson Knight's judgement that it 'reads rather as an effort to bind and clamp together a universe trying to fly off into separate bits; it is an accumulation of magnificent fragments'.[5] The pastoral tradition is not enough, in Hunt's opinion, to justify the variety of *Lycidas*, and he argues instead – or perhaps in addition – for the poem's belonging to the tradition of the Italian canzone, as developed both in practice and theory by Dante and Tasso. This involves the expansion of lyric poetry to include not only the middle style, which is the level of expression appropriate by conventional standards to its own sweetness and decorative nature, but also the more astringent emotions and tempestuous material associated with the high styles of epic and tragedy. It is an attempt, that is to say, to release the lyric from a narrow, and somewhat belittling, conception of what constitutes the lyrical, and to endow it with a 'Pindaric' strength and variety capable of including the whole range of human thought and emotion. As part of his argument Hunt also refers to Minturno's advocacy of digressions and Dante's suggestion (interpreted in a rather 'free', speculative manner) that the composer of the canzone has a certain kind of music in his mind, even though the finished poem may be independent of musical setting. Out of these suggestions for enhancing the lyric comes the idea of a poem which alternates between different areas of meaning and tonality of expression, exemplified in *Lycidas* in particular by the alternation of ruthful dirge and passionate, indignant outbursts

such as that of the St Peter passage (ll. 108–31). For Hunt this
gives the poem something of an Aristotelian tragic grandeur,
with dirge and indignation functioning as the equivalent of pity
and fear. The structure is such as to excite these emotions, but
also resolve them in a cathartic climax which 'ends by purging
these disturbances of mind and bringing us to final calm'.[6] That
the poem nevertheless remains pastoral in form is accounted for
by the fact that Milton is not yet sure enough of himself to
venture on full tragic expression. He prefers a mixed form which
allows him to break out into the higher style and subject-matter
of tragedy while keeping his feet on the traditionally lowly
ground of pastoral. *Lycidas* is thus 'a pastoral lyric on classical
and Italian models, musically contrasted in the tragic mode'.[7]

   Persuasive as Hunt is, his argument for the influence of a new
conception of the canzone is interesting rather than conclusive.
The idea of a nominally humble form which is yet pregnant with
the utmost seriousness and eloquence is already present in the
pastoral tradition as Milton inherited it. What he may have
gained from the Italians were the confidence, and some technical
hints, to help him to exploit this idea to the full. But the further
suggestion made by Hunt – prompted by, rather than following
inevitably from, the study of the canzone – that *Lycidas* effects
something like an Aristotelian tragic catharsis, raises important
questions about the interpretation of the poem as lyric tragedy.
Hunt even goes so far as to suggest, though with some hesitation,
that the rudiments of a tragic plot, complete with 'recognition'
and 'reversal', can be detected in *Lycidas*. The poem, he main-
tains, begins with an initial tragic change of fortune, with
Lycidas fallen from high promise to premature death by drowning. This is cause for grief and anguish, the very pressure of
which, however, leads to a second change: what was 'sunk low' is
found to be 'mounted high'. This is the true 'reversal' in which
the outcome is the opposite of what was expected; and it is
accompanied by the 'recognition' that Lycidas has not been
cheated of, but has actually achieved, his proper reward – in
heaven rather than on earth. Hunt concedes that the weakness of
such a plot, by Aristotelian standards, is that it apparently
involves the less tragic ascent from misery to happiness instead
of the essentially tragic fall from happiness to misery; but this
weakness is overcome by Milton's contriving to offer both: the

tragic fall succeeded by, and converted into, the gaining of a different and greater happiness.

Other critics have noted tragic elements in *Lycidas*, but the distinctive feature of Hunt's analysis is that it takes the poem beyond elegy to a tragic structure of Aristotelian proportions. Milton himself is conscious that he is in some sense overstepping the normal limits of his chosen form, as he indicates when, after allowing his fears of early death and unfulfilled promise to sweep him away, he deliberately turns back to the pastoral world:

> O fountain *Arethuse*, and thou honour'd floud,
> Smooth-sliding *Mincius*, crown'd with vocall reeds,
> That strain I heard was of a higher mood:
> But now my Oate proceeds.
>
> (85–8)

And after the St Peter outburst there is an even more marked self-checking and return to the norm of pastoral:

> Return *Alpheus*, the dread voice is past,
> That shrunk thy streams; Return *Sicilian* Muse.
>
> (132–3)

However, despite their appearance of spontaneous eruption, these outbursts are controlled and subordinated to a preconceived view of the place that suffering has within a divinely ordained scheme of human life, i.e. to a specifically Christian theology. Hunt's concession that the Aristotelian 'plot' of *Lycidas* is ultimately of the comic rather than tragic kind makes a more profound difference than he seems to appreciate. The structure of the poem cannot even be regarded as a highly condensed form of the Greek trilogy such as the *Oresteia*, in which tragedy erupts, but is at length harmonised and brought to reconciliation. Nor does it follow the pattern of *The Winter's Tale*, which at its mid-point modulates from tragedy to comedy, transforming destruction into regeneration. *Lycidas* is more a process of education. If it aims at catharsis, the kind of catharsis envisaged is that implicit in the final Chorus of *Samson Agonistes* – one that results from the final triumph of true understanding over misunderstanding of God's ways:

> All is best, though we oft doubt,
> What th' unsearchable dispose
> Of highest wisdom brings about,
> And ever best found in the close.
>   (1745–8)

This brings God's servants 'new acquist / Of true experience' and consequent 'peace and consolation' and 'calm of mind all passion spent' (1755–8). *Lycidas* constantly has a similar end in view. It progresses through a series of adjusted understandings to its formally and theologically predetermined vision; and it ends on a similar quietened note.

The poem begins in the first person: 'Yet once more . . . / I com to pluck' (1–3), and the speaker is 'I' throughout most of the poem. In the last paragraph, however, the pronoun is 'he', and Milton distances the figure who has uttered the preceding words to 'the uncouth Swain' (186). 'Uncouth' is not the modern 'graceless'; it may mean 'unknown', but more probably means 'rustic' in the sense of 'untutored, untaught, unskilled'.[8] This agrees with the pastoral convention that the poet is a simple shepherd singing a naive rural song; but, combined with the change from 'I' to 'he', it also serves to detach Milton from the speaker (or singer), and perhaps from that part of his own self which expresses its anguish, and makes its protests, in the main body of the poem. Certainly, the opening paragraph associates the speaker with unreadiness and immaturity. He has come to pluck the sacred laurel, myrtle and ivy before their berries are ripe, i.e. before he himself is sufficiently mature. This is usually taken as a comment on Milton's own sense that he is not yet fully prepared for the serious business of poetry; but such a reading is not incompatible with the view that the premature plucking is also a way of characterising the speaker as inadequately equipped either in skill, or understanding, or both. However, the advantage of the second view is that it allows the poem to work in terms of the situation it creates, without going behind that situation to the author's personal, but undivulged, circumstances. The speaker is then seen as conscious of insufficiency, but compelled by grief

('Bitter constraint, and sad occasion dear' emphasises the emotional compulsion), and by his sense of what is due to a dead fellow shepherd–poet, to speak out prematurely. Such an admission conditions all that follows; it is a tacit warning that emotion may be stronger than reason, and that immature feelings may need to be judged as such. And, further to strengthen the point, the poet for whom the speaker grieves is 'dead ere his prime' (8), and bears the name of a Vergilian poet who also deprecates his own immaturity. 'Lycidas' is the speaker:

> et me fecere poetam
> Pierides, sunt et mihi carmina, me quoque dicunt
> uatem pastores; sed non ego credulus illis.
> nam neque adhuc Vario uideor nec dicere Cinna
> digna, sed argutos inter strepere anser olores.
> (Eclogue IX, 32–6)

> ['Me too have the Muses made
> A poet; I too have my songs: yes, even I am called
> A singer by the shepherds, but I heed not what they say.
> For surely naught have I yet sung worthy of Varius
> Or of Cinna, a mere cackling goose among melodious swans.']

In other respects, too, the opening paragraph hints at what is to come. To develop Hunt's musical analogy, it is a prelude sounding in subdued manner the tonalities which are to receive louder and more sustained treatment later in the poem. Violence, of anguish and of protest, is anticipated in phrases such as 'harsh and crude' and 'forc'd fingers rude' and in the emphatic verb, 'Shatter'. The funereal sound of 'sad occasion dear' (its alliterative 'd' echoed in 'disturb your season due') leads to the elegiac repetition of

> For *Lycidas* is dead, dead ere his prime
> Young *Lycidas*,
>
> (8–9)

announcing the theme of untimely death which is to reach its climax in the more sharply expressed resentment of 'the blind *Fury*' in lines 75–6; and the lilting rhythm and repeated 'w's of

> He must not flote upon his watry bear
> Unwept, and welter to the parching wind
>
> (12–13)

initiates the water/weeping motif which, with many variations, recurs throughout. The poem itself as a musically inspired elegy is hinted by the conventional 'singing' of the poet–shepherd, while the ability of this supposedly humble pastoral to soar to the greatest heights is suggested by the compliment to Lycidas as one who knew to 'build the lofty rhyme' (10–11). And in the closing line of the paragraph ('Without the meed of som melodious tear') the tragic abandonment of Lycidas' body to the rolling waves and 'parching wind' is countered by yet another allusion to the musical nature of the poem itself, and the interaction of 'meed' and 'melodious' suggests the transformation of grief into harmony and ultimate reward. ('Meed' also anticipates the 'fair Guerdon' of line 73, which is frustratingly snatched away, and the contrasted heavenly 'meed' of line 84.)

After this prelude the elegy proper begins with a chord on the strings of the lyre symbolising the banishing of the speaker's diffidence ('Hence with denial vain'). If this is achieved, however, it is only because the Muses have been invoked as the inspirers of his song, with allusions to Aganippe and Helicon appropriate to the classical convention, but tactfully phrased to imply that the religious reality beneath the convention is Christian (hence 'sacred well' and 'seat of *Jove*', where 'Jove' is accepted Renaissance locution for 'God'). This is also the reality beneath the elegant convention observed in lines 19–24: the speaker is fulfilling the Christian duty to do unto others as he would have them do unto him.

First the speaker celebrates the memory of his friendship with Edward King, the 'Young *Lycidas*' of the poem, against a background of beneficent nature. He alludes to his and King's time as students at Cambridge, but in the generalising terms of the pastoral which allow a wider meaning. Similarly, the conventional 'Rural ditties' which are 'Temper'd to th'Oaten Flute' (32–3) represent the poetic exercises of Milton and King, but with a power of suggestion which more direct reference would lack: the flute made of natural material symbolises the harmony of poetry and the natural world; and the audience which listens to these 'ditties', including '*Satyrs*' and '*Fauns*' as well as 'old

Damoetas', suggests the integrated world of which such poetry is a part. It is an idealised world, as the pastoral traditionally is, close to the mythical Golden Age; and if it seems a nostalgic conception, that, too, has its appropriateness. The perfect innocence of such friendship is charming, but also a sign of immaturity. It will inevitably prove to be fragile.

The change therefore in the next paragraph, though abrupt, is not without poetic logic. The ideal is bound to succumb to the real, and this has already been anticipated. The incantatory formula,

> But O the heavy change, now thou art gon,
> Now thou art gon, and never must return!
>
> (37–8)

recalls the funereal tone of lines 8–9, and the images of decay and destruction which follow are related to the shattering of the leaves (5) compelled by the 'sad occasion' of the poem. Within this paragraph, however, nothing is said that cannot be contained by the traditional sympathy of nature with the dead shepherd to be found in pastoral elegy. There is increasing sharpness of anguish towards the end of the paragraph, with the harsh sound and greater violence of 'killing as the Canker' and the images of 'Taint-worm' and 'Frost' (once more echoing the theme of premature death), but it is not till the fifth paragraph, introduced by the questioning of the Nymphs, that this consciousness of destruction begins to take on the character of doubt and protest. The absence of the Nymphs when 'the remorseless deep' closed over Lycidas' head gives a first hint of the failure of providence, but with the short line, 'Ay me, I fondly dream!' (56), a more bitter note is struck, followed by the passionately broken syntax of:

> Had ye bin there – for what could that have don?

The archetypal poet, Orpheus himself, could not be saved by his mother, Calliope, from the wild, irrational violence of the Bacchanals who tore him limb from limb, much less the immature Lycidas. This brings providence still more into question. Milton does not mention the Bacchanals directly, referring only to 'the rout that made the hideous roar' (61); but, as J. B. Leishman argues, this is a strong rather than a weak periphrasis, by which the unnamed attackers are 'thrillingly evoked'.[9] It is also a periphrasis that stresses the injustice of the Bacchanals' enmity (they resented Orpheus' grief for his lost wife) and the uncontrolled extravagance of their rage. In a cancelled line – 'when she [Calliope] beheld (the gods farre sighted bee)' – the ineffectualness of divine foreknowledge was specifically referred to as well. Milton removed it, perhaps because its explicitness came too soon; but the thought was evidently in his mind, and in the final version the repeated emphasis on the helplessness of 'the Muse her self' (58–9), coupled with the horrific image of Orpheus' 'goary visage' rolling down the Hebrus (62–3), still projects an intense feeling of doubt with regard to divine providence.

It is this which breaks out into open protest in the paragraph beginning, 'Alas! What boots it with uncessant care' (64 *et seq.*). The speaker gives vent to his emotion with something of the extravagance of the 'I' in George Herbert's 'The Collar', and with a similarly implied effect of distortion. Following on the reference to Orpheus, it is clearly false to speak of 'the homely slighted Shepherds trade' (65). Even though Orpheus is treated unjustly, as the supreme exemplar of the 'Shepherds trade' he enjoys a brilliance of reputation quite inconsistent with the use of 'homely' and 'slighted'. The speaker is, of course, thinking of contemporary neglect of the poet – for which, again, there is ample pastoral precedent, notably in Spenser's 'October', where the Orphic power of poetry is rejected by an ignorant society. But at this stage the speaker is tempted to go along with such an attitude ('Were it not better don as others use'). 'Shepherds trade' may also refer to the work of the priest as well as that of the poet. If so, the speaker's exaggeration is still more marked; the work of the priest should transcend worldly regard. For both poet and priest the speaker seems to be craving a fundamentally inappropriate reward; and though this does not make his anguish spurious, it gives a strong suggestion of immaturity of understanding. The answer to his protest is already implicit in the way it is made.

Again, the idea that fame is the spur which drives the noble spirit on to labour and self-denial (70–2) is commonplace, and so, equally, is the Christian response that eternal rather than temporal fame is what finally matters.[10] Thus the crisis represented by death cutting off reward, which forms the climax of the speaker's protest, is essentially a crisis for Milton's imagined speaker rather than for Milton himself. It is placed and judged by the language. The jejune notion of snatching at a bright, glittering prize suggested by

> But the fair Guerdon when we hope to find,
> And think to burst out into sudden blaze
> (73–4)

already asks for the scornfully phrased retribution it gets:

> Comes the blind *Fury* with th' abhorred shears,
> And slits the thin spun life.
> (75–6)

This is less the language of tragic canzone than of tragic satire. The antithesis between 'abhorred shears' and 'thin spun life' emphasises the tragic fragility of the thread by which human life hangs, but it also mocks the ambition which would trust itself to anything so frail and vulnerable to such clumsy attack. The use of 'blind *Fury*' is especially significant. 'Fury' is a conflation of Fate and the Furies; it is Milton who 'adds blindness, not a recognized attribute of either Fate or Fury, because she seems, at this stage in the poem's development, to act without discrimination'.[11] The phrase (perhaps borrowed from *Gorboduc*[12]) is self-consciously histrionic – seriously tragic only to those who are themselves 'blind' in that they cannot recognise Fate as subordinate to God. The comparatively brief reply of Phoebus is therefore enough; and he does almost as much by his soothing touching of 'my trembling ears' (77) as by what he says. His argument merely adjusts the scale of values from temporal to eternal, reminding the speaker of the true and everlasting principle by which fame is a 'plant' that does not grow 'on mortal soil' but 'lives and spreds' in the sight of Jove. Limited human perception is put in its place by the perfect knowledge and judgement which pronounces with final emphasis: 'Of so much fame in Heav'n expect thy meed' (84).

'Phoebus' and 'Jove' are Christ and God respectively, but they retain their pastoral names in this pastoral poem because pastoral offers a screen from the direct, as yet unbearable, revelation of the full divine truth. We may ultimately see 'face to face', but for the time being we 'see through a glass, darkly',[13] as befits immature understanding. After the pronouncement of Jove, therefore, the poem retreats from its 'higher mood' (87) to the conventional procession of the mourners, questioning each one about the drowning of Lycidas, with echoes of the stormy language of the preceding paragraph, muted and softened, however, by the pastoral context. But in parallel with the earlier questioning of the nymphs leading to the death of Orpheus this stirs a sense of the uncertainty of mortal life once more, and Lycidas' loss at sea despite the calmness of the water ends the paragraph in disturbed language foreign to that of pastoral smoothness:

> It was that fatall and perfidious Bark
> Built in th' eclipse, and rigg'd with curses dark,
> That sunk so low that sacred head of thine.
> (100–2)

Some degree of extravagance returns in these lines. Maynard Mack comments: 'Literally [line 101] suggests that King's ship was foredoomed to sink by malign supernatural influences'; but he then goes on to offer a figurative interpretation in terms of the curse of the Fall.[14] The literal meaning will do quite well, however. The blaming of the ship is a superstitious explanation springing again from immaturity, its seemingly tragic quality (it echoes passages in *Lear* and *Macbeth*[15]) something which expresses the speaker's distress sincerely enough, but also recalls earlier histrionic outbursts. True understanding comes only from the Christian vision which the poem as a whole expresses.

The pastoral procession continues in conventional style with Camus; but with St Peter, 'The Pilot of the *Galilean* lake' (109), its smoothness is again broken by the most passionate and disruptive outburst of all. The theme is now the loss of good shepherds (priests more than poets this time) and the injustice of apparently leaving the field free for the bad. The language is again that of tragic satire, overflowing with contempt for the greedy self-seekers who only care

> to scramble at the shearers feast,
> And shove away the worthy bidden guest.
> (117–18)

But this is not superstitious misrepresentation. It must be conceded that Milton, not simply St Peter, is in deadly earnest. He
writes lines of forceful vituperation, as bitingly energetic as
anything in his own controversial prose and abounding in active
verbs ('Creep and intrude', 'climb', 'shove away') and adjectives
of studied vulgarity ('lean and flashy', 'scrannel', 'wretched')
which communicate his disgust with great power. Most brilliant
of these contemptuous phrases is the at first sight absurd 'Blind
mouthes!' (119). The misappropriation of the adjective compels
attention to the spiritual blindness it condemns, and the reduction of bad shepherds to mere mouths succinctly dismisses them
as self-indulgent travesties of their vocation.

This is not the language, however, of wisdom and insight. It
still has an element of exaggeration – exaggeration which may,
indeed, work as satire, but which leaves the reader (as even the
best satire usually does) with a sense that truth has been over-
shot, or at least presented partially from a limited human
standpoint. Milton surely identifies more with this spokesman
than with the 'I' who is generally the speaker in *Lycidas*, and the
separation of the two may be intended to give St Peter a status
free from the suggestion of immaturity associated with the
normal speaker, so that his criticism of the corrupt clergy is not
impaired. None the less, St Peter's is the voice of a limitingly
righteous indignation which can only express a part, not the
whole, of the Christian truth. In this connection it is perhaps
significant that the St Peter digression does not culminate like
the 'blind *Fury*' digression, in the intervention of a divine figure
evoking a transcedent vision of truth. It mounts to a passionate
denunciation of 'the grim Wooĺf', but then breaks off with the
resounding, but, it would seem, deliberately cryptic lines:

> But that two-handed engine at the door,
> Stands ready to smite once, and smite no more.
>
> (130–1)

Among the many explanations of this passage [16] the most generally accepted is that it alludes to the sword of Michael (thus
anticipating the reference to the angel at line 163) conflated with
the figure in Revelation 'likc unto the Son of man' (1:13) out of
whose mouth 'went a sharp twoedged sword' (1:16), and who
urges, 'Repent; or else I will come unto thee quickly, and will

fight against them [i.e. backsliders in the church] with the sword of my mouth' (2:16). Such an interpretation does, as a matter of fact, provide a shadowy structural parallel to the conclusion of the 'blind *Fury*' digression, since Phoebus in the earlier passage is identified with Christ and the figure with the two-edged sword also resembles Christ. But the avoidance of explicit statement is more evident, and the answer to the doubt that has been raised is more oblique – if the apparent threat of retribution can be regarded as an answer at all. More probably, we may have to recognise that no completely satisfactory answer to the problem of corruption in the church can be given while the tone of voice remains that of the indignant St Peter. Its lack of serenity and detachment, though it does not diminish the force of the criticism it makes, remains a disabling flaw that still awaits correction. It is cogent, but still not yet the medium of true wisdom.[17]

The return at line 132 to the sweeter tone of pastoral yet again may be seen as contributing to – though not in itself able to effect – the necessary correction of St Peter's indignation. The myth of the disappearing and reappearing River Alpheus provides a useful means to this end. It is an elegant way of signalling the resumption of pastoral convention once more, and it also hints, through the story of Arethusa's escape from violation, at the inimical strain in 'the dread voice' which 'shrunk' Alpheus' streams. A region of valleys is evoked, 'where the milde whispers use' (136), and the tender and fertile associations incorporated in the diction ('wanton winds', 'gushing brooks', 'green terf', 'honied showres' and 'vernal flowres'), together with the specific contrast in line 138 between 'fresh lap' and 'swart Star' and the elaboration of the traditional flower catalogue in lines 142–50, create an atmosphere of rest and recuperation which is a counterbalance to the withering zeal of St Peter.

This in its turn verges a little too much on the prettily sentimental – in, for example, the self-consciously artificial decoration of 'the well attir'd Woodbine' and 'every flower that sad embroidery wears' – and the catalogue is judged within the poem itself as the work of 'frail thoughts' which 'dally with false surmise' (153). The tonal change which the pattern of the poem now leads the reader to expect is towards tragic reality once more, introduced by the exclamation, 'Ay me!' (154), and focussing on the body of Lycidas:

> Where thou perhaps under the whelming tide
> Visit'st the bottom of the monstrous world.
>
> (157–8)

The impressive geographical sweep from 'the stormy *Hebrides*' (156) to St Michael's Mount, with the archangel looking towards Spain (161–2), seems to take the poem still further away from pastoral tenderness, but reaches its climax in the prayer to Michael to 'Look homeward Angel now, and melt with ruth', coupled with the dolphins, as representatives of sympathetic nature, being asked to 'waft the haples youth' (163–4). Strength thus joins with sweetness in grieving over the lost Lycidas.

But as there was an abrupt, but poetically logical, change at line 37 from the idealised world of youth to 'the heavy change' of Lycidas' death, so now there is a change, sudden but fundamentally in harmony with what has been implicit all along, from grief to rejoicing:

> Weep no more, woful Shepherds weep no more,
> For *Lycidas* your sorrow is not dead.
>
> (165–6)

The poem soars from the depths where the corpse is sunk 'beneath the watry floar' (167) to the height of the heavens, as physical death is transmuted into spiritual life. The pattern of fall and rise which is recurrent throughout the poem becomes a fall that is rhythmically completed in the vision of a regenerate and redeemed Lycidas sharing the company of the blessed. His natural home is light and joy, which his tragic sinking beneath the waves can only deny him temporarily, as the sun itself sinks to rise again:

> So sinks the day-star in the Ocean bed,
> And yet anon repairs his drooping head,
> And tricks his beams, and with new spangled Ore,
> Flames in the forehead of the morning sky:
> So *Lycidas* sunk low, but mounted high.
>
> (168–72)

The waters which seemed to have destroyed him, and the wetness of tears which grief evoked, are transformed, like the sinking and rising pastoral Alpheus, into the 'other streams' (174) and the spiritual '*Nectar*' (175) of heaven. In this new state the tears are forever wiped from his eyes, and Lycidas himself becomes, in a Christianised version of the deification of Vergil's Daphnis, 'the Genius of the shore' who will be 'good' – Vergil's 'bonus' – 'To all that wander in that perilous flood' (184–5). But this transformation is now attributed specifically to Christ, in a manner which relates his saving power to triumph over death by water: 'Through the dear might of him that walk'd the waves' (173) – thus putting the finishing touch to the Christian answer to Lycidas' drowning which has been implicit throughout the poem.

The use of the phrase 'dear might' for Christ's redemption power is a significant periphrasis. As Woodhouse and Bush note, 'The allusion to Matt. 14. 25–31 is intended to remind the reader of the whole incident, including the role of Peter, already associated with the Sea of Galilee . . . and carries more than one suggestion.'[18] Peter's temerity in trying to emulate Christ by also walking on the waves illustrates both his wish to demonstrate faith and his failure to sustain that wish in the face of tempest. Yet it is still Christ who saves him. The 'dear might' may therefore be seen as a power which is loveable and loving, but also 'dear' in the complex senses of dangerous to emulate and, because of the Crucifixion by which Christ allowed himself to sink and rise again in order to save man, a power which it costs Christ 'dear' to exercise. This power, via the allusion to Matthew, is also one that Christ manifests by walking quietly on the turbulent seas, while Peter's loud boldness proves in the end to lack the quiet calm of true faith. All of which is highly relevant to *Lycidas*. In this poem it is the quiet and humility of pastoral that carries and contains its tragic-satiric outbursts; and, though it seems to provide an escape from higher things, through the Christianising of its motifs (which have lain dormant as if waiting for this to happen) pastoral becomes a vehicle for visionary exaltation. Its 'other groves, and other streams' are those of a refound paradise, but implicit in its earthly ones, and its own existence as a 'Song' sung by a poet–shepherd prefigures the 'unexpressive nuptiall song' (176) which Lycidas hears in heaven. Above all, it is in this transformed pastoral that the Christ figure, only touched on in veiled terms before, is made explicit as the supreme agent of transformation, and gives Lycidas his place 'In the blest Kingdoms meek of joy and love' (177).

In this line the adjectives balanced on either side of 'Kingdoms' have equal importance: 'blest' exalts spiritual above earthly kingdoms, while 'meek' recognises that the exaltation is paradoxically lowly rather than high and mighty; and the 'joy and love' which follow indicate that such kingdoms have to do not with power as domination, but as the expression of qualities of suffering and bitterness changed into their opposites.

Disturbance contained within, and overcome by, pastoral harmony, rather than cathartic purging of grief, is also the implicit theme of the poem's finale. Here the 'uncouth Swain' is clearly in his traditional pastoral setting once more, singing 'to th'Okes and rills' (186). There is a brief rehearsal of the compassion and anxiety which have been the subject of the poem:

> He touch'd the tender stops of various Quills,
> With eager thought warbling his *Dorick* lay;
>   (188–9)

but it is bound within a more regular rhyme-scheme than the poem has hitherto shown ('These lines, which . . . make a stanza of *ottava rima*, furnish a narrative epilogue'[19]), and its context is the quiet progress of the day: the song began as 'the still morn went out with Sandals gray' and now ends as the sun lengthens its shadows and drops 'into the Western bay' (187 and 190–1). Given the well-established pattern of the poem, however, sinking inevitably suggests rising and renewal as well, and that expectation is not disappointed in the final couplet:

> At last he rose, and twitch'd his Mantle blew:
> To morrow to fresh Woods, and Pastures new.
>   (192–3)

'At last he rose' indicates the simple act of the shepherd's standing up, but in conjunction with the beginning of the previous line ('And now was dropt'), and the image of the sun to which that refers, it reverberates with larger meaning. The symbolic blue of his 'Mantle' likewise signifies hope. In the very last line the pronoun 'to', doubled in effect by Milton's separated spelling of 'To morrow', gives a forward impetus which suggests that this end is another form of beginning, and this is reinforced by 'fresh' and the conclusion of the line, and the whole poem, on the word 'new'. The final emphasis is thus firmly on new life, ensuring that the poem ends on the rising note which has repeatedly triumphed over the falling tragic strain.

Milton was nothing if not a careful and conscious artist. Close reading of *Lycidas* amply confirms this. The literary echoes, as J. B. Leishman has shown, reveal how much his poetry is the distillation of all that has gone before him in the tradition he chooses to follow, and the organisation of his own verbal structures confirms the sense that for him poetry is not so much self-expression as a vessel for carrying and containing personal emotion and relating it to a larger impersonal design. His work is premeditated, though not in a way that denies spontaneity. With Milton what counts is the kind of valuation accorded to spontaneity. As 'eager thought' it demands an outlet. Thus grief, compassion, anxiety, resentment, indignation – and even, perhaps, a degree of self-pity – are all to be found in *Lycidas*: they are natural, human emotions which demand release. But Milton always has in mind a more-than-human standard by which such spontaneous material is judged as incomplete, and ultimately immature; and that standard is the Christian one that sees through anguish to divine order.

To be more precise, art and Christianity are, for Milton, complementary. Artistic control is the means whereby the poet echoes within his own work the providential principle which his faith tells him permeates the actual world. The 'well' of inspiration springs 'from beneath the seat of *Jove*'. Consequently, the tragic is from the beginning something which has already been transcended – a compelling element in human experience, but by virtue of its human, and therefore fallible, nature, requiring to be placed in the context of a more inclusive, revealed pattern.

To this extent *Lycidas*, despite its tragic material, is not a tragic poem. The cathartic structure which Clay Hunt finds in it is really the structure demanded by a transcendent vision. The experience of reading the poem is not one of pity and terror faced and accepted as the devastating emotions which the conditions of human life make inevitable. Instead, it is the experience of being conducted through painful illusions, i.e. improperly understood responses to what is felt to be the 'fatall and perfidious

Bark' of destruction, but which the true aesthetic-cum-spiritual understanding of the poem as a whole resolves into the higher 'unexpressive nuptiall Song' celebrating the hidden, but beneficent, ways of providence. Grief becomes irrelevant: 'Weep no more, woful Shepherds weep no more.' The glorified Lycidas is no subject for lament; and though the proneness to grieve which is natural to imperfect human beings is fully recognised, the 'uncouth Swain' is educated to a higher, and ultimately more truthful, level of understanding.

But if *Lycidas* is not lyric tragedy, it is nevertheless a profound influence on the shape of lyric tragedy which comes after it. Shelley, Tennyson and Arnold draw on the same pastoral tradition, and the way it has been modified by Milton is a pervasive pressure on their own handling of it. His beliefs, however, are less fully shared. His pattern of fall and rise continues to exert a strong emotional appeal, but doubt gives the rise a poignant uncertainty which intensifies rather than transcends tragedy. All seek consolation, but none with the confidence that Milton does.

3 Shelley, Tennyson and Arnold: the Pastoral Elegy and Doubt

Two recent commentators on Shelley's *Adonais* have made a point of reminding their readers that it is not a Christian poem. Jean Hall warns us that Shelley's 'immortal world is not to be construed literally. After all, *Adonais* is a poem of immortality written by an atheist.'[1] She also quotes from Shelley's *Essay on Christianity* to show that what attracts him to the Christian belief that decaying mortality may be transformed into glorified immortality is not its theological, but its imaginative, truth. Likewise Richard Cronin, though emphasising Shelley's debt to the 'Christianised pastoral elegy', insists:

> Shelley was not a Christian; *Adonais* is not a Christian poem. *Adonais* works towards a consolation for the fact of death without reliance on any received dogma. It is a Christian pastoral elegy from which all Christian theology has disappeared.[2]

Hall and Cronin are right; but their denials have to be made precisely because of the strongly Christian flavour that the poem possesses. Although it offers no Christian heaven, it generates an enthusiastic, other-worldly religious fervour, and seeks to transfer the dead Adonais to what is at least 'an Heaven of Song' (413) in a way that is very reminiscent of the Christian answer to the grief aroused by death. Shelley takes as his acknowledged literary model Moschus' 'Lament for Bion', which he quotes from in his Preface, and details are also borrowed from Bion's

'Lament for Adonis', but his spiritual models are to be found in those Renaissance elegies which adapt the deification of Daphnis to Christian purposes, and which culminate in *Lycidas*. The pagan consolations of fame or release from the miseries of life are not enough; Shelley's urge is towards something like the Christian transcendency and transformation, and there are even moments when he verges on Christian doctrine.[3] His Platonism cannot, of course, be ignored. Intellectually this provides the most serious element in *Adonais*. But it is the Christian elegists that lead him emotionally.[4]

The atheism makes a considerable difference, however. *Adonais*, like *Lycidas*, is, in Shelley's own phrase, 'a highly-wrought *piece of art*',[5] but the art is not the medium of a faith that controls and directs it, as happens in *Lycidas*. On the contrary, Shelley constructs from within the poem itself – its own verbal materials and their literary and emotional overtones – a subjective, substitute faith, and it is this which he uses to counter the anguish that is overcome in Milton by his allegiance to the Christian faith. If Shelley rejoices, it is as a result of a process even more marked than T. S. Eliot's of 'having to construct something / Upon which to rejoice'.[6] The poem is almost uniquely self-supporting. Even its grief, though arising from the untimely death of Keats, as the Preface announces, at the hands of 'savage criticism',[7] gives the impression of being generated within the poem, and it is consoled and transcended by a purely imaginative form of truth which is equally self-bred. A consequence of this self-generating and self-transforming poetry is that it is also fragile and unstable. The relationship between human limitation and divine inspiration which gives *Lycidas* its fluctuating movement is thus echoed in the rhythm of *Adonais*, but without the certainty of belief which controls and directs the education of the 'uncouth Swain' in *Lycidas*. In the latter the transcendence of tragedy is guaranteed by the sure interaction of art and faith; in *Adonais* it remains partly ambiguous, and the very fervour of assertion betrays doubt almost as much as it generates ecstasy. *Adonais* is therefore more truly lyric tragedy than *Lycidas*. The absence of Christian belief, despite the presence of Christian feeling, lets in the anxiety that is calmed in *Lycidas*.

The characteristic movement of Shelley's stanzas is volatile and uncertain. In the very first there is apparent contradiction between opening and close:

> I weep for Adonais – he is dead!
> Oh, weep for Adonais! though our tears
> Thaw not the frost which binds so dear a head!
> And thou, sad Hour, selected from all years
> To mourn our loss, rouse thy obscure compeers,
> And teach them thine own sorrow, say: with me
> Died Adonais; till the Future dares
> Forget the Past, his fate and fame shall be
> An echo and a light unto eternity!

The emphasis, to begin with, is on grief for the loss of Adonais
which must be vented even though it can do nothing to restore
him; and this is to be reinforced by the lamentation of the Hour
in which he died and all its 'obscure compeers'. But when the
Hour is given words to express its grief they turn into an
affirmation, not only of Adonais' memory throughout time –
defiantly proclaimed in 'till the Future *dares* / Forget the Past',
but also of his symbolic relationship to 'eternity', the reverberant
word on which the stanza ends.

In the second stanza the movement is, if anything, still less
certain. Urania (Shelley's Muse-like Venus, mother and lover of
his poet-Adonais) is questioned, as the Nymphs are questioned
in *Lycidas*, lines 50–5. The implication seems to be that she was
absent at Adonais' death when she might have saved him by her
presence; but, as the lines following the question show, in a sense
she was with him (and in a sense especially relevant to this
poem, where Adonais is the Young Poet and Urania his inspiration) by attending to his death-defying poetry:

> With veiled eyes,
> 'Mid listening Echoes, in her Paradise
> She sate, while one, with soft enamoured breath,
> Rekindled all the fading melodies,
> With which, like flowers that mock the corse beneath,
> He had adorned and hid the coming bulk of death.
>
> (13–18)

The rekindling of Adonais' poetry 'with soft enamoured breath'
conveys a warmth which contrasts sharply with the tears of the
first stanza that could not thaw the frost binding his head. It
may be necessary to explain this by distinguishing between the

dead poet and his living poetry; but the fact that the poetry can live in this way already modifies the grief caused by his death. But this suggestion of vitality is then countered by the epithet 'fading'; and though the synaesthetic fusion implicit in 'melodies' being likened to 'flowers' hints at an imaginative reality transcending, and therefore well able to 'mock', the dead corpse, their function as a means of merely adorning and hiding the deliberately gross 'bulk' of death again reduces the sense of creative energy living in the poetry.

In stanza IV, as Cronin has shown, Shelley employs a kind of rhetorical sleight of hand which causes the reader to take the personal pronoun of line 29 ('He died') as referring to Adonais, but which proves, as the syntax unfolds, to be a reference to Milton.[8] Again, the effect of this is to shift the stanza from one attitude to its opposite – in this case from what seems to be renewed urging of weeping:

> Most musical of mourners, weep again!
> Lament anew, Urania! – He died
> (28–9)

to the ringing declamation that [Milton's] 'clear Sprite', with an unmistakable echo of 'the clear spirit' of *Lycidas*, line 70, 'Yet reigns o'er earth; the third among the sons of light' (36). In stanza IX, on the other hand, the urge yet again to weep, in the first line, immediately gives way to an intellectualising of the conventional 'flocks' of pastoral poetry as the 'quick Dreams' and 'passion-winged Ministers of thought' which Adonais nurses in his mind – a marvellous way of celebrating his creative power. But in the middle lines of the stanza the syntax passes over to the negative, and, instead of activity which is 'quick', 'living' and 'kindling', we have flocks that 'droop' and 'mourn'

> Round the cold heart, where, after their sweet pain,
> They ne'er will gather strength, or find a home again.
> (80–1)

A similar pattern could be traced in other stanzas, not always involving such a contradiction as that of stanza I, but at least warming and then chilling the reader's feelings as the glory or vitality of Adonais is alternated with the deprivation of his

death. Frequently, as in stanza IX, the quickened feeling for
Adonais serves only to make his loss the keener. The poignancy
of tragedy is heightened. But the emotions generated are again
unstable and ambiguous. In the sequence of stanzas VI–VIII, for
example, tenderness, pathos, even a degree of sentimentality, are
first evoked through the image of Adonais as the 'nursling' of
Urania's 'widowhood', growing

> Like a pale flower by some sad maiden cherished,
> And fed with true love tears, instead of dew.
>
> (48–9)

Then the flower image develops into a sterner one of bud nipped
by frost – reminiscent of the frost that could not be thawed in
stanza I, which culminates in a tragic image of waste: 'The
broken lily lies – the storm is overpast' (54). Next, a personification of 'kingly Death' opens stanza VII, as the scene moves to
Adonais' grave in Rome, where

> He came; and bought, with price of purest breath,
> A grave among the eternal.
>
> (57–8)

'Eternal' in this context could be either a tribute to Adonais like
that which ends stanza I, or an ironic reference to the false
grandeur of Rome and Romans, anticipatory of that which is to
come in stanzas XLVIII–L, where Rome is 'at once the Paradise, /
The grave, the city, and the wilderness' (433–4). Change comes
again with the exhortation:

> Come away!
> Haste, while the vault of blue Italian day
> Is yet his fitting charnel-roof!
>
> (58–60)

The mood seems now to be one of serenity and elegiac beauty,
and leads the stanza to a conclusion of 'deep and liquid rest,
forgetful of all ill' (63). But the macabre hint conveyed by
'charnel-roof' – a slightly dissonant undertone in these lines –
becomes a garish theme of Gothic horror in stanza VIII:

> Within the twilight chamber spreads apace,
> The shadow of white Death, and at the door
> Invisible Corruption waits to trace
> His extreme way to her dim dwelling-place.
>
> (65–8)

This again, however, is softened by 'pity and awe'; and the whole sequence is brought to a close as the personified Hunger is temporarily held at bay

> till darkness and the law
> Of change, shall o'er his sleep the mortal curtain draw.
>
> (71–2)

Such flickering variations of tone can be successfully carried by Shelley's verse because of its imprecise and ductile quality; but they leave – and perhaps are meant to leave – a disturbing sense of attitudes unfocussed and unstable. One possibility is to see them as a secularised equivalent of the Christian emphasis on the instability of all things earthly, comparable to Henryson's 'Nocht is 3our fairnes bot ane faiding flour',[9] the purpose of which is to bring about renunciation of the world and concentration on heavenly things. Some support for this view can be derived from the structure of the poem. Until stanza XXXVIII the current of grief seems to turn round and round on itself, continually renewed by the repetitive formulae characteristic of lyric tragedy, and of pastoral elegy in particular ('I weep. . . . Oh, weep. . . . Most musical of mourners, weep again. . . weep anew. . . . Ah, woe is me. . . . Woe is me. . . . *He* will awake no more, oh, never more'). Stanza XXXVIII opens, however, with a renunciation of worldly grief:

> Nor let us weep that our delight is fled
> Far from these carrion kites that scream below
>
> (334–5)

and this radical change of stance is accompanied with a quotation from the Christian burial service:

> Dust to the dust! but the pure spirit shall flow
> Back to the burning fountain whence it came,

A portion of the Eternal, which must glow
Through time and change, unquenchably the same,
Whilst thy cold embers choke the sordid hearth of shame.

(338–42)

Then, with a conscious echo of Milton's 'For Lycidas your sorrow is not dead', Shelley declares:

Peace, peace! he is not dead, he doth not sleep –
He hath awakened from the dream of life –

(343–4)

and the rest of the poem is an extended version of Milton's lines on Lycidas in heaven – though in Shelley's case they are lines which repeat and elaborately re-present motifs from earlier stanzas within *Adonais* as they are seen to be transformed by the light of 'the Eternal'.

What this view underestimates, however, is the tragic sense of finality which, notwithstanding the fluctuation of attitude and sentiment, haunts the whole of the first part of the poem and is particularly strong in stanzas XVIII–XXI. Milton may well have provided the source for these lines as well – though not the Milton of *Lycidas*, but of a powerfully tragic moment in *Paradise Lost*, Book III when Milton laments his own blindness:

Thus with the Year
Seasons return, but not to me returns
Day, or the sweet approach of Ev'n or Morn.

(40–2)

Milton's sense of deprivation is acute: he is 'from the chearful waies of men / Cut off' (46–7) and the book of nature is for him 'expung'd and ras'd / And wisdome at one entrance quite shut out' (49–50). But, characteristically, this tragic moment is not allowed to stand on its own, uncorrected; Milton's faith compels him to find a counterbalance which is more than compensation:

So much the rather thou Celestial light
Shine inward, and the mind through all her powers
Irradiate, there plant eyes, all mist from thence

Purge and disperse, that I may see and tell
Of things invisible to mortal sight.

                                                    (III, 51–5)

Shelley also has an equivalence to this, but it is deferred to his
last ecstatic stanzas. His development at this stage of *Adonais* is
rather different. He begins, as Milton does, with the negative:

Ah woe is me! Winter is come and gone,
But grief returns with the revolving year.

                                                    (154–5)

But his expansion – one of the most intensely beautiful passages
in the poem, continuing through two stanzas – seems almost to
lose sight of the grief that is said to return as it elaborates the
'quickening life' of nature which is subject to constant renewal.
The energy of this passage, however, only serves to throw into
greater contrasting relief the extinction of such an imaginative
consciousness as that of Adonais, which makes it possible to be
aware of the living mutability of matter:

Nought we know dies. Shall that alone which knows
Be as a sword consumed before the sheath
By sightless lightning? – th'intense atom glows
A moment, then is quenched in a most cold repose.

                                                    (177–80)

This is a realisation of death that poses the most serious threat to
man's sense of meaning in life. The death of the shepherd–poet
whose 'flocks', as we have seen in stanza IX, are the 'quick
Dreams' of poetry itself, raises the spectre of an imaginative
death extinguishing all humane consciousness, including even
the grief that such horror arouses. By implication, what Shelley
has already written may lose its ardour and collapse into mean-
inglessness, all distinctions be levelled, and the very course of
time become a dreary, pointless sequence like that expressed in
Macbeth's 'Tomorrow and tomorrow and tomorrow':

Alas! that all we loved of him should be,
But for our grief, as if it had not been.

And grief itself be mortal! Woe is me!
Whence are we, and why are we? of what scene
The actors or spectators? Great and mean
Meet massed in death, who lends what life must borrow.
As long as skies are blue, and fields are green,
Evening must usher night, night urge the morrow,
Month follow month with woe, and year wake year to sorrow.
                                                    (181–9)

No answer to this crisis is immediately forthcoming. The finality of Adonais' death ('*He* will awake no more, oh, never more!', 190) only produces the intensified lamentation of Urania. But with the procession of mourner-poets and the indignation felt at the critic whose insensitivity is held responsible for Adonais' fate a different sense of life and death begins to develop, from which an answer is finally able to emerge. The notorious Shelleyan self-portrait of stanzas XXXI–XXXIV eleborates the poet as a figure of alienation in a hostile world, and leads on to the condemnation of Adonais' murderer in terms of a life which is not worth living:

Live thou, whose infamy is not thy fame!
Live! fear no heavier chastisement from me,
Thou noteless blot on a remembered name!
But be thyself, and know thyself to be!
                                                    (325–8)

Such 'life' is merely a travesty of the word. By emotional logic, therefore, it is unnecessary to weep for one who has 'fled / Far from these carrion kites that scream below' (334–5), and, calling his Platonism in aid, Shelley is able to define the life of the world and the critic as the dream from which Adonais has woken to the Real. The tables are turned, and the physical corruption previously associated with the body of Adonais is now associated with us and the phenomenal world that we inhabit: '*We* decay / Like corpses in a charnel' (348–9), while 'He has outsoared the shadow of our night' (352), and 'lives', and 'wakes', so that ' 'tis Death is dead, not he' (361).

From stanza XXXIX onwards there are frequent echoes of images and motifs developed in the earlier part of the poem, as Shelley seeks to transform the material associated with what is now seen as a life-in-death world into appropriate imaginative substance for expressing the essentially living world to which Adonais has been translated. In stanza XLI, for example, 'Turn all thy dew to splendour' (363) recalls the association of dew with tears in

> 'See, on the silken fringe of his faint eyes,
> 'Like dew upon a sleeping flower, there lies
> 'A tear some Dream has loosened from his brain'
>
> (85–7)

and the 'dew all turned to tears' of line 144; as well as the washing of Adonais' limbs 'from a lucid urn of starry dew' (91). And the last lines of the same stanza, urging the Air to withdraw its scarf of mist from the Earth and 'leave it bare / Even to the joyous stars which smile on its despair!' (368–9), reverse the pessimism of the conclusion to stanza III, where 'Death feeds on his mute voice, and laughs at our despair.' The reference to the stars likewise takes up the reiterated star theme of lines 91, 174–5 ('Like incarnations of the stars . . . they illumine death') and 222–3 (' "Leave me not wild and drear and comfortless, / "As silent lightning leaves the starless night!'), and leads in its turn to stanza XLVI, where Adonais becomes the Vesper of those who are 'inheritors of unfulfilled renown', and to the closing lines of the poem:

> Whilst burning through the inmost veil of Heaven,
> The soul of Adonais, like a star,
> Beacons from the abode where the Eternal are.
>
> (493–5)

In stanzas XLVIII–LI Shelley also takes up again the theme of Rome, which he had touched on in stanza VII in connection with the grave of Adonais, and develops from it a contrast between the mere wrecks of time and the resting place of Adonais which now represents a 'shelter' and a desirable goal which none should fear to reach. This is followed immediately by the great Platonic passage of stanza LII:

> The One remains, the many change and pass;
> Heaven's light forever shines, Earth's shadows fly;

Life, like a dome of many-coloured glass,
Stains the white radiance of Eternity,
Until Death tramples it to fragments. – Die,
If thou wouldst be with that which thou doest seek!
Follow where all is fled!

The purpose here is still to transform what has gone before – in this instance both the morbid death associations of Adonais' corpse in stanza VIII and the 'deaf and viperous murderer' who is the fatal critic in stanzas XXXVI–XXXVII. The urge to 'Die, / If thou wouldst be with that which thou doest seek!' is not a recommendation of suicide, but an act of imaginative identification – a dying into light which is a climbing of the Platonic ladder back from the delusive 'many' to the real 'One'. Finally, in stanza LIII the departure of Adonais, which is now a signal to Shelley's own heart to follow where his hopes have already gone, is seen as a light 'past from the revolving year' (472), recalling, and contrasting with, 'the revolving year' of stanza XVIII which brought new life to the natural world, but only grief to the poet.

All this is effective in helping to create the impression of the poem as an intricately interlinked verbal and thematic structure, in which the later apotheosis can be seen as an organic transmuting of material contained in the earlier stanzas. Nevertheless, the result is not, as it is in *Lycidas*, to make the transition from grief to joy seem convincingly part of a firm, integrated vision. In Shelley's favour it can be said that his elegy is more exploratory than Milton's, and his triumph less of a foregone conclusion. His vision is of a creative power, in which Adonais as poet shares, which struggles with recalcitrant matter to achieve beautiful form. All is emergent, not preordained:

He is a portion of the loveliness
Which once he made more lovely: he doth bear
His part, while the one Spirit's plastic stress
Sweeps through the dull dense world, compelling there
All new successions to the forms they wear;
Torturing th'unwilling dross that checks its flight
To it's own likeness, as each mass may bear;
And bursting in it's beauty and its might
From trees and beasts and men into the Heaven's light.

(379–87)

This, of course, is a loaded language, derogatory to the world and attributing dominant, compulsive power to 'the one Spirit', but its surging, forward movement suggests a free, apocalyptic energy rather than a disciplinary imposing of order. The goal, however, remains imprecise; the fulfilment towards which the poetry so breathlessly urges is impossible to grasp. Words lose their referential value, and interact with each other to create their own metaphorical meaning – which compels admiration for a magnificent *tour de force*, but leaves doubt and uncertainty to continue to breed as they do in the earlier stanzas.

In fact, uncertainty remains the key-note even of the final, ecstatic stanza:

> The breath whose might I have invoked in song
> Descends on me; my spirit's bark is driven,
> Far from the shore, far from the trembling throng
> Whose sails were never to the tempest given;
> The massy earth and sphered skies are riven!
> I am borne darkly, fearfully, afar;
> Whilst burning through the inmost veil of Heaven,
> The soul of Adonais, like a star,
> Beacons from the abode where the Eternal are.
>
> (487–95)

The goal is 'Heaven' and 'the Eternal', but whether these words invoke religious faith or affirm a specific philosophical commitment, though they clearly have Christian and Platonic overtones, it is impossible to say. Their prime function is to give emotional and imaginative stimulus. The real centre is the poet himself. He declares himself to be caught up in the process he has been creating, and, as in some tragic tempest, he is 'borne darkly, fearfully, afar', losing touch with all familiar landmarks. The transformation of Adonais which he himself has imagined, following literary precedent, but rejecting its conclusion, provides him with a kind of direction, and a kind courage. But it does not preside like Milton's Lycidas as 'the Genius of the shore', and there is no guarantee that it will 'be good / to all that wander in that perilous flood' (*Lycidas*, 183–4). The comfort Adonais offers is simply that of being a poet whose poetry splendidly endures, and can thus reassure Shelley about the value of the creative process. It is no longer the comfort of arriving at a secure harbour.

Shelley is outwardly certain, but the texture of his poetry reveals
him to be somewhat less sure of himself. Tennyson in writing his
elegiac poem, *In Memoriam*, on the death of Arthur Hallam, is
much more openly diffident. The poem is not, in fact, one poem,
but a series of variable lyrics, reflecting different attitudes and
moods. Tennyson remarked that 'the different moods of sorrow
as in a drama are dramatically given';[10] and within the work itself
definitiveness and completeness are renounced:

> If these brief lays, of Sorrow born,
>   Were taken to be such as closed
>   Grave doubts and answers here proposed,
> Then these were such as men might scorn:
>
> Her care is not to part and prove;
>   She takes, when harsher moods remit,
>   What slender shade of doubt may flit,
> And makes it vassal unto love:
>
> And hence, indeed, she sports with words,
>   But better serves a wholesome law,
>   And holds it sin and shame to draw
> The deepest measure from the chords:
>
> Nor dare she trust a larger lay,
>   But rather loosens from the lip
>   Short swallow-flights of song, that dip
> Their wings in tears, and skim away.
>   (Section 48)

To some extent this is attributable to modesty, for many sections
of *In Memoriam* do deal with 'Grave doubts', and do attempt 'to
part and prove'. Also, though it does move as a very tentative
sequence of impulsive lyric utterances ('Short swallow-flights of
song') rather than with the sustained progression of 'a larger
lay', it nevertheless develops its own implicit narrative line, and
its sections vary in length from as few as three four-lined stanzas
to as many as thirty-six, with a roughly corresponding variation
in range and comprehensiveness.

The truth is that in *In Memoriam* Tennyson far from denies

himself the breadth and seriousness of epic or tragic writer, and yet he devises a form which enables him to claim, as he does in Section 48, that he should not be judged by such intellectually rigorous standards, or by such criteria of wholeness and consistency, as we bring to the integrated long poem. His form combines firmness with uncertainty – or, as Alan Sinfield expresses it, the Augustan 'artifact' with the Romantic 'linnet'.[11] Compared with the great elegies which precede it – those by Milton and Shelley in particular – it is more private and personal; and yet it rapidly became, after its first publication in 1850, the most celebrated of Victorian poems, on the strength of qualities that were not misread into it, but belong to it by its own nature. It is both private and public: as Robert Pattison remarks, 'although *In Memoriam* is the chronicle of a personal grief, it is also a very public poem, and much of its power derives from a resonance between the poem's sincere, lyric plaints and its universal, bardic utterances'.[12] However, the relationship between these two elements is not simple. The individual poems were composed over an unusually long period of more than seventeen years, and Tennyson maintained that he did not write 'with any view of weaving them into a whole, or for publication, until I found that I had written so many'.[13] It would seem, though, that the printed sequence roughly follows the compositional sequence,[14] and on the strength of this it can be said that there is a general movement which begins with intensely personal and private grief for the death of Hallam, but gradually widens out to include more public concerns, with a corresponding change to 'philosophical' acceptance of death and religious consolation. To this extent the pattern of *In Memoriam* is that sanctioned by *Lycidas* and the Christianised pastoral elegy. But there is no sudden reversal. Although Tennyson mentions a dramatic quality, it is of a non-Aristotelian kind which follows, not a controlling plot-structure, but the seemingly random impulse of emotion.

To complicate matters, Tennyson's own attitude towards the balance he achieved in *In Memoriam* seems to have varied. Judging by the so-called 'Introductory stanzas', dated 1849, by the time he came to actual publication he doubted if the work was sufficiently disciplined. It might seem like a series of personal outpourings inappropriate to a supposed Christian, and he therefore prayed the 'Strong Son of God, immortal Love' to whom the stanzas are addressed:

> Forgive these wild and wandering cries,
>   Confusions of a wasted youth;
>   Forgive them where they fail in truth,
> And in thy wisdom make me wise.
>
> (41–4)

But in Section 1 (described by Shatto and Shaw as 'the genuine introductory poem')[15] he is apologetic without being so guilt-ridden. The poised tension here achieved is more representative of the work as a whole:

> I held it truth, with him who sings
>   To one clear harp in divers tones,
>   That men may rise on stepping-stones
> Of their dead selves to higher things.
>
> But who shall so forecast the years
>   And find in loss a gain to match?
>   Or reach a hand thro' time to catch
> The far-off interest of tears?
>
> Let Love clasp Grief lest both be drown'd,
>   Let darkness keep her raven gloss:
>   Ah, sweeter to be drunk with loss,
> To dance with death, to beat the ground,
>
> Than that the victor Hours should scorn
>   The long result of love, and boast,
>   'Behold the man that loved and lost,
> But all he was is overworn.'

This is subtly compounded of contradiction. The firm beginning, 'I held it truth', leads the first stanza to a mounting climax ('men may rise . . . to higher things'), with a retardation on 'dead selves' serving as a spring to the concluding phrase; but the interruption provided by the allusion to Goethe ('with him who sings / To one clear harp in divers tones') suggests a unified truth which has a more complex relation to variety. As one moves to the second stanza this complexity is increased by the change of tense in the two questions. 'But who *shall*' makes one retrospectively aware of the past tense in the first line, and so of the possibility that what was held to be 'truth' then may not be so in the future. The antithesis in the first stanza between 'dead selves' and 'higher things' is also echoed in that between 'loss' and 'gain' in line 6, but in a way that throws doubt on the rising movement; and this is further undermined by the uncertainty of investment in the future conveyed in lines 7–8, and the slightly absurd effect created by the image of catching tears. The seemingly confident opening thus disturbed, the third stanza moves into the contrary affirmation of an emotional conservatism rather than progress. Love is urged to cling to Grief, not advance beyond it, as a means of keeping both alive; darkness is urged to retain its paradoxically glowing blackness; and the stanza mounts to a very different climax from that of the first as a violent grief wantonly casting aside all control is evoked through the images of drunkenness, dancing and frantic beating on the ground. However, the run-on from the third to the fourth stanza gives this climax, too, an altered effect. The implication of the comparative 'sweet*er*' is brought out by the clauses following 'Than', with the result that the seemingly drunken abandonment of lines 11–12 emerges, not as an absolute in itself, but only as something to be preferred to the scornful triumph of 'the victor Hours' boasting of their power to wear away feeling and leave the barrenness of emotional exhaustion. The total effect, therefore, is that the initial assertion of belief in man's capacity to profit from his misfortunes is not rejected outright, but one is compelled to recognise the psychological necesssity of grief and the humanising force even in what seems wild and irrational.

Accordingly, grief is given its head in *In Memoriam*, but within the loose overall constellation of lyrics of which the work consists. As might be expected, the most passionate distress occurs in the earlier-numbered sections – 2, 7, 11 and 16, for example. It is possible to isolate these from the rest, and read them as poignant moments of pain. In particular, Section 11, with its parallelism and repetition of 'Calm', mounting to the sudden cancelling of all soothing effect in the last two lines ('And dead calm in that noble breast'), seems to create a self-enclosing rhetoric of its own; and the dramatic vignette of Section 7 – which presents the 'I' of the poem haunting the street where the house of his dead friend stands – culminates in a resonant bleakness which seems to have tragic finality:

And ghastly thro' the drizzling rain
On the bald street breaks the blank day.

In such poems Tennyson's auditory powers – his sense of
rhythm, delicate use of sound effects, and memorable control of
cadence – are at their height. He is said to have read his poetry
aloud in an incantatory manner, and it is easy to imagine these
sections of *In Memoriam* being almost sung to their passionately
musical conclusions.[16] Love clasps Grief, and neither is drowned. Like
Keats, Tennyson keeps alert to 'the wakeful anguish of the soul'.

But to read these poems in isolation would be to ignore the
wider perspective which is also implicit in Section 1, and which
Tennyson takes some care to maintain by establishing links with
the surrounding poems. The calm of Section 11, for example,
reaches out to 'the bounding main' in its third stanza, becomes
'Calm on the seas' in the first line of the last stanza, and
contrasts in the final lines, as already noted, with the 'dead calm'
of Hallam's sea-borne corpse 'Which heaves but with the heav-
ing deep'. It is thus kept in relationship to the group of poems
dealing with the return of the body by ship and the ambiguous
comfort (expressed, as it happens, in one of the first of the *In
Memoriam* sections to be written, no. 18) to be derived from its
being laid to rest 'in English earth'. It also has a relationship
with Section 15, but one which is based on contrast: the reiterated calm of 11 is something spread throughout Tennyson's
native Lincolnshire Wolds, and, though the time is autumn, 'the
faded leaf' and 'chestnut pattering to the ground' and 'leaves
that redden to the fall' are all a harmonious part of it. In 15 this
changes to a stormy, wind-swept scene of late autumn on the
verge of winter, with tragically destructive overtones – 'The last
red leaf is whirl'd away', the trees of the forest are 'crack'd', and
all reaches its climax, as Sinfield has shown, in an image of
sunset symbolic of the poet's grief-stricken feelings.[17]

In Section 16 both Sections 11 and 15 recalled. The 'calm
despair' of Section 11, line 16 and the 'wild unrest' of Section 15,
line 15 are caught up together in the opening stanza of Section
16 in questions that may be regarded either purely rhetorical or
as giving expression to genuine uncertainty:

What words are these have fall'n from me?
Can calm despair and wild unrest

> Be tenants of a single breast,
> Or sorrow such a changeling be?

Other questions follow – the entire section consists of unan-
swered questions – which suggest the alternative possibilities
that these are but surface images disturbing the 'deep self' of
sorrow no more than reflections in 'some dead lake', or that the
shock of Hallam's death has confused the poet like a wrecked
ship that 'staggers blindly ere she sink' and made him

> that delirious man
> Whose fancy fuses old and new,
> And flashes into false and true,
> And mingles all without a plan?

By such means the isolated moments of Sections 11 and 15
become aspects of a troubled self poised in uncertainty as to the
permament truth of suffering, and yet intensely reverberant, for
the time being, with the feeling of desolation and loss.

Doubt becomes for Tennyson a vital element in the preserva-
tion of integrity, without which the wider consolation that the
work as a whole seeks to attain would be worthless. In Section 96
he finds this quality of doubt in Hallam, and it increases, not
diminishes, his respect for his dead friend. The music of Hallam's
thought was discordant, Tennyson says, but he 'ever strove to
make it true', and 'At last he beat his music out' – which leads to
the paradoxical lesson that

> There lives more faith in honest doubt,
> Believe me, than in half the creeds.

It is intellectual difficulty in accepting Christian dogma that is
here specially referred to, and the facing of such doubts becomes
an important part of the inwoven texture of *In Memoriam*. But,
interesting as these doubts are in the context of Tennyson's own
life, and in the history of Victorian intellectual life generally, it is
the urgency of personal grief, notwithstanding conventional
teachings, which constitutes the kind of 'doubt' most relevant to
the poetic structure of the work. Its emotional integrity depends
on its willingness to resist the pressures towards conformity
embodied, for example, even in the well-disposed friend who

writes, in Section 6, that 'Other friends remain' and 'Loss is common to the race'. That Tennyson almost certainly has in mind the similar advice given to Hamlet by his mother (*Hamlet*, I.ii.68–73) is suggested by the parallel play on the word 'common':

> And common is the commonplace,
> And vacant chaff well meant for grain.
>
> That loss is common would not make
> My own less bitter, rather more:
> Too common!

He extends the implications in a different way, however, from Hamlet by suggesting in a series of ballad-like instances of dramatic irony how the experience of joy and expectation being converted into a sense of loss and barrenness is something universal, but not therefore less real. He runs close to sentimentality in the individual stories, but he is saved by the strength of his wider purpose, which is to stress that such recognition of the 'common' ought not to devalue grief, but rouse even greater horror at the thought that human life recurrently exemplifies the same suffering. The implication is that the right way to respond to Hallam's death is not to blunt the feelings which it arouses, but to feel it more keenly, till the keenness reveals the nature of the human lot.

Against this, however, might be set the assertion in the longer, more meditative Section 85 that 'I count it crime / To mourn for any overmuch'. This is perhaps the Victorian voice of Tennyson speaking. He does have such a voice; and, indeed, it is essential to the successful balancing of 'voices' in *In Memoriam* that platitude, and the rejection of platitude, should both be internalised within the poet, for otherwise it might become a poem of protest rather than a series of elegies. Nevertheless, taken in its context, 'I count it crime' can be seen as only provisional endorsement of conventional wisdom, complementary to, rather than inconsistent with, the theme of 'Let Love clasp Grief'. These words are addressed to another friend, who is seen as a possible candidate for the place that Hallam once held in the poet's affections. They are preceded by 'I woo your love' – a simple and direct statement of positive feeling, and they form part of the gradual process by which in the latter sections of the work the exclusive intensity of grief in the earlier sections is modulated into an acceptance that life goes on, and that society still has its legitimate demands from the griever. But it is made equally plain that the new friendship can never be a complete substitute for the old; and that the old is not decayed, but – with a shift to the present tense which is increased in emphasis by the syntactic crossing of the stanzaic gap – was such

> A friendship as had master'd Time;
>
> Which masters Time indeed, and is
> Eternal.

The seasonal theme, running throughout *In Memoriam*, is caught up in this, too, as the poet insists that the 'victor Hours' resisted in Section 1 are still as ineffectual here:

> The all-assuming months and years
> Can take no part away from this:
>
> But Summer on the steaming floods,
>   And Spring that swells the narrow brooks,
>   And Autumn, with a noise of rooks,
> That gather in the waning woods,
>
> And every pulse of wind and wave
>   Recalls, in change of light or gloom,
>   My old affection of the tomb,
> And my prime passion in the grave.

In a fiction that is again somewhat sentimentally Victorian, but not debilitating, Tennyson imagines the dead Hallam watching him 'from the quiet shore', and urging him to find a new friend. This is a way of reconciling persistent devotion to Hallam with the conventional demand that he must wean himself from grief; but by the acknowledgement that this *is* fiction:

> So hold I commerce with the dead;
>   Or so methinks the dead would say;
>   Or so shall grief with symbols play
> And pining life be fancy-fed

we are led back to the authenticity of a feeling that cannot so easily be appeased. Compromise is reached, new friendship is offered; but on the understanding that it cannot have the wholeness of what was offered in youth to Hallam. It will be an 'imperfect gift', which is to be seen – in a further variation on seasonal change – as an autumnal primrose, 'The primrose of the later year', which does not participate in the full regeneration of spring, but is valued, nevertheless, 'As not unlike to that of Spring'.

In his discussion of *In Memoriam* A. Dwight Culler considers why Tennyson, though in the elegiac tradition, declines to use the form of the pastoral elegy, and concludes that it is because his poetry is 'gradualist rather than catastrophic'.[18] The cautious double negative ('not unlike') with which Section 85 ends is in accordance with this gradualist view, as is the second friendship, sincerely offered, but also frankly allotted a place inferior to the first. Even the Epilogue, which is probably addressed to the same person as Section 85 (he is now, in fact, cementing the bond of friendship through marriage to the poet's sister),[19] can be seen as modifying the ecstasy and optimism expected of epithalamia by presenting this spring of human love as the generation of some distant rather than immediate fruitfulness – setting it in a context in which not only the present actions of the participants, but their whole lives are looked back upon from some future vantage point, and seen as 'seed' of some ultimate 'flower and fruit' to come. Thus, if a pastoral elegy reversal is implicit, it is thrown forward into a distant future, and associated, in the very last words of *In Memoriam*, with that

> one far-off divine event,
> To which the whole creation moves.

However, vestigial elements of the pastoral elegy do remain in *In Memoriam*, and they are of two kinds: (1) the 'low' pastoral, which is a retreat for humility; and (2) the 'high', which looks back to a Golden Age in comparison with which ours is a fallen world. Section 21 illustrates the first. There the 'I' of the poem is a shepherd piping on a rustic, home-made instrument, which is symbolically made from the grasses growing on Hallam's grave. He is rebuked by unsympathetic voices that tell him he makes 'weakness weak', or that 'He loves to make parade of pain', or question whether a time of social upheaval and scientific change is suitable for 'private sorrow's barren song' – to which the 'I' replies:

> Behold, ye speak an idle thing:
> Ye never knew the sacred dust:
> I do but sing because I must,
> And pipe but as the linnets sing.

His activity is on a continuum with that of Nature, and, as befits his grassy pipe, it blends with the peculiarly lyrical evocations of landscape, weather, trees and birds which most strongly express his 'private sorrow', but also by their very intensity and beauty tacitly refute the charge of barrenness. Grief has a kind of life which is not cultivated for ulterior motives: 'I do but sing because I must'; though the accusation of making 'parade' is perhaps articulated to ward off the recollection that some pastoral elegies are, indeed, more demonstrations of their authors' skill than expressions of genuine pain. In satisfying this personal need, however, the 'I' of 'low' pastoral also manages to give private sorrow a natural justification and to suggest that it satisfies a natural human need. It blends with the life of Nature, and gives almost literal accuracy to the poet's claim that:

> I take the grasses of the grave,
> And make them pipes whereon to blow.

The poet also sings to 'him that rests below' – Arthur Hallam, also characterised as 'the sacred dust'. Within the 'low' pastoral of Section 21 these phrases are no doubt simply to be read as expressions of the intensity of the poet's feeling for his lost friend; but their idealising tendency also provides a link with the 'high' pastoral as it appears, for example, in Section 23. There the mutually vitalising quality of this friendship is expressed in a language of personification which creates 'lands where not a leaf was dumb', 'lavish hills' that 'would hum / The murmur of a happy Pan', and Thought that

> leapt out to wed with Thought
> Ere Thought could wed itself with Speech.

And it culminates in an idealised vision of youthful enthusiasm, debate and poetry which has the aura of an Arcadian Golden Age:

> And all we met was fair and good,
> And all was good that Time could bring,
> And all the secret of the Spring
> Moved in the chambers of the blood;
>
> And many an old philosophy
> On Argive heights divinely sang,
> And round us all the thickets rang
> To many a flute of Arcady.

The next section, no. 24, modifies this. It shows Tennyson aware of the possibility of exaggeration:

> And was the day of my delight
> As pure and perfect as I say?

and in another series of speculative questions he asks himself whether his tendency to idealise the past is due to 'the haze of grief' or man's inveterate habit of seeing things at a distance in rosier terms than when they were present. That he can ask such questions – even though he leaves them without a definitive answer – provides some sort of guarantee that he is not deluded by grief into accepting a fantasy version of the past; or, at least, that he is conscious how his Golden Age might be regarded by more detached observers. By allowing such reasonable doubt, however, his idealisation is released from merely biographical significance, and given a wider poetic meaning. Hallam, and the youthful friendship Tennyson enjoyed, or imagines himself as having enjoyed, with him, comes to represent a human potentiality which is tragically frustrated by the cutting short of his young life, much as King poetically transmuted into Lycidas, and Keats into Adonais, had represented lost possibilities of fulfilment for Milton and Shelley respectively. The similarity is there, but the process with Tennyson is much more tentative – much more punctuated with relapses into doubt and simple, seemingly inconsolable grief; and much more prolonged. The fluctuations and sheer length of *In Memoriam* place a realistic distance between the Golden Age and the idealised figure whose portrait, with sound judgement on Tennyson's part, is delayed until the closing sections of the work. That judgement may be less than completely reliable in some of the details of Sections 109 and 113 (the exalted domesticity of 109, for example, and the 'potent voice of Parliament' imagined for Hallam in 113 suggest the inflated virtues of obituary), and Tennyson is not at his best, to twentieth-century taste, in either the generalised optimism of Section 118, or the hymn-singing accents of 126. But, despite such flaws, the conversion of Hallam in these final sections into the complete man, who is also (with a slight reminiscence of Lycidas as 'Genius of the shore') reassuring guardian of an ultimately benign future, is acceptable, because it is seen as the end of a slow, uncertain process; and because, even in its most emphatic assertions, it still retains something of the poignancy of recognised wish-fulfilment:

> Dear friend, far off, my lost desire,
>   So far, so near in woe and weal;
>   O loved the most, when most I feel
> There is a lower and a higher;
>
> Known and unknown; human, divine;
>   Sweet human hand and lips and eye;
>   Dear heavenly friend that canst not die,
> Mine, mine, for ever, ever mine;
>
> Strange friend, past, present, and to be;
>   Loved deeplier, darklier understood;
>   Behold, I dream a dream of good,
> And mingle all the world with thee.
>
> (Section 129)

The language here is the language of Victorian devotional literature; Hallam is almost an intermediary between God and man. But what are we to make of this markedly religious element in *In Memoriam*? In what is probably the most quoted of all essays on the work, T. S. Eliot makes two related, but not quite identical, comments on its religious quality. Noting that Tennyson's contemporaries seemed to have regarded it 'as a message of

hope and reassurance to their rather fading Christian faith',
Eliot remarks, 'Nevertheless, I get a very different impression
from *In Memoriam* from that which Tennyson's contemporaries
seem to have got. It is of a very much more interesting and tragic
Tennyson.' The second comment is to the effect that *In Memoriam* can 'justly be called a religious poem', but that 'It is not
religious because of the quality of its faith, but because of the
quality of its doubt.'[20] In so far as these comments suggest that
the poetry is better when expressing grief for the death of
Hallam, and an accompanying uncertainty about divine providence, than when it is voicing the kind of consolation expected
by Victorian readers, they are probably true. The nearer *In
Memoriam* approaches to a tragic vision, the greater is its intensity. But to call it a religious poem on the strength of the quality
of its doubt, and specifically not on the quality of its faith, is to
muddy the meaning of 'religious' too much. The other remark
that it reveals a more 'tragic' Tennyson makes better sense. The
religious side of the poem corresponds to that poignant attempt
to reconcile grief with a justification of the ways of God to men
which links the Golden Age dream of youthful friendship with
Hallam to the Hallam who later emerges as a type of ideal man,
prefiguring an ultimate condition when the 'I' of the poem will
see – though now he only sees 'in part' –

> That all, as in some piece of art,
> Is toil cöoperant to an end.
>   (Section 128: 234)

The essential strength of the poem, however, is to be located in
the tension which exists between its tragic and religious elements. The tradition of Christian pastoral elegy calls for the
tragic to be resolved by the religious; and Tennyson makes one
feel his own longing for this, as well as the pressures exerted on
him by the Victorian world he inhabits to contrive such a happy
ending. But the integrity of his feeling refuses to be violated.
What results, therefore, is a series of lyric cries and rhetorical
gestures kept in tentative relationship to each other, and with the
slowly healing process of time as the means by which it is
envisaged that the religious will eventually supersede the tragic.
    Unlike *Lycidas*, however, *In Memoriam* never quite brings the 'I'
of the poem to the point where he can say: 'Weep no more.' In

Section 130 he addresses Hallam in a fashion that comes very close to this:

> Far off thou art, but ever nigh;
> I have thee still, and I rejoice;
> I prosper, circled with thy voice;
> I shall not lose thee tho' I die.

But the accents are still those of a lover longing to persuade himself that it is possible to speak in this way to the dead loved one. Their certainty is mixed with uncertainty; they belong with the 'truths' of the next, and final, Section, no. 131,

> that never can be proved
> Until we close with all we loved,
> And all we flow from, soul in soul.

The vagueness of such a formulation allows both doubt and affirmation equal value.

Both 'The Scholar-Gipsy' and 'Thyrsis' are elegiac poems in the sense that they are suffused with a melancholy regret for a time, as Tennyson expresses it, when 'all we met was fair and good'; but 'Thyrsis' is more specifically an elegy for the death of Arnold's friend, Arthur Hugh Clough. Like *Lycidas* and *Adonais*, rather than *In Memoriam*, it is not a closely personal poem. Arnold himself thought that not enough was said in it to warrant his sending it to Clough's widow – though he may also have felt some embarrassment with regard to the criticism of his friend which it implies.[21] What the poem mainly laments is the youthful world, particularly associated with their wanderings in the Cumnor Hills, which he and Clough shared during their undergraduate days at Oxford. It is in this respect that it is closely allied with 'The Scholar-Gipsy'. Both poems lament the disappearance of what Wordsworth calls 'the visionary gleam', though both also retain, through the shared symbol of the scholar who deserts Oxford, the vestiges of an 'unconquerable hope' – a phrase from 'The Scholar-Gipsy' (211), but reminiscent of Milton's 'unconquerable Will' (*Paradise Lost*, I.106) – which is able to feed the present with consolation as well as regret. For Arnold, even more than for Shelley, the Christian counterpoise to tragedy is invalid, but the drive towards compensation so firmly embedded in the pastoral elegy makes him cling to a belief in some vital link which still connects the present with the past; or, at least, to a belief in the imagination's power, through idealisation of the past, to relieve the barren consciousness of the present. A separation between present and past is undeniable, and with it comes a sense of tragically disabling loss; but its impact is softened by nostalgia and sentiment, muting the tragic feeling to tenderness, and allowing hope to be sustained.

The passage in Glanvill's *The Vanity of Dogmatizing* which gave Arnold the hint for his scholar-gipsy relates how the fugitive was spotted by two former friends, who hear from him

> that the people he went with were not such impostors as they were taken for, but that they had a traditional kind of learning among them, and could do wonders by the power of imagination, their fancy binding that of others: that himself had learned much of their art, and when he had compassed the whose secret, he intended, he said, to leave their company, and give the world an account of what he had learned.[22]

Since Arnold is known to have toyed with such titles as 'The first mesmerist' and 'the wandering Mesmerist',[23] this 'secret' may well have been hypnotism; but in 'The Scholar-Gipsy', although the passage is fairly faithfully reproduced at lines 41–50, the secret acquires a more inspirational character: 'But it needs heaven-sent moments for this skill' (50). Its precise intellectual meaning is obscured, and its imaginative quality allowed to flourish as an elusive aura surrounding the figure of the scholar-gipsy himself. He becomes the emanation of an idyllic landscape, symbolic of the tender, relaxed, but potentially creative, moments of life. He has left Oxford, and he also avoids all forms of noisy human contact. It is in a characteristically quiet, sheltered, lonely situation that the 'I' of the poem thinks of him:

> Or in my boat I lie
> Moored to the cool bank in the summer-heats,
> 'Mid wide grass meadows which the sunshine fills,
> And watch the warm, green-muffled Cumner hills,
> And wonder if thou haunt'st their shy retreats.
>
> (66–70)

'Shy' indicates both the secluded quality of the scenes the scholar-gipsy haunts and the character of the scholar himself. He favours retreat ('For most, I know, thou lov'st retiréd ground!', 71) and is associated with flowers, streams and mysterious darkness; his typical situation is to be lying back in a punt, trailing his fingers in the water, with flowers in his lap which have been gathered (the word 'shy' is repeated) 'in shy fields and distant Wychwood bowers' (75–9). He belongs to the past, having died long ago and been buried, again typically, 'in some quiet churchyard',

> where o'er thy unknown grave
> Tall grasses and white flowering nettles wave,
> Under a dark, red-fruited yew-tree's shade,
> (138–40)

but he still appears, fitfully, on the edge of society, glimpsed for a moment, and then vanishing – a romantic figure, with 'dark vague eyes, and soft-abstracted air' (98–9). He has thus already achieved his own peculiar version of the immortality which Milton's Lycidas and Shelley's Adonais do not achieve (or are not seen as achieving) until the end of their respective poems. It is a quite different kind of immortality, however, more akin to that of Keats's nightingale; its essential quality is not suffering transformed, but immunity from suffering:

> – No, no, thou hast not felt the lapse of hours!
> For what wears out the life of mortal men?
> 'Tis that from change to change their being rolls;
> 'Tis that repeated shocks, again, again,
> Exhaust the energy of strongest souls
> And numb the elastic powers.
> (141–6)

He belongs with the pastoral Golden Age:

> O born in days when wits were fresh and clear,
> And life ran gaily as the sparkling Thames;
> (201–2)

and he has a healthy single-mindedness which contrasts sharply with 'this strange disease of modern life, / With its sick hurry, its

divided aims' (203–4). Moreover, the poet encourages this elus-
iveness, as closer contact with the modern world would only
infect him with its fever. The 'shy' source of life which the
scholar-gipsy represents must be kept inviolate.

The vision embodied in the scholar-gipsy might thus seem to
be an escapist one. He is urged repeatedly to 'fly' life as we know
it, and plunge more deeply 'in the bowering wood' (207). But it
would be inaccurate to term the poem itself 'escapist'. Its focus is
on the contrast between the scholar-gipsy's visionary world and
the condition which he is urged to fly. The climactic moments
are those, expressed in distancing, but also moving, images from
classical literature, in which the visionary encounters the modern – with a pang of recognition which is attributed to the
visionary's representative, but which also seems to waken a
momentary tragic consciousness in the poet himself.

The first of these images is that of the betrayed Dido of
Vergil's *Aeneid*, Book VI, turning away from Aeneas in Hades:

> Still fly, plunge deeper in the bowering wood!
>   Averse, as Dido did with gesture stern
>   From her false friend's approach in Hades turn,
> Wave us away, and keep thy solitude!
>
> (*S-G*, 207–10)

The Vergilian passage which this echoes (VI. 469–73) has what
may seem an incongruous severity. Dido is rock-like in her
implacability. The scholar-gipsy is merely urged to wave us
away and keep his solitude; and in the next stanza the impetus of
the syntax is maintained with a positive force which turns
defensive retreat into a kind of creative renewal:

> Still nursing the unconquerable hope,
>   Still clutching the inviolable shade,
>   With a free, onward impulse brushing through,
>   By night, the silvered branches of the glade –
>   Far on the forest-skirts, where none pursue,
>   On some mild pastoral slope
>   Emerge, and resting on the moonlit pales
>   Freshen thy flowers as in former years
>   With dew, or listen with enchanted ears,
> From the dark dingles, to the nightingales!
>
> (211–20)

The stanza becomes increasingly ecstatic, but also voluptuous, as it progresses, and the strong placing of 'Emerge' and 'Freshen' at the beginning of lines 217 and 218 almost erase the memory of Dido's hostility; but the intensely Keatsian final line topples the ecstacy over into a melancholy which allows the under-lying anguish to be felt, and leads, in the following stanza, to renewed awareness of the 'strong infection of our mental strife' (222) and a still more Keatsian fear that in contact with us the scholar-gipsy's

> glad perennial youth would fade,
> Fade, and grow old at last, and die like ours.
> (229–30)

The second, and much more extended image, stretching over two stanzas, is that of the Tyrian trader, the source of which is Herodotus.[24] This, too, is ambivalent in that 'the merry Grecian coaster' freighted with its 'amber grapes, and Chian wine, / Green, bursting figs, and tunnies steeped in brine' (238–9), and the Greeks who sail in her – 'The young light-hearted masters of the waves' (241) – scarcely seem equivalents for the modern world of 'sick hurry' and 'divided aims'; and yet the indignant reaction of the 'grave Tyrian trader' is offered, in the formal analogy of the long-tailed simile, as a parallel to the reaction urged on the scholar-gipsy in the face of the modern world. On the other hand, 'the dark Iberians' towards whom he sails, in order to open up a new, more honest commerce, are certainly to be seen in the same romantically idealised terms as the scholar-gipsy and his associated scenes of pastoral seclusion. They are 'Shy traffickers' (249), recalling the 'shy retreats' and 'shy fields' earlier in the poem, and the remote region which they inhabit, on the fringe of the then known world, corresponds to the 'retiréd ground' loved by the scholar-gipsy.

That the simile partly fits and partly does not may perhaps be explained if it is seen in a more historical perspective. The Greeks parallel our world only in the sense that they represent a new dispensation, replacing an older one which is ill-fitted to resist, but has a stronger hold on the imagination and is nostalgi-cally regretted. The new men are associated with sunrise and 'an emerging prow' (233), and they carry a wealth of new goods, but their methods are stealthy and their confidence that of 'intrud-ers'. The older Tyrian instinctively recognises a kind of cunning superiority which he is ill-equipped to combat, and which he will not stoop to try, and so indignantly seeks for new markets. Yet even on this interpretation the simile includes elements, especially towards its close – which is also the climax and close of the poem – which are suggestively different from the manner in which the scholar-gipsy's relation to the modern world has previously been presented. The Tyrian heads, not to a haven such as 'the bowering wood', but towards a region of storm: 'To where the Atlantic raves / Outside the western straits' (246–7); and the Iberians, though 'shy', come 'down cloudy cliffs, through sheets of foam' (248). The final line, 'And on the beach undid his corded bales', hints at the beginning of a new trade, 'without the least instance of dishonesty on either side' perhaps,[25] but, if so, it is trade sought out by the Tyrian with effort and risk. It is his 'indignant' answer to despicable rivals.

As with the Dido simile, there is a hint of tragic feeling in the Tyrian trader's response to the 'young light-hearted' Greeks. They represent something apparently attractive and successful in which, however, he foresees a tragic end; and it may well be that Arnold wishes us to see them as the beginning of a new era, of which the modern world is the final outcome – with the tragic comment which that also implies. But we cannot be sure. The poetry hovers between different possible meanings and different moods, as it does throughout the poem. The inclemency of the modern world is deeply felt – the more so by contrast with the idealised youthful freshness of the scholar-gipsy; but Arnold's response seems to hesitate between the finality of tragedy and a regretful melancholy which tinges its sadness with the hope that retreat may be the source of new life.

In 'Thyrsis' there is again an incipient tragic awareness, but the wish to find consolation and hope also intervenes once more to prevent a full acceptance of the tragic implications. Its opening is on a sadder, more prosaic, note than that of 'The Scholar-Gipsy': 'How changed is here each spot man makes or fills!' Although the earlier poem juxtaposes a seventeenth-century fancy with modern reality, the sense of time bringing change and destruction is stronger in 'Thyrsis'. The countryside celebrated in 'The Scholar-Gipsy' is also that of 'Thyrsis' (though now Oxford itself also shares in the timelessness of idealised youth); but the pleasure it once gave to Arnold and Clough jointly has been undermined by time and the death of the latter, and

perhaps more insidiously – though this is only delicately hinted –
by changes in Arnold's friendship with Clough which occurred
even before his death. Arnold's involvement with the world
increasingly separates him from the joys of Oxford and Cumnor,
but Thyrsis/Clough 'of his own will went away' (40).[26] He
allowed himself to be seduced by what seems to be presented as
unnecessarily gloomy views:

> Some life of men unblest
> He knew, which made him droop, and filled his head.
> He went; his piping took a troubled sound
> Of storms that rage outside our happy ground;
> He could not wait their passing, he is dead.
>
> (*Th*, 46–50)

But the sense that Arnold's own departure was inevitable, while
Thyrsis' was not, is curiously at odds with the tone in which
Thyrsis' crisis is expressed. The image of storms raging 'outside
our happy ground' which Thyrsis could not simply wait and
allow to pass, and the suggestion that he was too deeply troubled
by knowledge of 'Some life of men unblest' to be content with
their pastoral retreat, makes Thyrsis sound much more like
Keats's tragic visionary 'to whom the miseries of the world / Are
misery, and will not let them rest'.[27] By comparison Arnold's regret
that 'My pipe is lost, my shepherd's holiday!' (37) seems trivial.

But, of course, 'Thyrsis' is not biography. It does not, as far as
the poetry is concerned, greatly matter whether Arnold is being
fair to Clough. What matters is that he imagines such restless-
ness, and tries to contain it within his pastoral structure. It
represents a discord in his own mind, which is a problem for him
to cope with in this poem; and the way he goes on to do so hints
that he is less easily able to dismiss it than the stanza on Thyrsis'
departure suggests. Once again simile, as in 'The Scholar-
Gipsy', reveals much. The stanza on Thyrsis' departure is
immediately followed by the formal 'So, some tempestuous morn
in early June', and the image of the cuckoo calling in the
untimely storm, along with 'the volleying rain and tossing breeze',
that '*The bloom is gone, and with the bloom go I!*' (51–60). The call is
meant to be understood as a false alarm; the cuckoo, like
Thyrsis, has been unnecessarily scared, and is rebuked for being
a 'Too quick despairer' (61). Nevertheless, the despair is suspiciously

like the poet's own. The deeper note of storm is not easily
dismissed as an illusion. Even though the cuckoo will return,
Thyrsis will not; and the hopes of recovery sanctioned by the
pastoral tradition are now no longer valid:

> Alack, for Corydon no rival now!
>   But when Sicilian shepherds lost a mate,
>   Some good survivor with his flute would go,
>   Piping a ditty sad for Bion's fate;
>   And cross the unpermitted ferry's flow,
>   And relax Pluto's brow,
>   And make leap up with joy the beauteous head
>   Of Proserpine, among whose crownéd hair
>   Are flowers first opened on Sicilian air,
>   And flute his friend, like Orpheus, from the dead.
>   (81–90)

This is a deeply attractive, but, in the modern world, unbeliev-
able, myth. There is no redemption of this kind possible. Proser-
pine has never heard 'of our poor Thames' (98), and therefore,
'Well! wind-dispersed and vain the words will be' (101). The
classical pastoral is only a charming illusion, and, for Arnold,
there is no alternative such as the Miltonic power of faith, or
even the Shelleyan power of imagination. The sudden storm-like
catastrophe may be a false alarm, but it has radically disturbed
the pastoral calm of the mind. It serves as an introduction to an
insidious force which works perhaps more slowly, but, in the
end, more devastatingly, by sapping the recuperative power of
consciousness:

> Yes, thou art gone! and round me too the night
>   In ever-nearing circle weaves her shade.
>   I see her veil draw soft across the day,
>   I feel her slowly chilling breath invade
>   The cheek grown thin, the brown hair sprent with grey;
>   I feel her finger light
>   Laid pausefully upon life's headlong train;
>   The foot less prompt to meet the morning dew,
>   The heart less bounding at emotion new,
>   And hope, once crushed, less quick to spring again.
>   (131–40)

Here Arnold breaks through to the tragic recognition of the human condition which Keats encounters in the Odes. Though not the most richly 'poetic' of the stanzas, it is the most deeply moving. It recalls the prosaic opening, and seems at last to be the realisation of the saddening truth which has lain dormant in the poem since then (but which, perhaps, Thyrsis/Clough had known, despite the pretence that this was false knowledge). Arnold is still left, however, with his own personal myth of the scholar-gipsy. This, too, takes one back to the opening stanzas, and, in particular, to the 'single elm-tree bright / Against the west' which Thyrsis and the poet prized dearly, and which, while it stood, signified to them that 'Our friend, the Gipsy-Scholar, was not dead' (26–30). After the failure of the pastoral redemptive theme it reappears in the poem as 'the tree-topped hill' and 'the Fyfield tree' which keep the poet's questing power alive (102–10); and in his feeling of defeat by the sapping disillusionment of time he is suddenly reminded of it again when the troop of hunters causes him to fly into a farther field, much as the scholar-gipsy had done. The old ties of association revive. The tree is the principle of continuity expressed in the questing spirit, handed on from scholar-gipsy to Thyrsis and the poet, which, although Thyrsis is now dead, the poet, with the aid of Thyrsis' memory, is still able to renew; and it is with the affirmation of this continuity, in the form of the dead friend's whispering to the poet, that 'Thyrsis' ends:

> Why faintest thou? I wandered till I died.
> Roam on! The light we sought is shining still.
> Dost thou ask proof? Our tree yet crowns the hill,
> Our Scholar travels yet the loved hill-side.

The previous development given to the symbol of the elm, and its link with the earlier poem, 'The Scholar-Gipsy', combine to give this ending a certain rhetorical persuasiveness. But, on reflection, it seems to be rather too much of a conscientiously constructed device, like the symbol of the river in George Eliot's *The Mill on the Floss*, intended to bring about a comforting conclusion that replaces adult division by the harmony of child-hood, or youth. Arnold would have us believe that the tree, and 'this rude Cumner ground' to which it belongs, still 'a virtue yields' (220) which enables him to face 'the great town's harsh,

heart-wearying roar'(234); but the poem's emotional orientation is split between the youthful vision of the scholar-gipsy and
the tragic undertone which breaks the surface at lines 131–40.
The failure of pastoral consolation, in a poem which employs the
pastoral elegy conventions, is the more telling comment on its
meaning. This tacitly admits the breakdown of the traditional
means by which the mind has tried to heal its wounded consciousness; and in the face of this larger breakdown Arnold's
private attempt to construct a consolatory myth from the scholar-
gipsy and the elm tree is bound to seem slight and ineffective.
But this does not make 'Thyrsis' itself a poetic failure. The
weakness of its attempt to fashion a substitute consolation makes
the underlying anguish which prompts it all the more evident.
By comparison with *Lycidas* and *Adonais* it is a diffident and
almost apologetic poem; and, though it has more in common
with *In Memoriam*, it is also lacking in the subtle orchestration of
voices that enables Tennyson to bring the private and the public
into such fine imaginative balance. But the very fragility of its
achievement, poised as it is between a wistful looking to the past
and a reluctant commitment to the present, gives it a pathos that
comes very near, if it does not quite realise, the tragic.

4 Wordsworth: 'The still, sad music of humanity'

Wordsworth offers both a general and a more personal experience of tragedy, though the two are closely linked, since it is the collective sense of individual privations and misfortunes which gives rise to the general awareness of tragedy. They merge together in a pervasive sense of the insecurity of human life, which in 'Tintern Abbey' he calls 'The still, sad music of humanity'. Individual happiness can be intense and pure, and as such it is to be rejoiced in; and Wordsworth celebrates it in verse which, at times, seems almost naively selective. But this is only a way of reaffirming that spontaneous pleasure, especially in childhood, is a necessity of life. It is on a par with the sense he enjoyed when he himself was a child that death could not touch him personally, recorded in a note on the Immortality Ode:

> Nothing was more difficult for me in childhood than to admit the notion of death as a state applicable to my own being. . . . But it was not so much from feelings of animal vivacity that *my* difficulty came as from a sense of indomitableness of the spirit within me.[1]

If the emphasised '*my*' suggests that a distinction is being made between the youthfully idealistic poet and the rest of humanity, Wordsworth hastily corrects this by adding: 'To that dream-like vividness and splendour which invest objects of sight in childhood, every one, I believe, if he would look back, could bear testimony.'[2] Such a condition is not seen as something private and peculiar, nor as one of deplorable illusion; and yet the adult mind must also recognise it as temporary and immature. It is right and necessary for the child, and the adult should keep alive a sympathetic understanding of the child's state of mind – as Wordsworth does, for example, in 'We Are Seven'. But, for the

89

adult, recognition of the fragility of this condition is also essential. He must see beyond it without becoming patronisingly
superior to it. Indeed, 'The Child is father of the Man'; and at
least one of the meanings of that paradoxical statement is that
superiority lies with the child. The problem for the adult is to
place his sense of the fragility of the child's vision in proper
perspective. He may all too easily exaggerate the child's innocence so that it becomes a sentimentalising of immaturity and a
travesty of wisdom, for wisdom is necessarily a product of
experience. Wordsworth commits this error in stanza VIII of the
Immortality Ode, and Coleridge rightly condemns such phrases
as 'Mighty Prophet! Seer blest!', applied to the 'little Child', as
'*mental* bombast'.[3] On the other hand, the adult may fall into the
opposite error by dwelling too pathetically on the sorrow and
suffering which inevitably accompany maturer awareness. Here
the Wordsworthian sympathy with private pain and bereavement can lead, as it does in such lyrical ballads as 'The Thorn'
and 'The Mad Mother', to an emotional plangency which alien-
ates the reader by too openly demanding his sympathy as well.
The right balance is not easy to find. It requires both immediacy
and restraint, passionate involvement and a degree of coolness
and detachment – the finding, in fact, of a certain tone of voice
which reconciles the private and the universal in a wisely tragic
harmony; and Wordsworth's contribution to lyric tragedy may
be regarded as his working towards this end, whether or not he
ever fully achieves it.

In 'Tintern Abbey' Wordsworth's aim is to connect youth and
the more sobered maturity of later years in a perspective that
gives each its proper validity. 'Youth' and 'maturity' are, of
course, relative terms. Wordsworth wrote the poem in 1798,
when he was 28 years old, and the two visits to the Wye valley on
which he meditates were separated by no more than five years.
But the opening, with its deliberately pleonastic insistence on the
passage of time –

> Five years have past; five summers, with the length
> Of five long winters!

seems to stretch those five years to an eternity which makes the difference between earlier and later much more profound than the change from 23 to 28 years old might suggest. Both summers and winters are mentioned, but, thanks to the sense of extension created by the *traductio* of 'length' and 'long', it is the winters which receive particular emphasis. The effect is to imply a long wintering of the spirit as taking place during those intervening years which radically alters the climate of the soul. This carries over into the second paragraph, with its spells 'in lonely rooms, and ' 'mid the din / Of towns and cities', its 'hours of weariness', and its accumulated consciousness of 'the burden of the mystery' and 'the heavy and the weary weight / Of all this unintelligible world' (25–40).

Time thus brings a change to more tragic understanding. However, to isolate the phrases which have this tragic import is to distort the effect of the poetry into which Wordsworth has woven them. The full line, for example, in which 'hours of weariness' occurs, reads: 'In hours of weariness, sensations sweet'. The almost Augustan balance of the phrases creates a modified effect, in which the sadness of experience is countered by recollections of a more innocent time. And when not only the line, but more of the complete syntactical context is restored, the effect is still more intricate:

> These beauteous forms,
> Through a long absence, have not been to me
> As is a landscape to a blind man's eye:
> But oft, in lonely rooms, and 'mid the din
> Of towns and cities, I have owed to them
> In hours of weariness, sensations sweet,
> Felt in the blood, and felt along the heart;
> And passing even into my purer mind,
> With tranquil restoration.
>
> (22–30)

'in lonely rooms, and 'mid the din / Of towns and cities' and 'In hours of weariness' now appear only as interruptions in a flow, originating in the initial 'beauteous forms' of the Wye valley, that brings 'sensations sweet' pouring into the whole physical and mental complex of the poet's being, and culminating in

'tranquil restoration'. Likewise, the cluster of tragically coloured
phrases in lines 38–40 is contained within the 'blessed mood'
(the containment emphasised by the repeated relative conjunc-
tions, 'In which. . . . In which') which has the same source of
origin, and leads on ultimately to the transcendent vision which
ends the entire paragraph:

> While with an eye made quiet by the power
> Of harmony, and the deep power of joy,
> We see into the life of things.
>
> (47–9)

An overall harmony is created out of disharmony, and a sense of
continuity (which Arnold no doubt admired, and tried to imitate
in 'Thyrsis') is achieved.

The harmony is none the less made possible only by the
wisdom of the more mature Wordsworth. The reviving power of
innocence seems to subordinate experience to itself, but its
capacity to do so derives from the larger vantage point that
experience provides. The voice is that of the older Wordsworth,
rejoicing that he still finds within himself something of his
younger response to the landscape, but presenting what he sees
in the changed perspective of the present. Thus, even in the
opening descriptive paragraph the pervasive greenness (specifically associated with 'unripe fruits' at line 12) is suggestive of a
younger world consciously recognised as such, and the fanciful
element in

> These hedge-rows, hardly hedge-rows, little lines
> Of sportive wood run wild
>
> (15–16)

presents the hedges almost as if they were mischievous children
at play. They are seen by the poet ('Once again I see', 14) from a
vantage point which is concretely given in the passage ('I again
repose / Here, under this dark sycamore, and view', 9–10), and
which further suggests the watchful, indulgent eye of the adult
on his younger, less responsible self. The maturer being is now
more of an observer, and less of an active participant, than he
was five years earlier. As he moves on, in later lines, to recon-
struct his younger self (though even as he does so, he admits

that, strictly speaking, this is impossible: 'I cannot paint / What then I was', 75–6), he admits that his passionate involvement with nature was of a different kind from what it is now:

> The sounding cataract
> Haunted me like a passion: the tall rock,
> The mountain, and the deep and gloomy wood,
> Their colours and their forms, were then to me
> An appetite; a feeling and a love,
> That had no need of a remoter charm,
> By thought supplied, nor any interest
> Unborrowed from the eye.
>
> (76–83)

He warms to his subject, and, despite what he has just said, almost paints what he previously was with a power that gives it a re-awakened reality; but the absence of 'need of a remoter charm / By thought supplied' hints at a lack in such complete abandonment to the immediacy of sensual experience which points inevitably forward to the judgement on it which comes in the next sentence:

> That time is past,
> And all its aching joys are now no more,
> And all its dizzy raptures.
>
> (83–5)

The 'joys' and 'raptures' were real and substantial, but their qualification by 'aching' and 'dizzy' condemns them as intemperate. They self-centredly lack conscious awareness of pain and suffering, and thus are 'thoughtless' (90) both in the sense of being unreflective and lacking in human sympathy.

What follows is the central statement of 'Tintern Abbey', correcting this thoughtlessness with an elegiac gravity responsive to the outside world:

> For I have learned
> To look on nature, not as in the hour
> Of thoughtless youth; but hearing oftentimes
> The still, sad music of humanity,

> Nor harsh nor grating, though of ample power
> To chasten and subdue.
>
> (88–93)

Precisely what gives rise to this music is not specified, nor quite
why it is 'Nor harsh nor grating', and when Wordsworth goes on
to couple it with the pantheistic lines that speak of 'a sense
sublime / Of something far more deeply interfused' (95 *et seq.*) it
is not clear if this is a perception that is generated by his now
awakened sensitivity to the 'still, sad music'. But there is at least
a sense that the mind has moved on to a much more serious level
of response, created by the impressive accumulation of natural
phenomena which reaches its climax in

> A motion and a spirit, that impels
> All thinking things, all objects of all thought,
> And rolls through all things.
>
> (100–2)

The agents of thought and the objects of thought are now felt to
be manifestations of a common power, which the insistent 'all'
persuades one is all-inclusive, and the final sentence of the
paragraph extends this feeling, with further repetition of 'all' in
lines 104–5, to the formation of a bond between nature and 'all
my moral being' (111).

  This may be regarded as eloquent assertion rather than a
convincing demonstration of a natural-human continuity leading to deeper moral insight. The important thing for Wordsworth's purpose, however, is not the strength or weakness of his
philosophical position so much as the impression he creates of
greater maturity transcending the egotism of youth. Moreover,
he is willing to admit the vulnerability of the wisdom that he
claims to have reached with maturer years. Having concluded
his long, corrective paragraph with such an impressive climax of
moral affirmation, he immediately concedes the possibility that
what he has claimed might not be so:

> Nor perhance,
> If I were not thus taught, should I the more
> Suffer my genial spirits to decay.
>
> (111–13)

This is both admission and affirmation. The verb 'decay' is negatived. Corruption will not be allowed. But the word is very different from those which surround it, and, though it is introduced only to be rejected, it is enough to remind the reader of a destructive alternative that might be the real one. His defence against it is the presence of his sister, Dorothy, by his side, acting as a living reminder of his self of five years previously:

> in thy voice I catch
> The language of my former heart, and read
> My former pleasures in the shooting lights
> Of thy wild eyes.
>
> (116–19)

He can behold in her what he once was, and so, in another fashion, connect the present with the past. At first, this would seem to contradict the theme of deepened, maturer wisdom; as if what Wordsworth is most anxious to protect is the responsiveness of his earlier youthful self, immature though it may be – as if he fears that fading of 'the vision splendid' into 'the light of common day' about which he is so pessimistic in the fifth stanza of the Immortality Ode. But he has in mind a subtler relation between past and present. He looks forward to a time in the future when 'these wild ecstasies' of Dorothy's (which he does not judge, but which inevitably recall the 'dizzy raptures' of 'thoughtless youth' earlier in the poem) 'shall be matured / Into a sober pleasure' (138–9), i.e. she will have reached the stage which he has now reached in the present; and then, he half proclaims, half fervently prays,

> with what healing thoughts
> Of tender joy wilt thou remember me,
> And these my exhortations!
>
> (144–6)

In other words, it is not so much the Dorothy of the present, re-incarnating his earlier immaturity, that consoles him, as her presence, guaranteeing the reality of a living connection between past and present, and his own faith in the maturing process, which he envisages for Dorothy as well as himself.

What is less secure in 'Tintern Abbey' is the 'cheerful faith,

that all which we behold / Is full of blessings'. Like the knowledge 'that Nature never did betray / The heart that loved her'
(122–3), this is naive assertion, lacking the subtler perspective
which Wordsworth gives to his belief in the maturing process. (A
more complex recognition, that the natural world is what man
makes· it, seems to be implied in lines 105–7, but is not developed.) Nature, he says, buttresses that faith, makes it immune
to evidence of human wickedness:

> for she can so inform
> The mind that is within us, so impress
> With quietness and beauty, and so feed
> With lofty thoughts, that neither evil tongues,
> Rash judgements, nor the sneers of selfish men,
> Nor greetings where no kindness is, nor all
> The dreary intercourse of daily life,
> Shall e'er prevail against us, or disturb
> Our cheerful faith, that all which we behold
> Is full of blessings.
>
> (125–34)

This is a manifest self-contradiction; or if it is not, it requires the
kind of justification that Milton carefully and painstakingly
provides, but which Wordsworth, it seems, is quite blithely
prepared to omit. Despite the assertion to the contrary, the
catalogue of evils does 'disturb' – even if it is so held within the
negatived syntax that it does not 'prevail'. And it disturbs in a
way that ties it in with other disturbances throughout the poem:
'the heavy and the weary weight / Of all this unintelligible
world' (39–40), 'the fretful stir / Unprofitable, and the fever of
the world' (52–3), which have gone before; and the 'solitude or
fear, or pain, or grief', and the separation from Wordsworth,
perhaps by his death, which are imagined as possibilities for
Dorothy in subsequent lines (143, 146–9). These are details
which give flesh and blood to 'The still, sad music of humanity'.
Without them the claims for a maturer understanding would be
meaningless. It is true that Wordsworth continually seeks (as we
have seen by examining lines 25–7 in their context) to subordinate such sad experience to a more 'serene and blessed mood',
but this cannot be equated with a simple view that 'all which we
behold / Is full of blessings'. The excuse for such a statement

might be that it is intended merely for the immature Dorothy's consumption, and that Wordsworth does not offer it as his own mature view (or even as a view that, in the future, will be appropriate to the sadder, but wiser, Dorothy that she will then become). Certainly, it is not the view implicit in the poem's grave and saddened language. That includes, not excludes, disturbance; it is the language of thoughtfulness rather than thoughtlessness.

The disturbing of 'cheerful faith' is much more directly, and, it must be said, more honestly, approached in 'Resolution and Independence'. The alternation of youthful thoughtlessness with more mature awareness here becomes an alternation of moods within the present consciousness of the poet, with a manic-depressive seriousness that brings him much closer to the intensity of tragic experience. There is a superficial resemblance between the role of the old leech-gatherer speaking to the poet and that of the maturer self reviewing his younger self in 'Tintern Abbey'; but the meeting with the leech-gatherer is presented in a way that makes him only a limited example of the wisdom of experience. The essential dialogue is that which goes on in the poet's own mind, and its subject is that of *Lycidas* and *Adonais* – the mortality of the poet:

> I thought of Chatterton, the marvellous Boy,
> The sleepless Soul that perished in his pride;
> Of Him who walked in glory and in joy
> Following his plough, along the mountain-side:
> By our own spirits are we deified:
> We Poets in our youth begin in gladness;
> But thereof come in the end despondency and madness.
>   (43–9)

The first line of the poem speaks of a storm that has lasted all night, but this has been succeeded by a day of exceptional beauty, the delicacy and wonder of which fills the rest of the stanza and the whole of the next. In the third the poet introduces himself as a traveller on the moor, responding to this scene with the carefree happiness of a boy:

> The pleasant season did my heart employ:
> My old remembrances went from me wholly;
> And all the ways of men, so vain and melancholy.
>
> (19–21)

For a while it is as if the youthful thoughtlessness of 'Tintern
Abbey' has been recaptured. But the opening line was ominous,
as is the present suggestion of exemption from tragic awareness.
The very intensity of joy begets its opposite, and 'blind thoughts'
come rushing in. The poem enacts a kind of secular Fall, an
introduction to, and darkening of, that 'Chamber of Maiden-
Thought' which Keats speaks of in his letter to Reynolds,[4] with
an accompanying recognition that bliss may be replaced by
'Solitude, pain of heart, distress, and poverty', and, in stanza VI,
a degree of self-rebuke by the poet for his own egotistical heed-
lessness. This, in its turn, ushers in the stanza on Chatterton,
which is at once an act of outgoing sympathy for another, and an
expression of anxiety for himself – both the Aristotelian pity and
the Aristotelian fear.

The 'despondency and madness' of stanza VII thus appear as
the climax of a Fall into tragic awareness of the human condition. But the words also suggest a condition that might be
regarded as pathological. Wordsworth is not sure that the tragic
response is either right or justifiable; and it is for this reason
perhaps that he chooses this moment to introduce the old
leech-gatherer, with a suggestion of something providential in
their meeting:

> Now, whether it were by peculiar grace,
> A leading from above, a something given,
> Yet it befell.
>
> (50–2)

Their encounter becomes a corrective of the poet's seemingly
unbalanced response. By the end of the poem the old man's
stoicism is seen as offering some kind of rebuke to the poet's
indulgence in gloomy thoughts, and an example of the 'resolution and independence' which he should take as his moral guide.
The concluding words are, in fact, a moral lesson on these lines:

> 'God,' said I, 'be my help and stay secure;
> 'I'll think of the Leech-gatherer on the lonely moor!'
>
> (139–40)

This has its real, practical point, and the title of the poem would seem to underline it. Yet the core of the poem is to be found in the actual encounter as it is presented in stanzas IX–XIX, and in the peculiar reaction of the poet to the old man. The moral lesson drawn at the end seems largely irrelevant to this. The leech-gatherer's firmness in pursuing his task, in spite of the increasing difficulties in his way, hardly seems to register on the mind of the poet: he asks about it, but fails to attend to the answer; he eagerly renews his question at line 119, and, as if with an indulgent smile at the absent-mindedness of the poet, the old man 'did then his words repeat' (120); but still it seems that the poet does not really listen, and the old man, 'having made a pause, the same discourse renewed' (133). Indeed, what prompts the renewal of the poet's question is nothing in what the old man says, but the return of his own 'former thoughts':

> the fear that kills;
> And hope that is unwilling to be fed;
> Cold, pain, and labour, and all fleshy ills;
> And mighty Poets in their misery dead.
>
> (113–16)

The poet is 'Perplexed, and longing to be comforted' (117). What, in effect, he seeks from the old man is some explanation of the human condition which can support and console, but at the same time he tacitly recognises that no conscious explanation will, or can, be forthcoming from such a source. Only when transformed by the imagination can it speak effectively to the poet; and then, of course, it becomes the poet speaking to himself.

Such transformation is already suggested by the curious epic simile which presents the impression that the old man creates in the poet's mind when they first meet (interestingly, Wordsworth later chose this simile to illustrate what he calls 'the conferring, the abstracting, and the modifying powers of the Imagination'[5]); and it is made more explicit in stanza XVI, where the old man's capacity to give strength is specifically associated with his becoming a dream-like figure from another world:

> The old Man still stood talking by my side;
> But now his voice to me was like a stream
> Scarce heard, nor word from word could I divide;

And the whole body of the Man did seem
Like one whom I had met with in a dream;
Or like a man from some far region sent,
To give me human strength, by apt admonishment.
                                                    (106–12)

After the renewed question reality is again transferred to the
'mind's eye' rather than the physical eye, and there the old man
seems to

                                                    pace
About the weary moors continually,
Wandering about alone and silently.
                                                    (129–31)

He becomes a symbolic figure, with the timelessness of an
essentially imaginative creation, focussing in himself all that
'troubled' (128) the poet, but at the same time able to reassure
by virtue of his transcendent reality. Whether that reassurance is
of the kind offered by Keats's Grecian urn, or, as Wordsworth's
letter to Sara Hutchinson suggests, of a specifically religious
kind,[6] the poem itself does not narrowly define. It is true that the
old man is identified as a moral agent at the end of the poem, but
at the cost of a certain anti-climax. Here he seems a more
vaguely potent and mysterious figure, whose message cannot be
verbalised ('nor word from word could I divide') – a creation of
language, and yet not to be tied to the statements made by
words. Biographical evidence suggests that he corresponds to a
man actually known to Wordsworth, but this particular figure
has his context only in the poem in which he is created, and
comes into being only as a consequence of the crisis evoked in the
opening stanzas.

This is not to say that Wordsworth is indifferent to the plight of
the leech-gatherer. On the contrary, when his imagination works
upon the figure of the old man to create the strangely transforming simile of stanzas IX–X, it incorporates the physical disability
and miseries of old age into the image, with moving humanity:

His body was bent double, feet and head
Coming together in life's pilgrimage;
As if some dire constraint of pain, or rage
Of sickness felt by him in times long past,
A more than human weight upon his frame had cast.

(66–70)

If the figure is a visionary one, then it is a vision, prompted, certainly, by the 'despondency' of the poet, but also having its origin in sympathy with real human suffering. This is at least akin to the tragic awareness that takes its stimulus from pain, exposing itself, in King Lear's words, 'to feel what wretches feel'.[7] But poise between self-absorption and other-directed awareness remains the curious quality of 'Resolution and Independence'. It finds its way to an intimation of tragic grandeur by using the leech-gatherer as material for the transforming imagination; ordinary humanity and compassion are not in themselves enough.

For Jonathan Wordsworth, however, it is just such compassion that gives tragic distinction to 'The Ruined Cottage'. He argues that, although many of Wordsworth's solitaries are generalised figures, Coleridge's criticism, that he and Goethe 'are always, both of them, spectators *ab extra* – feeling *for*, but never *with*, their characters',[8] is quite unjustified with regard to characters like the Old Cumberland Beggar, the Discharged Soldier, Michael and Margaret, the heroine of 'The Ruined Cottage'. Of the latter poem, in particular, he says: 'It shows in Wordsworth a humanity, an insight into emotions not his own, that is wholly convincing – places him, perhaps unexpectedly, among the very few great English tragic writers.'[9] This is an extraordinarily high claim, and whether one feels it to be warranted perhaps depends, in the last resort, as Jonathan Wordsworth disarmingly admits, on personal response. But there is also the question of whether it is quite the sort of judgement that the poem invites. Does the poem really aspire towards a totally tragic effect? Or does it – in spite of compassion which is probably stronger than that displayed in 'Resolution and Independence' – seek to qualify, and even to some extent deflect, the reader's tragic response?

Jonathan Wordsworth writes that 'There seem to be two forms of tragedy – or at least two extremes – the fight against odds . . . and the tragedy of waste. . . . In a curious way *The Ruined Cottage* unites the two.'[10] Of these two claims the claim that it embodies 'the fight against odds' is more difficult to accept than 'the tragedy of waste'. The story of Margaret's decline after her husband abandons her suggests passive acquiescence rather than resistance. It is true that she does not immediately give way to despair on learning that her husband has left her. She continues to work and care for her children, for a time, and she is almost obsessive in her enquiries of passers-by as to the whereabouts of her husband. On the Pedlar's third visit – by which time, however, she has begun neglecting the child so much that it indulges in a pathetic echoing of its mother's grief – her husband's clothes still hang ready in their usual place, as if she expects him to return at any moment. But there is no impression of her struggling against hostile forces. The successive stages of her decline are beautifully presented, but it is a process to which she gradually yields herself; and – to the detriment of the poem's effect as tragedy – her devotion to her husband seems to sap her will, resulting eventually in a death-wish rather than a struggle made futile by the sense of impossible odds. On the other hand, there is more to be said for the poem as a tragedy of waste. The sense that something of great value is being lost is heightened by the degree to which the life shared by Margaret and her husband is represented as initially one of healthy, active, mutually loving co-operation; and her continuing devotion to him, even when he has behaved so irresponsibly, reveals a capacity for love which is made the more moving by the circumstances which frustrate it. Nevertheless, even this might seem to many readers pathetic rather than tragic; and there are times when Margaret's condition seems the consequence of a lack of ordinary common sense.

'The Ruined Cottage' is not, in fact, a straightforwardly tragic poem. On the contrary, it is almost an investigation into the validity of tragic feeling; and, at the same time, an education of the reader's emotional response. Jonathan Wordsworth is justified, at least as far as this poem is concerned, in saying that it is tragic if you find it tragic. Wordsworth's art is aimed at inducing a feeling which will make the reader prepared to accept Margaret's experience as tragic; it creates a 'still, sad music' conducive to thoughtful rather than thoughtless response. But, also, by incorporating the listener within the poem, as the poem's 'I', and giving the narration of Margaret's history to the older, wiser, but more detached, Pedlar, Wordsworth holds back from complete endorsement of it as tragedy.

The opening paragraph of 'The Ruined Cottage' is given over to natural description.[11] Its first line is, ' 'Twas Summer and the sun was mounted high.' But that impression of strong, warm light, made in a short, simple, uncomplicated sentence, is checked and qualified through the next seventeen lines with 'shadows dappled' and a transition to 'dewy shade', bird-song, and the viewpoint of a relaxed, 'dreaming' man lying in an oak-tree's shade, which concludes with the scene's being represented as 'made more soft, / More soft and distant'. This change is echoed in the next two paragraphs, which introduce the two characters who are to be, respectively, listener and narrator of the tale of Margaret. The listener, the poem's 'I', is weary, hot, and plagued with insects. He finds the narrator, the Pedlar, by the ruined cottage in shade that recalls the dappling effect of the opening paragraph:

> His eyes were shut,
> The shadows of the breezy elms above
> Dappled his face.
>
> (46–8)

And the listener-to-be, though himself 'With thirsty heat oppressed', is glad to see the Pedlar's hat 'Bedewed with waterdrops, as if the brim / Had newly scooped a running stream'. From this contrast between the listener's heated irritation and a more pleasantly dappled context it is a comparatively smooth step to the focussing of his attention on the dilapidated building, Margaret's ruined cottage, and his being gradually drawn by the Pedlar, who claims, 'I see around me here / Things which you cannot see' (67–8), into sympathetic awareness of its human significance. As the tale unfolds, however, the listener is drawn in so far that at the end his involvement is much greater than the Pedlar's. His own initially heated condition compared with the Pedlar's sheltered situation is thus prophetic. The Pedlar has to cool his heat by urging that sorrow should be limited, and subordinated to a philosophical understanding of life as 'passing shews of being' (522). Finally, the opening paragraph is recalled in the closing pastoral epilogue (reminiscent of the end of *Lycidas*), but with the high-mounted sun now changed into the 'declining' sun that 'shot / A slant and mellow radiance' (526–7), and the motifs of shade and bird-song recapitulated in a gentle climax of distance and softness.

What Wordsworth is doing is voiced for us by the Pedlar in his first speech. We are being offered the plain, unadorned telling of an ordinary human tale, free from the gratuitous excitements of sensation or horror, but, for all that, belonging to a long-sustained tradition of elegy which deepens our awareness of the human condition:

> The Poets, in their elegies and songs
> Lamenting the departed, call the groves,
> They call upon the hills and streams to mourn,
> And senseless rocks – nor idly, for they speak
> In these their invocations with a voice
> Obedient to the strong creative power
> Of human passion. Sympathies there are
> More tranquil, yet perhaps of kindred birth,
> That steal upon the meditative mind
> And grow with thought.
>
> (73–82)

To become more thoughtful is to become more conscious of 'the still, sad music of humanity'. It is to acquire – or, at least, approach nearer to – the tragic understanding that enters feelingly into the reality of suffering, but also accepts the fact of its being woven into the fabric of general life, in which the particular human life has only a part. This implies an attitude of delicate poise, which can easily unbalance into excess of pathos, or too calm a philosophic detachment. In this sense 'thought' can be both creative and destructive, and in this poem we experience variations on it which involve both aspects. The ideal balance tips towards neither extreme, but in practice the poem involves both; it is in the distribution of awareness across the whole range of the poem, giving the reader a salutary experience of organised checks and balances, that the right quality of 'thought' is achieved.

The humanising view of thought is expressed by the Pedlar near the beginning of the Second Part:

But we have known that there is often found
In mournful thoughts, and always might be found,
A power to virtue friendly; were't not so
I am a dreamer among men, indeed
An idle dreamer. 'Tis a common tale
By moving accidents uncharactered,
A tale of silent suffering, hardly clothed
In bodily form, and to the grosser sense
But ill adapted, scarcely palpable
To him who does not think.

                                        (227–36)

In this context 'mournful' is not morbid. 'Mournful thoughts'
are those which are adjusted to the realities of suffering, and
therefore do not prompt despair or cynicism. As such, they are
the agents of moral awareness. It is thoughts of this kind that the
unsensational tale of Margaret is intended to awaken. Its ability
to do so, however, depends on the reader's sensitivity and
emotional maturity. The Pedlar – and Wordsworth is, surely,
with him at this point – here comes near to begging the question,
since he seems almost to be asking for the quality of response
which the telling of the tale is supposed to generate. But, as in
life, we do not learn, and then apply; learning and application
continuously interact. Although the tale may be 'scarcely palpable / To him who does not think', there is no Calvinistic divide
between the elect thinkers and the damned non-thinkers. The
reader is, in reality, being exhorted to encourage his own better,
thinking self – to put himself into a sympathetic frame of mind so
that the poem can do its beneficent work on him.

   The effect of suffering on Margaret illustrates the destructive
meaning of thinking. On his second visit to her the Pedlar finds
her absent from the cottage. Her garden shows neglect, and she
has left her child alone while she has been wandering abroad on
a quest, which she already knows to be futile, for news of her
husband. Even when brought into social intercourse she seems
to be refusing communication; and

                In every act
        Pertaining to her house-affairs appeared
        The careless stillness which a thinking mind
        Gives to an idle matter.

                                        (380–3)

This is 'thinking' that amounts to an obsessive consciousness; it does not deepen her understanding, but comes between her and the performance of necessary human tasks. It is a canker thoughtfulness which shrinks her humanity, and eventually eats her away to literal illness and death. The reader does not participate directly in this. Instead, he is the sympathetic observer of a corrosive process which he can see in a wider, tragic dimension; and he is also alerted to a kind of thoughtfulness which is the enemy of the tragic, in that it can turn consciousness into a disease. It would be better for Margaret if her 'careless stillness' were the carefree activity of an unthinking mind. That might be something that would 'grow' healthily 'with thought', as suggested by the Pedlar in his first speech. As it is, however, she is caught in a death-giving, rather than a life-enhancing, process, which is reflected in the organic deterioration of uncontrolled growth that goes on in and around her cottage as she neglects its upkeep.

It has been argued that what is death and deterioration for Margaret and for the cottage as a human habitation is still part of the continuity of natural life.[12] Animals find shelter in the ruined building and nature's abundance is evidenced in the proliferating 'willow-flowers and grass' (63). The tragic touch which 'moved' the listener's 'very heart' is 'The useless fragment of a wooden bowl' (91–2), this being the distinctively human tool. What the bowl symbolises, however, is the breaking of the 'bond / Of brotherhood', mentioned a few lines before (84–5), between man and nature, where the control traditionally exercised by man, as in Burgundy's speech in *Henry V* (V.ii.38–62), is a condition of civilisation. However, the social and cosmic implications of this, which are very much to the fore in Shakespeare, are only peripheral in Wordsworth. He mentions economic recession and war as causes of the husband's deterioration, but these seem little more than levers of the plot. His real interest is psychological – the imbalance in Margaret's mind and how it relates to what is, in effect, the reader's education. The 'bond / Of brotherhood' is the Wordsworthian concept of sanity. It implies a mental even more than an ecological balance, which can embrace the right use of tragic feeling. The purpose of this poem is to encourage its development, but with healthy, controlled growth.

Against the destructive 'thought' of Margaret, therefore,

Wordsworth sets the carefree thoughtlessness which can har-
monise with nature, voiced, at least for the time being (it is not to
be regarded as representing his whole view), by the Pedlar. At
the end of the First Part – just after Margaret's consciousness of
what lies beneath her husband's 'wild freaks of merriment' has
begun to make her 'heart bleed' (180–5) – the Pedlar breaks off
his own narration, as if to reject what he is saying as potentially
harmful to the bond between man and nature:

> At this still season of repose and peace,
> This hour when all things which are not at rest
> Are chearful, while this multitude of flies
> Fills all the air with happy melody,
> Why should a tear be in an old man's eye?
> Why should we thus with an untoward mind,
> And in the weakness of humanity,
> From natural wisdom turn our hearts away,
> To natural comfort shut our eyes and ears,
> And, feeding on disquiet, thus disturb
> The calm of Nature with our restless thoughts?
>
> (188–98)

This has something of the same theme, but not quite the same
tone, as 'The Tables Turned':

> Come forth into the light of things,
> Let Nature be your Teacher.

The Pedlar's plea for 'natural wisdom' has the advantage of
being only a moment in a longer poem, not that moment isolated
as a poem in itself. It is no more than a check in the poem's
larger progress. Accordingly, the Second Part of 'The Ruined
Cottage' opens with a comment on how the Pedlar's speech,
though spoken 'with somewhat of a solemn tone', quickly gives
way to 'easy cheerfulness', with the result

> That for a little time it stole away
> All recollection, and that simple tale
> Passed from my mind like a forgotten sound.
>
> (202–4)

Such relief – such springing back of the bent stem – is a welcome
and necessary reaction. Nevertheless, it does not obliterate the
disturbing power of the thoughtfulness that the Pedlar has begun
to provoke. In fact, it works with 'a heartfelt chillness' in the
listener's veins, so that the shade in which he is sitting seems too
cold, and he goes out for a while 'To drink the comfort of the
warmer sun' (216). This oscillation is not, however, mere garru-
lousness. It is a vital part of the poem's progress through balance
and counter-balance. Both warming and cooling are required, if
the right developing temperature is to be maintained.

The listener's interest being thoroughly aroused, it is he who
begs the Pedlar to resume his tale – which he does, rehearsing
Margaret's gradual decline to its culmination in her death five
lingering, winter-dominated years (the link with 'Tintern Abbey'
is significant) after his last visit to her. The effect on the listener
is exhausting. His emotional involvement leaves him in such a
state of 'weakness' that he lacks the power even to thank the
Pedlar. But as he leans over the garden gate and reviews the
woman's suffering, he seems to find both comfort in it and the
paradoxical satisfaction of blessing her 'in the impotence of
grief' (499–500). The implications of this seem both positive and
negative, as do his subsequent reactions:

> At length towards the cottage I returned
> Fondly, and traced with milder interest,
> That secret spirit of humanity
> Which, 'mid the calm oblivious tendencies
> Of nature, 'mid her plants, her weeds and flowers,
> And silent overgrowings, still survived.
>
> (501–6)

'Fondly' in this passage suggests both folly (reactivating the
previous 'impotence of grief') and affection (recalling the sense of
'a brother's love' which made the listener bless Margaret). The
'oblivious tendencies / Of nature' and her 'silent overgrowings'
recapitulate the process of decay rehearsed in the main body of
the tale; but 'calm' – and perhaps 'silent', likewise – modifies the
anguish that has been aroused, and brings it more into accord
with the 'milder interest' which the listener now feels. And, as
always, Wordsworth's syntax also contributes to the overall
effect of qualification and modification, by containing the re-

peated phrases beginning with ' 'mid' (and relating to natural indifference) within the more positive, though muted, statement that the 'secret spirit of humanity . . . still survived'.

The next words, introducing a further speech from the Pedlar, read: 'The old man seeing this resumed' (507). It is not altogether clear what 'this' refers to: it may be that the Pedlar is intuitively aware of the complex feelings at work in the listener, or it may be that he simply notices the 'survival' element. Either way, he chooses to encourage the listener's calmer tendencies, rather than 'the impotence of grief', and urgest him to be 'wise and chearful' (510). He repeatedly emphasises quietness: 'She sleeps in the calm earth, and peace is here' (512), and the beautiful image of the spear-grass 'By mist and silent rain-drops silvered o'er' is introduced to heighten the same theme ('So still an image of tranquility, / So calm and still', 517–18). The total effect is to lessen the urgency of feeling aroused by his story of human suffering, and to suggest to the listener that he should allow the same calming influence to work on him as the Pedlar himself had experienced when noticing the spear-grass:

> what we feel of sorrow and despair
> From ruin and from change, and all the grief
> The passing shews of being leave behind,
> Appeared an idle dream that could not live
> Where meditation was.
>
> (520–4)

The Pedlar concludes by saying, 'I turned away, / And walked along my road in happiness' (524–5). This suggests that tragedy has now been left behind. 'Thought' has been transmuted into 'meditation', and 'grief' into 'happiness'. But we are not necessarily blessed in the change. A distinction has to be made between what is artistically right for the conduct of the poem and feelings and attitudes which the reader may be expected to endorse. The entire development of Margaret's story, and the increasing thoughtfulness which it induces in the listener, is inconsistent with the more resigned attitude that reduces life to mere 'passing shews of being'. On the other hand, we do not exactly judge the Pedlar to be crass and insensitive – as the narrator of a story in which he himself has been to a considerable extent sympathetically involved he has acquired a hold on our respect which is too strong for that. His encouragement of the listener to distance his emotion recognises, and wisely accepts, the inevitability that intense emotional involvement will give way to a more ordinary level of response, and it is already to some extent foreshadowed in the way the listener's ultimate reaction is presented. Both the exclusiveness of tragic response, and the danger inherent in it that it may become fixated in something which is morbid rather than properly tragic, are thus tactfully resisted. Without endorsing what the Pedlar says, we can see its rightness and appropriateness in this context; and that it even contributes to, while seeming to reject, a sound tragic response.

5 Hardy: Illusion and Reality

Yea. Tragedy is true guise,
  Comedy lies.
    ('He Did Not Know Me')

But our eye-records, like in hue and line,
Had superimposed on them, that very day,
Gravings on your side deep, but slight on mine! –
Tending to sever us thenceforth alway;
Mine commonplace; yours tragic, gruesome, gray.
                    ('Alike and Unlike')

Both of these quotations come from poems in which, as so often with Hardy, there is a dialogue, actual or implicit, between opposed points of view, but which end, none the less, with a lapidary statement having the air of authoritative, sadly won wisdom. In 'He Did Not Know Me' the personified figure of Tragedy does not recognise Comedy, though she does recognise him, and it is Time who answers Comedy's bewilderment over this with the lines quoted above. In 'Alike and Unlike' the speaker is not identified (though according to F. B. Pinion it is Hardy's first wife, Emma[1]). However, a male–female exchange is again clearly implied; and of the two, nominally equal, impressions it is the woman's deeper and more tragically inclined, which is given the heavier emotional weighting. The title of this poem indicates that, objectively speaking, the two are witnesses of the same sight (Great Orme's Head, near Llandudno) – 'alike' in that respect, but 'unlike' in their responses to it. They endow the same landscape with diverse meanings; or perhaps they are conditioned by mental histories that give the same scene divergent associations for each of them. There is a pattern of community, followed by disunity, of impression, and this is echoed in the simple structure of the poem· the first stanza beginning, 'We watched the selfsame scene', and ending with it laid up 'As if for joint recallings by and by'; the second beginning with similarity, but ending with antithesis. Looked at more closely, however, what is observed in the first stanza tacitly endorses the 'tragic' interpretation: it consists of 'the magnificent purples' of the mountains, followed by the arrival of a storm – a typically Hardyan sequence of illusion followed by disillusionment, happiness by misery. That such a sequence should be built into something 'tragic, gruesome, gray' might suggest the distorting subjectivity of personal impression; but, on the other hand, that it should be put down as simply 'commonplace' suggests insensitivity. Indeed, to present the 'I' who is writing the poem as the comparatively indifferent one of the two borders on sardonic self-mockery, for to react as the 'I' is said to do is virtually to be disqualified from writing it. The comedy lies; the tragedy is the 'true guise'.

This represents a very different tone from the one cultivated by Wordsworth. It would appear, like Wordsworth, to allow for variable response, but in doing so it knows where the truth lies. Honesty demands that the underlying reality of the tragic be recognised, and there is little room for the Wordsworthian accommodation to 'years that bring the philosophic mind'.[2] Nevertheless, Hardy's poems reveal him in something of a dilemma with regard to tragedy. The form in which he most frequently presents tragic experience is that of a 'discovery' involving cold reality breaking through false, though passionately engaging, human sentiment. But again and again he denies that this is pessimistic. Above all, in the 'Apology' to *Late Lyrics and Earlier* he argues that, although 'some grave, positive, stark, delineations' are to be found among his poems, these are essentially explorations of reality, and, as such, they are 'the first step towards the soul's betterment, and the body's also'. He cites his own words in 'In Tenebris II' – 'if way to the Better there be, it exacts a full look at the Worst' – and glosses them as follows:

> that is to say, by the exploration of reality, and its frank recognition stage by stage along the survey, with an eye to the best consummation possible: briefly, evolutionary meliorism. But it is called pessimism nevertheless; under which word, expressed with condemnatory emphasis, it is regarded by many as some pernicious new thing (though so old as to underlie the Gospel scheme, and even to permeate the Greek drama); and the subject is charitably left to decent silence, as if further comment were needless.[3]

Rarely, however, do the poems rehearse their discoveries as necessary steps on the road to ultimate enlightenment. They end with themselves rather than point to some benefit or consolation to be gained from taking a full look at the worst. Indeed, at times Hardy draws a conclusion that even he would have to designate pessimistic; as he all but does in the sonnet which stands as the bleak, penultimate poem of the aptly titled *Winter Words*:

> We are getting to the end of visioning
> The impossible within this universe,
> Such as that better whiles may follow worse,
> And that our race may mend by reasoning.
>
> We know that even as larks in cages sing
> Unthoughtful of deliverance from the curse
> That holds them lifelong in a latticed hearse,
> We ply spasdomically our pleasuring.
>
> And that when nations set them to lay waste
> Their neighbours' heritage by foot and horse,
> And hack their pleasant plains in festering seams,
> They may again, – not warely, or from taste,
> But tickled mad by some demonic force. –
> Yes. We are getting to the end of dreams!

This is almost an endorsement of the doctrine of original sin, without the Christian corollary of the possibility of redemption implied in the parenthesis in the above quotation from the 'Apology'. Its tragic statement is bald and uncompromising, and it will not allow for myths or subjective magic that screen the truth. Whether or not based consciously on *King Lear*, it rejects, as Shakespeare's play does, the illusion that we may sing like birds in the cage, and forces us to recognise the inveterate evil which goes on – and will go on – destroying irrationally.

'We are getting to the end of visioning' makes a powerful statement of the tragic truth. However, its relationship to the rest of Hardy's tragic poetry, as its opening lines suggest, is more through its emphasis on illusion than its assertion of evil. It is the pang of broken dreams that most often provides the subject, and shapes the form, of his poems. This is especially true with regard to his love poetry. The deserted maiden of ballad tradition, who trusts her lover, but finds too late that men deceive, is an obvious enough topic; but Hardy specialises more in the lover who finds his previously idealised mistress becoming commonplace, as the veil of illusion is lifted from his eyes. 'At Waking' and 'Amabel' are typical examples. Both may be dismissed as studies in solipsism, or satires on the immature lover whose mistress is created out of the upward displacement of sexual desire; but Hardy knows what pain can, nevertheless, be generated in the breaking of such fragile illusions (and, perhaps more convincingly, he knows what their destruction can mean for the woman on to whom they are projected, as he shows in the tragi-comic treatment of 'The Gap in the White'). What justifies the otherwise exaggerated response is the glimpse which his experience gives the lover into the fallibility of his own consciousness. In suddenly seeing the adored woman as 'but one / Of the common crowd' he is chilled by the fear that whatever hope clings to may similarly fade:

> O vision appalling
> When the one believed-in thing
> Is seen falling, falling,
> With all to which hope can cling.
> > Off: it is not true;
> > For it cannot be
> > That the prize I drew
> > Is a blank to me!
> > > ('At Waking')

The mocking song-rhythm of 'Amabel' takes the experience more lightly. This 'I', more self-aware, proceeds neatly from the 'ruined hues' of '*My* Amabel', through the contemplation of a replacement lover who will celebrate her as '*His* Amabel', to the wry recognition of a continuous process that reduces her to merely '*An* Amabel':

> Knowing that, though Love cease,
> Love's race shows no decrease;
> All find in dorp or dell
> An Amabel.

Potentially, however, this paradox is more disturbing. That the death of an individual love is not the death of the species may seem to offer some kind of comfort; but it shows, in fact, uniqueness lost in a universal natural function, with the painful disillusionment only slightly disguised by the sardonic diction and rhyme.

Carried to extreme, this extinction of the individual in impersonal, universal process becomes anti-tragic in effect. Hardy's totally unWordsworthian sense of an uncaring, indifferent nature – nature as mere scientific cause and effect – theoretically, at least, nullifies the personal resonance which tragedy requires. Yet he rarely writes in the neutral manner that would seem to be appropriate to such a theme. The nearest that he comes to doing so is in the chill, but curiously moving, 'Proud Songsters'. The first stanza reads like a typical spring-time lyric, with the slight, but significant, modification that the birds sing as darkness comes on, and the fifth line ends with the verb 'wears' ('Pipe, as they can when April wears') – meaning, presumably, 'as the month of April advances', but also conveying the discordant impression that April is starting to show wear-and-tear. The second stanza, however, has no truck with the more romantic associations of Spring:

> These are brand-new birds of twelve-months' growing,
> Which a year ago, or less than twain,
> No finches were, nor nightingales,
>   Nor thrushes,
> But only particles of grain,
>   And earth, and air, and rain.

These 'songsters' seem more like market-garden produce, and in place of the first stanza's triumph over time ('As if all Time were theirs') these birds retreat back through their process of growth to when they were mere 'particles'. One critic suggests that this poem 'appears to insist on a totally reductive and disenchanted view of spring', but that the last three lines change the whole conception: 'The mechanism is suddenly refreshed and transformed.'[4] It is true that there is an unmistakable echo of Wordsworth's 'With rocks, and stones, and trees'[5] in the last line of 'Proud Songsters', and that 'rain' gives a final suggestion of fertility. But the word is conditioned by its context and grammatical relationship to 'particles'. The very idea of fertility is diminished in such a stanza: and the echo of Wordsworth serves mainly to summon up the attitude towards nature which this poem does *not* express.

In the poetry of the great Romantics, such as Wordsworth himself and also Keats, birds are carriers of strong personal feeling; and it must be conceded that Hardy, even in the depersonalising 'Proud Songsters', follows them in playing at least indirectly on such feelings. In a poem like 'The Bullfinches' he does this more directly. Here the birds speak with a human voice, perceiving each other as 'Brother Bulleys', and in the curious double negative of

> For we know not that we go not
> When to-day's pale pinions fold
> Where they be that sang of old

the ignorance of death appropriate to birds as such is set against the supposed consciousness that enables them to voice their ignorance. In the rest of the poem the bullfinches' spokesman reports what he has heard the fairies of Blackmoor Vale say of 'queenly Nature's ways, / Means, and moods', and here, too, there is an in-built contradiction. Nature is a Mother, and all living beings are her children (she calls them such), but, like Hardy's Immanent Will, she 'works on dreaming', ignorant, or heedless, of her offspring's well-being: 'All things making for Death's taking'. The personification of Nature which this poem presents is an essentially human response to human consciousness of insentient natural process – at once asserting it as the objective truth, and at the same time protesting against it in terms of a philosophical (or, more properly, religious) outlook which has conditioned man to expect loving parental care from his creator. Out of this tension comes a poem which, if not tragic, has tragic implications. The bullfinches accept their fate, although *as* bullfinches they have no awareness that they are accepting anything, while the account of what the fairies say both excites pity for the victimised condition of the birds, and expresses very human protest at the absence of divine benevolence.

Another bird poem, 'Winter in Durnover Field', again exploits the tension between human consciousness and the unconsciousness of birds to indict a scheme of things in which comfort is abitrarily withheld. The dialogue of the Rook, Starling and

Pigeon is played off against the stage-direction prefaced to the poem, which indicates that the ground has been recently sown with wheat, but is now 'frozen to iron hardness'. The birds are cheated of food, which is so near and yet so far. As in 'The Bullfinches', they are endowed with human feeling, both in the stage-direction, where they are said to walk about the cornfield 'wistfully eyeing the surface', and in the dialogue, where they animate the frost and call it 'cruel'; but in this poem the curtness of the birds' expression lends a stoic air to their complaints. The repetition imposed by the triolet form is technically sophisticated, but paradoxically creates an effect of primitive monotony which intensifies the sense that there is an absolute impossibility of the birds being able to satisfy their hunger. They seem caught in a hopeless situation, in which 'genial thawings' are mentioned only to be surrounded and lost again in the echoing sounds of 'Throughout the field I find no grain' and 'The cruel frost encrusts the cornland!' Landscape, weather, the irony of the birds' situation, and the contrastingly sophisticated demands of the poem's form thus combine to create an effective image of what is, again, an essentially human state of awareness.

In a note written in 1877 Hardy comments: 'An object or mark raised or made by man on a scene is worth ten times any such formed by unconscious Nature. Hence clouds, mists, and mountains are unimportant beside the wear on a threshold, or the print of a hand.'[6] The human mark in 'Winter in Durnover Field' may seem to be lacking, but the poem itself is that mark. It is an objective correlative for Hardy's sense of man's predicament. That he also felt strongly about animals and birds, and would probably have rejected the implication that they could only be taken seriously if humanised, is not irrelevant, for it helped, in this poem at least, towards greater distancing and control of the underlying human material. Though the birds mediate this material, they are also compassionately treated as birds. A similar effect of immediacy and distance combined is also achieved in the strange animal's-eye-view of Waterloo which is inserted as a moving tragic lyric in Part Third of *The Dynasts*.[7] Where Hardy deals more directly with a human situation containing figures of pathos such distancing is not always as

effectively managed. Its lack is felt even in such excellent poems
as 'Neutral Tones' and 'Beyond the Last Lamp'. Both gain from
the creation of a dramatic situation and evocative scene-setting
not unlike that of 'Winter in Durnover Field', though integrated
with the poems rather than prefacing them. In the case of
'Neutral Tones', however, the scene functions too blatantly as
pathetic fallacy. F. B. Pinion's comment that 'It is as if the poet
were trying to present a non-subjective impression'[8] is surely
wrong. The scene may be neutral in colour, but it is far from
neutral emotionally. Desolation is projected from the minds of
the disillusioned lovers on to their surroundings; and the season,
even more than in 'Winter in Durnover Field', is chosen for its
consonance with their mood. The simile in 'And the sun was
white, as though chidden of God' (re-emphasised later in the
poem by the reference to 'the God-curst sun') does little to add to
the visual effect, but much to intensify the sense of the bitterness
of the lovers. Another such simile occurs in the third stanza:

> The smile on your mouth was the deadest thing
> Alive enough to have strength to die;
> And a grin of bitterness swept thereby
> Like an onimous bird a-wing.

The bird here is a bird of ill omen; its function is to add to the
harrowing effect. The last stanza says that since the moment
recorded in the previous stanzas 'keen lessons that love deceives'
have recalled the scene and the woman's face to the poet's mind,
in something like a parody of Wordsworth's 'emotion recollected
in tranquillity'. But it seems rather as if subsequent experience
has thrown its veil over the past. Powerful as the poem is, it
reads more as the jaundiced memory of a saddened man than as
a moment recognised at a later date as marking the inception of
tragic vision.

   This is not quite so with 'Beyond the Last Lamp'. The
Wordsworthian recollection is at work here, too, from a retros-
pect of 'thirty years of blur and blot', and the damp, dreary
setting combines with the sad look of the lovers to create an
image of disillusionment:

> The pair seemed lovers, yet absorbed
> In mental scenes no longer orbed
> By love's young rays.

But there is both a more human, and less predetermined, focus. The lovers belong to the scene, and yet are entirely intent on themselves:

> Some heavy thought constrained each face,
> And blinded them to time and place.

And it is this very intentness that attracts the attention of the observer, puzzles his mind, and at the same time makes them real and individual to him. A weakness still remains, however, in the degree of the poem's subjectivity. Its situation is reminiscent of that of Tess and Angel Clare in Chapter 35 of *Tess of the d'Urbervilles*, but the poem is less specific than the novel. The picture of the lovers is vividly presented, but their misery is merely a question for speculation concerning 'things which had been or might be', and

> One could but wonder who they were
> And what wild woe detained them there.

Because he does not know what private suffering they brood on, the observer is able to fashion them as the more generalised 'That mysterious tragic pair', who continue, even after they are no longer physically present, to reverberate in his imagination. This gives the poem an undoubtedly haunting lyrical beauty, but the actual tragedy has to be taken on trust. We have only the observer's word for it; and though the human reality is more convincingly created than it is in 'Neutral Tones', a sense still remains that the poem is the projection of a mood rather than the means of embodying acutely felt tragic experience.

The greatest of Hardy's love poems have a much more specifically tragic situation inherent in them. These are the poems he wrote in 1912–13 after the death of his first wife, grouped together under the Vergilian epigraph, 'Veteris vestigia flammae'. The reference is to the feeling Dido still has for her dead husband, Sichaeus, even though she has just met and fallen in love with Aeneas. She wishes to remain true to Sichaeus' memory, but feels the stirring of what she had thought to be dead passion. This is at the beginning of Book IV of the *Aeneid*; by the end she has capitulated to the new love, been deserted by Aeneas, and committed suicide. Immediately, therefore, the

words relate to Hardy's loving memory of Emma and to the
poems as posthumous sparkles of his old flame; but they may
also have been associated in his mind with Aeneas' betrayal of
Dido and his own coolness towards, and virtual estrangement
from, Emma in the later years of their marriage. For the poems
are intensely confessional, both in the sense that they express
private and personal emotion, and that they are tacit admissions
of guilt. The allusion to Vergil helps to distance this theme,
however; and along with the other devices that Hardy uses –
especially the temporal perspective that enables him to colour
the past with the present, and the present with the past – it gives
him a means of controlling and directing his complex grief. His
situation loses none of its poignant personal immediacy, and
there is no attempt to work out Vergilian parallels; but the
subdued echo of one of literature's great examples of betrayal
gives a tragic resonance to his own story (as Arnold hoped it
would when he, more consciously and deliberately, alluded to it
in 'The Scholar-Gipsy').

However, the betrayal has to do, not only with Hardy's
treatment of his wife, but, even more so, with the loss of that
romantic 'magic in my eyes' which is celebrated in 'When I Set
Out for Lyonnesse'. It is another variation on the theme of
illusion and disillusion which runs through so much of Hardy's
poetry. The death of his wife seems to have revived memories of
their courtship and early love in the Cornish landscape where
they first met, and in March 1913 Hardy actually made a
sentimental journey to revisit the spots that were hallowed for
him by association with Emma. This becomes an integral part of
the 1912–13 poems. But it also stands for a youthful dream that
was dissipated in the long years of married life, and now enjoys
only a cruelly ironic revival in the mind of a remorseful and aged
widower. In giving expression to this curious revival Hardy
enjoyed a kind of poetic renaissance, but tragically coloured. As
he writes in the *Life* (attributed to his second wife, but virtually
by Hardy himself):

Many poems were written by Hardy at the end of the previous
year and the early part of this [i.e. 1913] – more than he had
ever written before in the same space of time – as can be seen
by referring to their subjects, as well as to the dates attached
to them. To adopt Walpole's words concerning Gray, Hardy

was 'in flower' in these days, and, like Gray's, his flower was
sad-coloured.[9]

Of these poems the nearest to traditional elegy, as Pinion
points out, is 'A Death-Day Recalled'.[10] Hardy asks, somewhat
rhetorically,

> Why did not Vallency
> In his purl deplore
> One whose haunts were whence he
> Drew his limpid store?

This reproach to the indifference of the Cornish valley to the
death of the woman so strongly associated with it in her lover's
mind recalls Milton's 'Where were ye Nymphs?' (*Lycidas*, 50)
and Shelley's 'Where wert thou mighty Mother?' (*Adonais*, 10);
but the facile trochees in which most of the poem is written
reveal that for Hardy there is no vitality in the pastoral convention of natural grief. It is an illusion belonging with the romantic
associations of the place. The reality is that 'these, unheeding, /
Listless, passed the hour.' What the poem offers is the pathos of
the isolated human feeling.

A facile rhythm as the carrier of futile romantic yearning is an
important element in certain other poems as well – notably
'Beeny Cliff', with its lilting

O the opal and the sapphire of that wandering western sea,
And the woman riding high above with bright hair flapping free,

and the dactylic plangency of the first stanza of 'The Voice':

> Woman much missed, how you call to me, call to me,
> Saying that now you are not as you were
> When you had changed from the one who was all to me,
> But as at first, when our day was fair.

But in the latter poem, in particular, there is a careful placing of
the yearning 'voice' that gives the poem a different, and more
tragic, perspective. It calls back into an idealised past, in which
the poet imagines the woman waiting 'as I knew you then, /
Even to the original air-blue gown!' But it is qualified by the

question, 'Can it be you that I hear?' and this continues into the
third stanza with the alternative possibility that it is only 'the
breeze' creating an illusion, the futility of which is beautifully
caught in the odd rhyme of 'listlessness' with 'wistlessness'.
Then comes a marked change of rhythm in the last stanza,
together with a much greater emphasis on the melancholy
soughing of the wind ('Wind oozing thin through the thorn from
norward'), which transforms 'the woman calling' into a mere
voice from the past, made all the more poignantly sad by the
late, autumnal, circumstances of the present.

It is this interplay of past and present, realised in more
complex fashion, that gives 'At Castle Boterel' its much more
movingly elegiac appeal. It opens in the present ('As I drive to
the junction of lane and highway'), but at what proves to be the
end of a sentimental journey – the one, in fact, that Hardy made
in 1913 – *à la recherche du temps perdu*. The poet's journey is in
drizzly weather, but as he looks back he sees on the slope of the
hill (and with a jump from one stanza to the next which
effectively dramatises the time-change) a very different scene,
from the past, which nevertheless seems to him part of the present:

> I look behind at the fading byway,
>   And see on its slope, now glistening wet,
>   Distinctly yet
>
> Myself and a girlish form benighted
>   In dry March weather.

The next sentence is in the historic present ('We climb the road /
Beside a chaise'), and then the poem switches into the past tense
('We had just alighted'). But the sense of the poet reflecting in
the present on what happened in the past is continued by such
interactions of tense as

> What we did as we climbed, and what we talked of
>   Matters not much, nor to what it led.

'To what it led' also points forward to the future (though a future
– presumably Hardy and Emma's marriage – which is now past
to the poet), and is further glossed as something stretching into
an indefinite future, beyond even that of the present:

> Something that life will not be baulked of
> Without rude reason till hope is dead,
> And feeling fled.

This 'filled but a minute', but it is singled out from both the past and future of 'that hill's story' as an almost timeless moment. To the poet, increasingly enraptured by this transcendent vision from the past, it now becomes possible to make a massive affirmation of the significance of subjective feeling in the face even of the awesome prospect of geological time:

> Primaeval rocks form the road's steep border,
> And much have they faced there, first and last,
> Of the transitory in Earth's long order;
> But what they record in colour and cast
> Is – that we two passed.

None the less, this is only personal impression. The next stanza opens with 'And to me' (echoing 'To one mind never', in the fourth stanza), thus narrowing what is to follow; and 'Time's unflinching rigour', though still contained within a clause that subordinates it to the emphatic present of the 'phantom figure' which 'Remains on the slope', takes on an ominously destructive power. In the final stanza we are back in the present of the first stanza, with the co-presence of the 'girlish form' of the second; but now it is 'shrinking, shrinking', and so is the strength of the subjective vision:

> I look back at it amid the rain
> For the very last time; for my sand is sinking,
> And I shall traverse old love's domain
> Never again.

The ending of 'At Castle Boterel' is an important qualification of the poem's carefully achieved balance between past and present. The middle stanzas affirm the abiding significance of subjective human feeling, much in the manner of Hardy's wartime poem, 'In Time of "The Breaking of Nations" '[11], and to that extent its theme is heroic rather than tragic. But the initial drizzle of the present, to which we return in the 'rain' at the end in association with the fading powers of old age, sets this humanist affirmation in a more sombre frame. The phrase, 'old love's domain,' likewise has a qualifying effect: its slight tinge of sentimentality is carefully judged, subtly undermining the splendid timelessness which the poet attributes to love in his more subjectively excited mood; and the plain finality of 'Never again' speaks both of approaching death and the end of romance. The poet's own present in these last lines becomes a present that has all the fragility of limited human life, and tacitly reminds us that the thrilling exploration of present, past and future time – and even the transcendence of time – are dependent on a frail decaying consciousness.

What is missing, however, from 'At Castle Boterel' is the sense of guilt attached to the *veteris vestigia flammae*, and because it is missing the poem is less tragic than others in the group which make its underlying present felt. In 'The Going', for example, the theme seems to be quite simply the unexpected death of the wife, which meant that there was no leave-taking between her and her husband; but the emotional reality beneath this surface is the husband's feeling of unpurged guilt:

> Why, then, latterly did we not speak,
> Did we not think of those days long dead,
> And ere your vanishing strive to seek
> That time's renewal?

The tragedy now is that the situation is irremediable – one of the most familiar, and perhaps commonplace, experiences of bereavement, but expressed by Hardy with an urgency that makes it new and keen:

> Well, well! All's past amend,
> Unchangeable. It must go.
> I seem but a dead man held on end
> To sink down soon. . . . O you could not know
> That such swift fleeing
> No soul foreseeing –
> Not even I – would undo me so!

Robert Gittings suggests that the actual death of Emma did not take Hardy by surprise in this way, that he deliberately turned his eyes away from her suffering during the last months of her life, and that his attention was already being given to the younger woman who was to become his second wife: 'His full guilt was too horrible to face.'[12] If so, the biographical information only spells out what, despite its lack of full frankness, is implicit in the broken rhythms, and the flat weariness and despair, of that last stanza. The hidden guilt seems more powerful than full confession could be.

The most moving of such poems is 'After a Journey'. This, once more, is a poem which slides between the past of Hardy and Emma's courtship and the present of his re-entry into her 'olden haunts'. The language is paradoxical: what he has come to 'view' is a 'ghost', which, contrary to the expectation set up by the verb, is neither visible nor invisible, but 'voiceless'; and yet, as in 'The Haunter', where the ghostly speaker is also Emma herself, is capable of murmuring reproaches:

What have you now found to say of our past –
   Scanned across the dark space wherein I have lacked you?
Summer gave us sweets, but autumn wrought division?
    Things were not lastly as firstly well
      With us twain, you tell?

When visible, that is when alive, this 'voiceless ghost' did have a voice, but the suggestion is that Hardy neither saw nor heard her. The voice that he now hears is really, of course, his own, speaking what his guilt tells him she might well have wanted to say to him. The fact that it is articulated in such decorously discreet Victorian language does not, curiously perhaps, emasculate the passage, but rather adds a sense of painful groping through euphemistic evasion to recognition of the truth. The reality of the poem is the buried discord that has lain between the man and the woman so long, but which death now makes it possible to begin disinterring.

Much in the poem is vaguely and imprecisely evoked, but appropriately so. It belongs to the evanescent memory-world, typified by the mist-bow shining above the waterfall 'At the then fair hour in the then fair weather' – where the repeated 'then fair' carefully differentiates the romantic past from the disillusioned present. It is this essentially subjective world – its subjectivity heightened by the ignorance of its 'flitting' nature attributed to the birds and seals in lines 25–6 – which provides the meeting-ground for the woman who was 'all aglow' in her youth, though

now a 'thin ghost', and the elderly man who 'frailly' follows her.
The idealised image of her, returning from across forty years,
dominates him and directs his sentimental pilgrimage; but he
does not resent this – indeed, the closing lines seem to represent
a willing immersion in the fantasy-world of the past:

> nay, bring me here again!
> I am just the same as when
> Our days were a joy, and our paths through flowers.

However, Hardy does not quite mean what this seems to say.
The poem is full of the sense of the ravages of time and guilt: 'the
dead scenes', 'the dark space' and the autumnal division of
stanza 2; the changes implied in stanza 3; and the inimical
coming of dawn and the louring of Life in stanza 4. All these
show that things are very different from what they were forty
years ago. It is the wish to reach back through the past to the
guiltless illusions of youth that is expressed by 'I am just the
same', and it is precisely the ghostly nature of that revisited past
which tacitly denies its truth. The poem is thus tragic because it
expresses the longing to atone for, and restore, the past, while
keeping its foundation in the sadly disillusioned present.

In the poems written after the death of his wife Hardy gives
intensely personal feeling tragic distance by setting it in the
perspective of time. Through the counterpointing of present loss
and the romance of youthful courtship, with the indirectly
communicated sense of long years between, tragic discovery and
reversal are both telescoped into a single lyrical utterance and
made to seem part of an inevitable process of disillusionment.
They suggest, as so often the novels do, Hardy's special gift of
universalising the private and domestic. Thus at the beginning
of *The Woodlanders* he writes of Little Hintock as being 'one of
those sequestered spots . . . where, from time to time, dramas of a
grandeur and unity truly Sophoclean are enacted in the real, by
virtue of the concentrated passions and closely-knit interdependence of the lives therein':[13] though it is in *The Mayor of Casterbridge* and *Tess of the d'Urbervilles*, rather than *The Woodlanders*
itself, that the integration of personal and universal is most

successfully accomplished. In the poems, apart from those in ballad form, Hardy does not have the narrative space in which to build up the kind of resonance achieved in the novels; but, as his use of Cornwall and courtship in the 1912–13 poems shows, its place may be taken by an implied narrative which links private details to a wider theme.

This is the kind of relationship to be found in 'During Wind and Rain'. Its theme is the great commonplace of mutability, realised in particular vignettes from the history of a family.[14] Each stanza is an image of domestic happiness, presented like a flash-back in a film, which, however, returns remorselessly at the end to a refrain summing up the passage of time, followed by a final line concretely recording its destructive effect in the present. In the first stanza the scene is a musical evening indoors; 2, 3 and 4 are all outdoors; and in 4 the family also moves house:

> They change to a high new house,
> He, she, all of them – aye,
> Clocks and carpets and chairs
>   On the lawn all day,
> And brightest things that are theirs.

The details are personal and intimate, though the members of the family are not specified, remaining generically 'They'. (There is, however, a ritual expansion to 'He, she, all of them' in the second line of stanzas 1 and 4, and to 'Elders and juniors' in stanza 2 and 'Men and maidens' in stanza 3.) Thus the poem seems to deal with humanity as such, but in terms of individuals familiar to us, and in scenes made lovingly real to us by emotionally significant details. The more, however, that these images claim our warm recognition, the more we are seared by the negating refrain and its following line. And the process is cumulative. Again and again creation is followed by destruction, the ritualised positives turning into a negative ritual that grates painfully on an increasingly involved observer; and the climax is the last and most painful image of all:

> Down their carved names the rain-drop ploughs.

The final lines of each of the preceding stanzas have been summaries of natural destruction, forms of the 'wind and rain' alluded to in the title. Here destruction overwhelms the human

beings, whose happiness has been repeatedly threatened, and
whose story is now seen to be completed by their reduction to
names on a tombstone down which the all-pervasive rain ironically 'ploughs'.[15]

'During Wind and Rain' derives its title from Feste's song at
the end of *Twelfth Night*, with its refrain, 'With hey, ho, the wind
and the rain'. It lacks the curious mingling of tragic and comic
which gives Feste's song its special flavour (the equivalent of
'With toss-pots still had drunken heads' is to be found in the
so-called 'rustic choruses' of *Far from the Madding Crowd* and *The
Mayor of Casterbridge*), but it is typically Shakespearean in its
locating of tragic feeling between natural forces and human
compassion. This is the most characteristic Hardy. But there is
also the Hardy who tries to give his immediate sense of disillusionment and destruction a vast, philosophical dimension. The
most obvious expression of this is his huge epic drama, *The
Dynasts*. It is also to be found, however, in some of his lyrics, and
especially in those which are prompted, like *The Dynasts*, by war.
Among these his poem on the Armistice which ended the First
World War, 'And There Was a Great Calm', attempts, not very
successfully, to give generalised expression to the theme of
war-weariness through the use of personified abstractions such
as Passion, Despair, Anger, Selflessness, and Lovingkindness
and the comments of the choric Spirits of Irony and Pity, which
are borrowed from *The Dynasts*. These seem portentously out of
place in the more intimate form of the lyric. Where the poem
does succeed, in an unusually bizarre way, is in its presentation
of the immediate effect of the cease-fire:

> Aye; all was hushed. The about-to-fire fired not,
> The aimed-at moved away in trance-lipped song.
> One checkless regiment slung a clinching shot
> And turned.

This suggests that war has reduced men to either instruments of
destruction ('The about-to-fire') or their targets ('The aimed-
at'), and even the release from fighting leaves them moving in an
unreal world of trance. Likewise, the regiment that fires its final
shot does so as if unable immediately to halt a mechanical habit.
Such a condition of virtually will-less automatism suits the poet's
vision of human beings dehumanised by 'a brute-like blindness',

the pointlessness of which can only make the Spirit of Pity whisper, 'Why?' But the absence of individuality in the victims leaves them as objects of pathos rather than tragedy. By serving the poem's idea they put the reader at too great a distance.

A similar criticism ought to apply to 'The Convergence of the Twain', Hardy's no less bizarre poem on the loss of the *Titanic*, sunk by an iceberg on its maiden voyage across the Atlantic in 1912. Like the later war poem it deals in personified abstractions – 'the Pride of Life', 'The Immanent Will' and 'the Spinner of the Years', and even the iceberg seems to join their company as 'A Shape of Ice'. It also creates its own specialised poetic diction in which the ship's boilers become 'Steel chambers, late the pyres / Of her salamandrine fires' and the ship itself 'This creature of cleaving wing'. All this is highly effective, however, in giving a serious mock-epic dimension to the *Titanic*, and intensifies the deliberate grotesqueness of the contrast, elaborated in the first five stanzas, between the flashy affluence of the ship and her position on the sea-bed, where the sea-worm crawls over her mirrors 'meant / To glass the opulent', her jewels 'Lie lightless, all their sparkles bleared and black and blind', and

> Dim moon-eyed fishes near
> Gaze at the gilded gear
> And query: 'What does this vaingloriousness down here?'

The ship is weirdly out of context in this setting, and it is Hardy's purpose to make the reader feel this as acutely as possible. It is in part a satire on 'human vanity', but not mainly so. The question which these five stanzas lead up to is one that Hardy intends his readers to ponder, and he provides an answer in the form of the tragic 'plot' which the rest of the poem recounts. The bizarre end already described is predetermined: the building of the ship goes *pari passu* with the making of the iceberg, and, though 'Alien they seemed to be', 'they were bent / By paths coincident / On being anon twins halves of one august event'. The actual catastrophe is announced only in the histrionic, but oblique, manner of the last stanza:

> Till the Spinner of the Years
> Said 'Now!' And each one hears,
> And consummation comes, and jars two hemispheres.

All this is deliberately plotted, a foregone conclusion; moreover Hardy does not mention the human victims of the disaster (even though the poem was originally written for a charity performance at Covent Garden in aid of their relatives). And yet in its total effect the poem does not seem coldly indifferent. It has a curiously moving human element in its use of the metaphor of marriage: the conventional reference to a ship as feminine is given more than conventional force, and the iceberg becomes 'a sinister mate / For her'. She is a great lady of fashion (the mirrors, jewels and 'gilded' gear' of the opening stanzas now take on a different meaning, and 'smart' in stanza VIII becomes peculiarly appropriate), destined for a misalliance that will bring only a tragic parody of 'consummation'.

One senses that the same experience of marital disharmony and disillusion lies behind 'The Convergence of the Twain' as behind the 1912–13 poems (though at the time of Hardy's writing it, April 1912, Emma was still alive). If so, that experience should not be evoked reductively – to rob the poem of serious concern with a great historical disaster. The effect, rather, is to bring public and private together in a uniquely telling way. The disillusionment centred on Hardy's own marriage, which is, in essence, the disillusionment with romantic love, gives its emotional colouring to the mocking consummation of a philosophical design. What is so painful is the recognition that providence is withdrawn – or, more precisely, was never there, but only projected by the human mind, as romantic glamour is thrown over youthful courtship only to be eroded in the inevitable course of life. The strength of 'The Convergence of the Twain' is that it succeeds in combining the sharpness of this disillusionment with the ironic grandeur of a public poem. Its weakness, on the other hand, is that it manages its distance and detachment just a little too well. It lacks the intimate domestic detail, and the sense of controlled, but not quite mastered, personal grief and guilt, which seem necessary to produce Hardy's most profoundly moving tragic lyrics. When reading it we can forget the frail fallibility of the man who wrote it, as we cannot when reading 'During Wind and Rain' and especially the poems on the death of Emma.

6 Edward Thomas: the Unreasonable Grief

Edward Thomas is strongly reminiscent of both Keats and Hardy. Keats is recalled in 'Blenheim Oranges' by the ambivalent image of apples that 'Fall grubby from the trees', and in 'The sun used to shine' by the mixture of ripeness and rottenness in 'the yellow flavorous coat / Of an apple wasps had undermined'.[1] Less immediately in terms of style, but with a similar sense of the organic process that makes death and life seem inherent in all seasons, Thomas also suggests Keats when in 'The Thrush', for example, the bird's song heard in November prompts reflections on its associations with April. The bird loses itself in the unconscious spontaneity of the present season, but the poet must recognise, and accept, the complexity of change:

> But I know the months all,
> And their sweet names, April,
> May and June and October,
> As you call and call
>
> I must remember
> What died into April
> And consider what will be born
> Of a fair November;
>
> And April I love for what
> It was born of, and November
> For what it will die in,
> What they are and what they are not.

The kinship with Hardy is obvious in the sonnet, 'February Afternoon', which broods on both the permanent rhythms of nature and the incorrigible human appetite for war, and ends with a very Hardyan divine indifference:

> And God still sits aloft in the array
> That we have wrought him, stone-deaf and stone-blind.

And in 'The New House' Hardy's sense of the interaction of past, present and future is echoed when the new occupier enters his dwelling and immediately hears the moaning of the wind, which foretells

> Nights of storm, days of mist, without end;
> Sad days when the sun
> Shone in vain: old griefs, and griefs
> Not yet begun.

Yet Thomas has his own voice. Both sets of echoes combine in him to reinforce that distinctive self-consciousness which is both a torment to him and the source of his own peculiarly tentative awareness of the tragic. The melancholy which is so persistent a feature of his poetry has the lush quality of Keats', and the bleak disillusion of Hardy's, but it is constantly undermined by self-analysis and self-doubt which make him question its validity. He shares their vision, but distrusts the rhetorical means that are available to him to express it. In particular, he is aware of himself as an alien (and here he may owe something to the Hardy of 'In Tenebris II') in a society that welcomes extrovert energy and success, but has little time for the 'unreasonable' despondency of a sensitivity such as his. He is unable, however, to respond to hostility with hostility. The openness of his mind makes him half-concede the criticism directed against him – indeed, it is criticism which originates as much from within as from without. At the same time his alternative vision is unremittingly present to his imagination, and insists on creating its own world. The only way to resolve his problem, therefore, is to include the terms of his dilemma within the poetry itself, reconciling denial and affirmation in a form that allows both.

This is what he does in 'Aspens'. It is a poem about the nature of his own imagination. The aspens are himself, as he confirms in a letter to Eleanor Farjeon: 'About "Aspens" you missed just the turn that I thought essential. *I* was the aspen. "We" meant the trees and I with my dejected shyness.'[2] The aspens at the crossroads 'talk together / Of rain', their soft, insistent whispering sound, suggestive of the insidious gossip of village women, in seemingly timorous contrast to the ringing, roaring noise of smithy and inn, which represents the boisterous, busy life of the community. But for all the loudness of this competition, 'The whisper of the aspens is not drowned'. It has power to call up a ghostly alternative, 'silent' smithy and inn; and in certain conditions of darkness and mystery (that, again, have Keatsian overtones) –

> In the bare moonlight or the thick-furred gloom,
> In tempest or the night of nightingales –

it can turn even the crossroads 'to a ghostly room'. As he makes this claim, which is an affirmation of the introspective poet's vision of a shadow side which social man prefers to ignore, his belief gathers strength, and leads, in the fifth stanza, to a seemingly confident assertion of creative power:

> And it would be the same were no house near.
> Over all sorts of weather, men, and times,
> Aspens must shake their leaves.

Characteristically, however, Thomas seems to become diffident in mid-sentence, and withdraws authority from the aspens, concluding with

> and men may hear
> But need not listen, more than to my rhymes.

The final stanza continues this undercutting:

> Whatever wind blows, while they and I have leaves
> We cannot other than an aspen be
> That ceaselessly, unreasonably grieves,
> Or so men think who like a different tree.

This seems to reduce the poet's vision to a compulsively irrational melancholy that can, after all, be dismissed by the more commonsense, daylight mind; but there is yet again a check in the closing line. 'Or so men think who like a different tree' reopens the possibility that the aspen vision may be valid, and even hints that rejection on the ground that its grief is unreasonable may itself be the product of fearful clinging to the social world of inn and smithy lest the 'ghostly' alternative take hold.

The fluctuating syntax of 'Aspens' thus has the effect of conceding the doubtful status of the poet's vision without yielding to the opposition it encounters. The melancholy menace of the aspens still persists in its disturbing challenge, but allowance is made for the possibility that it may be, as the remark to Eleanor Farjeon suggests, the consequence only of 'dejected shyness'. Such hesitancy is inseparable from the honesty with which Thomas tries to face his experience. He does not, of course, always achieve it. He sometimes slips into a sentimental view of death, as in 'The Child on the Cliff'; and sometimes he reverts, impressively, but archaically, to a more traditionally tragic-rhetorical posture, as in 'The Gallows'. But these are exceptional in their lack of self-critical tentativeness. More often, even when his mood is bleakly pessimistic, he discounts his own attitude, or introduces some other view to balance it. In 'Digging [I]', for example, where the major theme is the deathliness of autumn scents, he also includes a bonfire which

> burns
> The dead, the waste, the dangerous,
> And all to sweetness turns –

as well as a robin singing 'Sad songs of Autumn mirth'. In 'The Owl' also, though the bird's 'most melancholy cry' echoes the poet's hunger and weariness after a day straining against a cold North wind, it heightens his enjoyment of food and rest, and deepens his feeling for those who suffer more than he – a double effect which is concentrated in the double meaning of 'salted':

> And salted was my food, and my repose,
> Salted and sobered, too, by the bird's voice
> Speaking for all who lay under the stars,
> Soldiers and poor, unable to rejoice.

It is this more complex, mixed state of consciousness that gives Thomas' tragic lyrics their distinctive quality. It is present even in a poem like 'Rain', which, in its opening lines, seems to evoke complete despair:

> Rain, midnight rain, nothing but the wild rain
> On this bleak hut, and solitude, and me
> Remembering again that I shall die.

By itself this is a powerful, but narrowly exclusive beginning, over-insistent on the dark, wild downpour of rain and the isolated self-consciousness of the poet. However, to separate this from what follows is to distort the poem – though in a way that the verse seems to dictate, since the third line has the air of completing a statement and a cadence that falls to rest on the final 'die' (intensified by its internal rhyme with 'I'). But the sentence is not in fact complete. 'I' is also the subject in the next line of the verbs 'hear' and 'give', and the sentence gains a new momentum which carries it through to the end of the sixth line:

> And neither hear the rain nor give it thanks
> For washing me cleaner than I have been
> Since I was born into this solitude.

The brooding awareness of mortality continues with the negativing of these verbs; the poet is conscious that the time will inevitably come when he will not hear and not be able to give thanks. But simultaneously he suggests that in the present he does hear and does give thanks for a kind of purification that he receives from the rain. Moreover, the ultimate completion of the sentence by the word 'solitude' has the effect of qualifying the isolation which that word had conveyed in line 2. It seems a wiser, perhaps less lonely, form of solitude than it was before. At the very least, something has happened to mitigate its bleakness. This change makes the next line, which might otherwise seem a totally unjustified leap, more acceptable. Rain, the purifying agent, rather than the obliterating downpour, is, presumably, the force warranting the beatitude of 'Blessed are the dead that the rain rains upon'; and the sense of 'cleaner' (in 'washing me cleaner') perhaps carries over to the dead also, suggesting that they are washed free of guilt. On the other hand, their condition of blessedness may be simply their unconsciousness, which allows the rain merely to rain upon them without the tragic overtones it has for the poet in the opening lines. The tragic state is essentially one of consciousness of suffering, with which the poet identifies himself as if it were his own, but which also transcends the personal to become a sense of the human condition. With Thomas, in this poem, it takes the form of a recognition of the cleanness and simplicity of the dead, balanced, however, by a prayer that none whom he once loved may experience the same lacerating solitude. His own anguish is the means by which he enters the tragic state; but it remains a private state in that it is achieved through identification with others who are linked to him by personal feeling:

> But here I pray that none whom once I loved
> Is dying tonight or lying still awake
> Solitary, listening to the rain,
> Either in pain or thus in sympathy
> Helpless among the living and the dead.

Again, the pause at 'dead' creates an illusion of completion, which, however, is only temporary, for the sentence continues with two comparisons which first generalise, and then once more personalise, the experience. The first of these reaches tragic impersonality by imaging the consciousness of destroyed lives in a chillingly immediate form which also makes it part of the natural landscape:

> Like a cold water among broken reeds,
> Myriads of broken reeds all still and stiff.

The second seems to maintain the generalised momentum by using the same formula, 'Like', but swings back to the poet and his initial emphasis on the desolating rain:

> Like me who have no love which this wild rain
> Has not dissolved except the love of death,
> If love it be towards what is perfect and
> Cannot, the tempest tells me, disappoint.

Death unmitigated by any Christian or other religious consolation has a finality which in the absolute, tragic state of 'the tempest' is both end and consummation. It is the only ultimately illusion-free release, and Thomas seems to be accepting this with stoic resignation. There remains, however, the final addition to the sentence, in the clause beginning 'If'. This also recognises the coldness of such perfection and its incompatibility with the personal anguish and sympathy evoked in the body of the poem. It thus keeps another kind of feeling alive; without explicitly contradicting the poet's claim that he has no love which the wild rain has not dissolved, the final clause qualifies its title to the word 'love', and so tacitly pleads the case for a warmer, more human, kind of love.

Such love is always focussed on the imperfect. It is aroused by suffering and the desolating feeling that the consciousness of mortality entails, but it cannot be satisfied with the exclusiveness of tragedy. Thus in 'Liberty' Thomas entertains the idea of a freedom from blighting self-consciousness, only to reject it in favour of a Keatsian preference for 'pain' (in the process somewhat altering the import of the phrase he borrows from 'Ode to a Nightingale'); but then modifies 'pain' still further to include 'both tears and mirth':

> And yet I still am half in love with pain,
> With what is imperfect, with both tears and mirth,
> With things that have an end, with life and earth,
> And this moon that leaves me dark within the door.

Above all, love rejects the superficiality that goes with mere liking. If it goes beyond tragedy, it is not because it refuses the dark, lacerating involvement, but because it follows the lead of a wider commitment. In 'Roads', for example, Thomas begins by saying 'I love roads', and he recognises that, in the tragic time of war in which he is writing, 'all roads lead to France / And heavy is the tread / Of the living'. Yet the roads pre-exist, and outlast, the individual man's consciousness, and maintain a life for the dead which enables them to keep the poet company and populate his solitude. The men 'who like a different tree' in 'Aspens' may have reason on their side, but they would be incapable of such a vision.

In 'Old Man' this distinction between liking and loving is of crucial importance. *Artemisia abrotanum*, or southernwood, has various names including those with which the poem opens, 'Old Man, or Lad's-love', and these names the poet says, 'I like'; and yet, paradoxically,

> The herb itself I like not, but for certain
> I love it, as some day the child will love it
> Who plucks a feather from the door-side bush
> Whenever she goes in or out of the house.

The whole poem is one which involves a process of meditative discrimination, rather than logical distinction, between what is loved and what is merely liked. The child's 'snipping the tips and shrivelling / The shreds' of the shrub – which she does in an absent-minded way that the drifting syntax admirably echoes – releases the 'bitter scent'; and, as attention passes back from the child to the adult, it is this 'bitter scent' which provides a teasing continuity:

> I, too, often shrivel the grey shreds,
> Sniff them and think and sniff again and try
> Once more to think what it is I am remembering,
> Always in vain.

Although memory is defeated, the impulse given by the 'bitter scent' is so strong that the discrimination previously made between liking and loving swells up again in another shape:

> I cannot like the scent,
> Yet I would rather give up others more sweet,
> With no meaning, than this bitter one.

Liking appears to be superseded by the deeper compulsion of love, which has already been declared in the second paragraph, and which the child is subconsciously in the process of acquiring; and it is this compulsion that takes over in the final paragraph, immersing the poet in an overwhelming sense of loss:

> No garden appears, no path, no hoar-green bush
> Of Lad's-love, or Old Man, no child beside,
> Neither father nor mother, nor any playmate;
> Only an avenue, dark, nameless, without end.

If what is lost were more precisely identified, the poem might well be less hauntingly resonant than it is. This is the shadow side of consciousness hinted at in 'Aspens', where liking and reasonableness are irrelevant. It is a submerged area where the sharpest anguish has its source, and approachable not by will, but only by the groping, half-baffled pursuit of the 'bitter scent', which is the compulsive effect of love.

The goal to which love finally draws the poet in 'Old Man' is a dark, negative, but inexplicably potent, world; and in many of Thomas' poems there is a similar dark world complementary to, and often quietly dominating, consciousness. His most frequent symbol for this is the forest. In 'The Green Roads' it is the forest in which the green roads end, and where one dead oak 'in the middle deep' seems to brood over the rest of the trees. In 'The Dark Forest' it is almost 'a too obvious metaphor', as Thomas himself realised,[3] making the opposition between the flowers of the forest and those of 'outside' uncharacteristically rigid:

> Nor can those that pluck either blossom greet
> The others, day or night.

More typical is his use of the forest in 'The Other'. It begins: 'The forest ended.' The speaker, emerging from the forest, is happy to reach the light and hear bees, and smell grass

> because I had come
> To an end of forest, and because
> Here was both road and inn, the sum
> Of what's not forest.

But he immediately encounters people who ask if he passed that way the day before, and the refreshing sense of release expressed in the opening lines gives way to huddled cross-questioning (' "Not you? Queer." / "Who then? and slept here?" ') which ends abruptly with: 'I felt fear.' From here on, as Andrew Motion comments, 'Thomas reverses the roles usually allotted to self and image', acting as 'the pursuer rather than the pursued',[4] until his search for the man resembling himself leads to his entering an inn where the man loudly asks for him. For a moment their roles seem to revert to their traditional order, as the speaker is reproached by his quarry, but says nothing, and slips away. The previous pursuit is renewed in the final lines, but with the speaker now more cautious: 'I steal out of the wood to light'; and the final state of the relationship is summed up in an abrupt, uneasy closing couplet:

> He goes: I follow: no release
> Until he ceases. Then I also shall cease.

The speaker's initial emergence from the wood, when looked at retrospectively from the end of the poem, is recognised as misguidedly 'glad'. The darkness cannot be escaped; it must either pursue, or be pursued, in a continuous process that can only end with death. This clearly gives scope for a Jungian interpretation in terms of the interdependence of self and shadow-self; but, as so often with Thomas, the poem resists any one meaning. Its wandering search and awkward, almost unsociable, social encounters enact the tormented uncertainty of the speaker with regard to his relationship with his other self, and that in turn is reflected in his feelings towards darkness and the wood. There is one particularly powerful section (lines 61–90), just before his encounter with his 'man' at the inn, which seems to offer reassurance and serenity:

> I stood serene,
> And with a solemn quiet mirth,
> An old inhabitant of earth.

With an echo of Vaughan, he says that such times once seemed to him 'Moments of everlastingness', as if he had recovered a lost paradise of integrated consciousness. But they were essentially unstable, dependent on a spontaneity that had to be unaware of itself:

> And fortunate my search was then
> While what I sought, nevertheless,
> That I was seeking, I did not guess.

The very awkwardness of the syntax brings them down to earth, and in the next paragraph the speaker is back to what is the norm for this poem – the baffling search, which, even when it leads to a meeting, ends in nothing but reversal of roles and inarticulacy:

> what had I got to say?
> I said nothing. I slipped away.

'The Other' is concerned with the inherent instability of consciousness. The only real release from it is death: 'no release / Until he ceases. Then I also shall cease.' In the most tragic of Thomas' poems, 'Lights Out', that release becomes the central issue. He no longer vacillates. The forest is not an ambiguous alternative to daylight consciousness, but the final extinction of consciousness which is universal and inevitable:

> I have come to the borders of sleep,
> The unfathomable deep
> Forest, where all must lose
> Their way, however straight
> Or winding, soon or late;
> They can not choose.

It is the end of deception and of love, and of the opposites of despair and ambition, pleasure and trouble, whether 'sweet or bitter'. The speaker is willing to give up what is dearest to him for the sake of it; and, finally, he welcomes its obliteration of his self-consciousness.

'Lights Out' is thus one of the most direct of Thomas' poems, presenting the dark of the forest as a welcome relief from the uncertainties which torment him. It may easily be mistaken for the expression of a suicidal death-wish, but its date, November 1916, and its title remind us – though it must be admitted that there is nothing in the text that otherwise would tell us – that this is a war poem. The death he accepts is not to be self-inflicted. He does not mention fighting, much less his reasons for taking part in it (though that is done in one of the most thoughtful of poems to come out of the First World War, 'This is no case of petty right or wrong'). The poem simply takes the necessity for it, and its inevitable consequence, as granted, fusing his private situation with the universal inevitability of death. In this way what is a usually evaded reality is faced, and not only accepted in the knowledge that there is no alternative, but also embraced for what it can, and will, give. The strength of the poem is that, without undervaluing in a *contemptus mundi* spirit the things it recognises as bound to be lost, it can contemplate their loss in a positive manner. In an age of faith his acceptance might well have taken the form of accepting death as God's will; but for Thomas this becomes the secularised, though still religiously charged, image of the 'tall forest', of whose ominous dominion he can say:

> Its silence I hear and obey
> That I may lose my way
> And myself.

This echoes the first stanza, but with a difference. There losing one's way was part of a stoical acceptance of death; here obedience to the forest's commanding silence is accepted as a means to the end of losing both 'my way' and 'myself'. Loss is envisaged as potential gain. There is a sense of direction rather than mere capitulation. But, equally, there is no triumph, or even consolation as such. Death remains a form of losing.

In the best known of Thomas' war poems, 'As the team's head brass', there is more willingness to balance loss and gain; and the symbol of the wood is still further varied in meaning. At the beginning a pair of lovers disappear into the wood, and they reappear four lines from the end. In between the plough moves rhythmically back and forth from the wood, thus associated with love and creativity, to the lonely and more ominous figure of the soldier–poet sitting on a fallen elm, 'by a woodpecker's round hole'. Each time the ploughman reaches the poet's end of the field he pauses for conversation – starting with the elm which was blown down in a blizzard and is not likely to be moved till the war is over; next touching on the poet's own chances of being killed or wounded, and mentioning the death of the ploughman's mate in France, 'back in March, / The very night of the blizzard'; and finally commenting that all would have been different were it not for the war.

The scene and the dialogue are ordinary and familiar, almost to the point of banality, and yet they slowly build up a counterpoint of creation and destruction. For example, though the poet sits in its 'crest', the tree is dead, and the 'blizzard' which felled it is also equated with the war that killed the ploughman's mate. It thus contrasts with the wood of the lovers; but also, because of the woodpecker's hole, it has a kind of link with them. The very movement of the plough further echoes this suggestion of sexual procreation; while its 'narrowing a yellow square / Of charlock', together with the flashing of the brass, have both positive and negative implications.

Thomas himself is more detached in this poem that in 'Lights Out' – more able to balance the continuity of life against the discontinuity of war, and even ready to joke about his own chances of survival:

I could spare an arm. I shouldn't want to lose
A leg. If I should lose my head, why, so,
I should want nothing more.

And there is even the muted optimism of the ploughman's 'If we could see all all might seem good' (though it is only thrown in as a concession to conventional wisdom, which itself seems to be under threat). To this extent, 'As the team's head brass' is not a tragic poem, but a poem which sets tragedy in the wider context of nature's continual destruction and renewal. What it does not do, however, is to offer the prospect of renewal as an ultimate answer to destruction. The two processes seem to go on side by side, as they do in the final lines of the poem, where the lovers come out of the wood, and the horses begin their last stumbling movement along the furrows. They are held together in the poet's consciousness, but are not seen as parts of a meaningful overall design that reconciles him to his condition. If anything, the continuity of nature heightens his sense of isolation; the fact that the lovers move in and out of the wood so easily becomes merely an ironic comment on his own vulnerability as he sits 'among the boughs of the fallen elm'. His only resource is the creation of the poem itself, with its honest recognition of both the tragic and non-tragic elements in his situation. In this way he achieves a view that is free from the narrowness of self-consciousness, but also does justice to the pain which self-consciousness unavoidably generates.

7 D. H. Lawrence: Tragedy as Creative Crisis

Acceptance of death forms no part of Lawrence's view of tragedy. In a letter written in 1912, after reading Arnold Bennet's *Anna of the Five Towns*, he declares: 'I hate Bennett's resignation. Tragedy ought really to be a great kick at misery. But *Anna of the Five Towns* seems like an acceptance – so does all the modern stuff since Flaubert. I hate it. I want to wash again quickly, wash off England, the oldness and grubbiness and despair.'[1] And six years later, in the Preface to his play, *Touch and Go*, he formulates an alternative view of tragedy: 'Tragedy is the working out of some immediate passional problem within the soul of man.' It is a struggle in which profound beliefs are involved, and hence 'a creative activity in which death is a climax in the progression towards new being'. The note is strongly positive: he writes of 'the intrinsic tragedy of having to pass through death to birth', and of the possibility of knowing some happiness in the process – 'the very happiness of creative suffering'. Tragic defeat has no place in this conception. Indeed, by traditional standards it is a view that seems more heroic than tragic. Man is challenged to brace himself for an act of moral courage: 'The essence of tragedy, which is creative crisis, is that a man should go through with his fate, and not dodge it and go bumping into an accident.'[2]

Between these two statements come such novels as *The Rainbow* and *Women in Love*, and at least the first half of *The Lost Girl*, all of which deal with potentially tragic material in terms that protest against, and finally reject, the sense of defeat. *Women in Love*, for example, is almost traditionally tragic in its treatment of Gudrun and Gerald, but – in a pattern which Lawrence adapted from *Anna Karenina* – their relationship is balanced by that of Ursula and Birkin, as Anna and Vronsky are balanced by Kitty and Levin in Tolstoy's novel. The result is a tragedy of mutual destructiveness, which, however, is contrasted with, and clearly

144

judged inferior to, a tragedy of 'creative suffering' which passes through psychic death to at least the possibility of new life.

In Lawrence's poetry the corresponding volume is *Look! We Have Come Through!* (published in 1917). These are poems based on his elopement with Frieda, and the 'Argument' suggests another variation on the theme of 'creative suffering': 'The conflict of love and hate goes on between the man and the woman, and between these two and the world around them, till it reaches some sort of conclusion, they transcend into some condition of blessedness.'[3] Unfortunately, however, the sense of transcending is much too near the surface for the effect of tragedy, even by Lawrence's revised definition. There is too little to counter the fervour which, even in the midst of bitterness and struggle, constantly promises a triumphantly apocalyptic outcome. The sexual self-annihilation is too patently a means to an end, and the supposed suffering too much a matter of assertion to be convincing:

> Plunging as I have done, over, over the brink
> I have dropped at last headlong into nought, plunging
>   upon sheer hard extinction;
> I have come, as it were, not to know,
> died, as it were; ceased from knowing; surpassed myself.
> What can I say more, except that I know what it is to
>   surpass myself?
>
> It is a kind of death which is not death.
> It is going a little beyond the bounds.
>
> > ('Manifesto', VI)

The plasticity of the free verse which Lawrence employs in much of *Look! We Have Come Through!* allows free play to the ego; and, though in the best of these poems (such as 'The Song of a Man Who Has Come Through') the wave-like rhythm succeeds in transforming the reiterated 'I' so that it seems to be 'borrowed / By the fine, fine wind that takes its course through the chaos of the world', the freedom gained is too often a licence to hector the reader and strike rhetorical postures. The idea of 'creative crisis' prevents a sense of real crisis from taking hold, with the result that the tragic commitment is merely spurious. Suffering becomes a kind of medicine which is known in advance to be good for one:

> God, but it is good to have died and been trodden out,
> trodden to nought in sour, dead earth.
> quite to nought,
> absolutely to nothing
> nothing
> nothing
> nothing.   ('New Heaven and Earth',V)

The insistent repetition quite fails to carry conviction; and it is
no surprise that in the very next line absolute extinction is
reversed, and nothing brings everything:

> For when it is quite, quite nothing, then it is everything.
> When I am trodden quite out, quite, quite out,
> every vestige gone, then I am here
> risen, accomplishing a resurrection.

The weakness of such poetry is that it is extravagant in its
claims and yet remote from the actual suffering which it profes-
ses to transcend. It needs to become much more down-to-earth
before it can speak with conviction. Lawrence recognised this,
and in his later volume, *Birds, Beasts and Flowers* (1923) he
deliberately cultivates a tone which complements rapturous
assertion with colloquial casualness, and brings ecstasy into
touch with more commonplace reality. As he expresses it in 'St.
Matthew' (one of the four poems on 'The Evangelistic Beasts'):

> So I will be lifted up, Saviour,
> But put me down again in time, Master,
> Before my heart stops beating, and I become what
>   I am not.
> Put me down again on the earth, Jesus, on the brown soil
> Where flowers sprout in the acrid humus, and fade
>   into humus again.
> Where beasts drop their unlicked young, and pasture, and
>   drop their droppings among the turf.[4]

Thus 'Snake' balances evocative repetition, expressive of the
snake's mysterious underworld life, with the more prosaic voice
of the poet's daylight world; and 'Fish' makes delightful fun of
the self-conscious over-intensity of human love by exploring the curi-

ous sexlessness of the fish's sex-life in mock rhetorical questions:

> Who is it ejects his sperm to the naked flood?
> In the wave-mother?
> Who swims enwombed?
> Who lies with the waters of his silent passion,
>   womb-element?
> – Fish in the waters under the earth.
>
> What price *his* bread upon the waters?

Images are used that are both precise and ridiculous: the whine of the mosquito becomes its 'hateful little trump', and bats have 'Wings like bits of umbrella'. The baby tortoise is a 'brisk egg', and 'he scuffles tinily past [his mother] as if she were an old rusty tin'; and the wattles of a turkey 'are the colour of steel-slag which has been red-hot / And is going cold'.[5]

Yet none of this is whimsical or silly. Many of Lawrence's most serious poems are to be found in *Birds, Beasts and Flowers*. His witty, and sometimes bizarre, language is rather an extension of seriousness to include tone and attitude outside the conventionally solemn. He is still committed to his theme of tragedy as 'creative crisis', but now tries to give it a more concrete immediacy. In 'Almond Blossom', for example, though it is not an entirely successful poem, there is a new sense of creative flowering issuing from a hard, black, suffering shape. It has passages of unwarranted assertion and over-excited exclamation, but its essential vision is realised in the freshly particularised terms of

> Seeing iron break and bud,
> Seeing rusty iron puff with clouds of blossom.

As in 'St. Matthew', a distinctively human voice speaks, and rejects unballasted rapture. The blossom looks like 'Odd crumbs of melting snow', but it is earth-bred, not heavenly:

> But you mistake, it is not from the sky;
> From out the iron, and from out the steel,
> Flying not down from heaven, but storming up,
> Strange storming up from the dense under-earth

> Along the iron, to the living steel
> In rose-hot tips, and flakes of rose-pale snow
> Setting supreme annunciation to the world.

The language leaps from one extreme to another – from 'iron' and 'steel' to 'supreme annunciation' – but only as a mimesis of the organic process which makes the unlikely branch burst into pink blossom.

The almond's blossom is a flower born out of suffering – an intense struggle which is metaphorically fused with the agony of Christ on the cross, but remains natural rather than supernatural. This process is presented, in typically Lawrentian fashion, by means of overlapping repetition – a 'pulsing, frictional to-and-fro, which works up to culmination'.[6]

> See it come forth in blossom
> From the snow-remembering heart
> In long-nighted January,
> In the long dark nights of the evening star, and Sirius,
>   and the Etna snow-wind through the long night.
> Sweating his drops of blood through the long-nighted
>   Gethsemane
> Into blossom, into pride, into honey-triumph, into most
>   exquisite splendour.
> Oh, give me the tree of life in blossom
> And the Cross sprouting its superb and fearless flowers!
>
> Something must be reassuring to the almond, in the
>   evening star, and the snow-wind, and the long,
>   long nights,
> Some memory of far, sun-gentler lands,
> So that the faith in his heart smiles again
> And his blood ripples with that untellable delight of
>   once-more-vindicated faith,
> And the Gethsemane blood at the iron pores unfolds,
>   unfolds,
> Pearls itself into tenderness of bud
> And in a great and sacred forthcoming steps forth, steps
>   out in one stride
> A naked tree of blossom, like a bridegroom bathing
>   in dew, divested of cover,

> Frail-naked, utterly uncovered
> To the green night-baying of the dogstar,
>   Etna's snow-edged wind
> And January's loud-seeming sun.

The repetition is both incantatory and dramatic. The cumulative technique ('long-nighted January . . . the long dark nights . . . the long night . . . the long-nighted Gethsemane . . . the long, long nights') acts out the surging of the sap, and simultaneously casts an hypnotic spell on the reader which allows the insinuated language of crucifixion and resurrection, bridal and consummation, to blend with the Sicilian landscape and with the seasonal transition from winter darkness to spring sun. The whole passage is a rhetorical *tour de force*, but, unlike the rhetoric of 'New Heaven and Earth', it is tied in with the sensual reality of the tree and the metaphorical, but keenly felt, bloodshed of the Crucifixion. 'Something', it is conceded, 'must be reassuring to the almond', i.e. the 'creative' outcome of the 'crisis' is inherent in the tree's struggle, and this is reflected in the ecstasy which urges each phrase rhythmically forward; but the triumph does not seem to be an easy, foregone conclusion. The blossom is symbolic of pain, as well as resurrection. In subsequent lines it is imaged as 'Sword-blade born'; and in the closing words of the poem it is 'red at the core with the last sore-heartedness, / Sore-hearted-looking'. It pushes through to its crisis and emerges as creative affirmation, and is thus an example to man of the tragedy which passes through death to birth, and knows 'the very happiness of creative suffering'. But the poetry in which this process is embodied gives a sense of the agonising effort required to reach this end.

The most important of Lawrence's tragic poems are to be found in his posthumously published volume, *Last Poems*, and in particular in the group of poems clustered around 'The Ship of Death' which form a series of meditations inspired by Lawrence's consciousness of his own approaching death. These are heralded, however, by a minor, but significant, change in his attitude towards tragedy. A number of poems in *Pansies* (published in 1929, just nine months before his death) suggest a decline of interest even in 'creative crisis', and an impatience with the idea of tragedy altogether. 'Tragedy' seems merely 'a loud noise / louder than is seemly'; and in poems like 'The Death of Our Era', 'The New Word' and 'Be Still!' the apocalyptic fervour for renewal expressed in *Look! We Have Come Through!* and still evident in 'Almond Blossom', all but disappears, to be replaced by a sense of personal nothingness and the need for rest from the tragic struggle. Thus in 'Nullus' he feels that his 'whole consciousness is cliché', and must simply be given a rest – a post-tragic 'pause':

> There are said to be creative pauses,
> pauses that are as good as death, empty and dead as
>   death itself.
> And in these awful pauses the evolutionary change
>   takes place.
> Perhaps it is so.
> The tragedy is over, it has ceased to be tragic, the last
>   pause is upon us.
> Pause, brethren, pause!

Similarly, in 'After All the Tragedies Are Over –' Lawrence imagines a condition beyond that of tragedy:

> When love is gone, and desire is dead, and tragedy
>   has left the heart
> then grief and pain go too, withdrawing
> from the heart and leaving strange cold stretches of sand.

The faintest suggestion remains that the tide might flow in again, but that is entirely dependent on the moon: 'The beaches can do nothing about it.'

Some of these poems seem the work of a devitalised and despairing Lawrence. He was a very sick man at the time of writing them, and they may, to that extent, be discounted as the low moments of a man in poor health. But they also bring him a more convincing sense of tragic annihilation than he achieves in the reiterated 'nothing' of 'New Heaven and Earth'. They are expressions of a mood which seems to immobilise man – to force a halt, but also, perhaps without quite realising it, to revise and reassess the assumptions on which his energies have hitherto been based. As Lawrence hints, it is possible that they are 'creative pauses', essential elements in a process of 'evolutionary change', and that the resignation which leaves tidal flow to the moon is a necessary relinquishing of willed activity without which the deepest movements of the psyche cannot take place.

Considered in this light, they can, in fact, be seen as preliminaries to the kind of change that characterises *Last Poems*. Here Lawrence, though turning his attention once more to 'the intrinsic tragedy of having to pass through death to birth', identifies himself, as he would not allow himself to do before, with the outward flow of life towards death, and enacts a *rite de passage* which has a truer tragic authenticity, because its outcome is not optimistically prejudged. Such change requires, not the defeatist acceptance that he earlier so disliked in Bennett, but a willingness to submit to destruction without such impatient kicking against it.

Accordingly, the most satisfying poems in Lawrence's final volume are those which have a new-found quietness and delicacy – an unforced vitality submissive to the 'pause' in which vitality itself is on the brink of collapse. A perfect example is 'Butterfly', a poem which has a fragile and totally unpretentious beauty. The butterfly is an ancient symbol for the soul, but it is not till the third-from-last line ('Farewell, farewell, lost soul!') that Lawrence makes this symbolism explicit. Prior to that the setting is simple and natural, and the repetitive technique subdued enough to acquire cumulative effect without intrusive insistence. Gradually, however, the butterfly's intermediate, autumnal position – between the warmth of the house and garden and its impending journey seaward on the mountain wind 'polished with snow' – makes itself felt as an expression of the advent of death. The vivid particularity of its settling on the poet's shoe and sipping the dirt, and, in the third stanza, the arch-like downward path of its flight as it is carried by the wind, give the butterfly an immediacy which makes the imminence of its departure (which is also the poet's own departure into death) that much more poignant. The fluttering rhythms, counterpointed with the poem's air of relaxed restfulness, indicate a poise between motion and stability which, together with the black spots against the whiteness of the butterfly's wings and the warm redness of the geraniums against the cold of the wind outside the garden, recalls the balance of fruitfulness and decay in Keats' 'To Autumn'. But, as in Keats, this balance is also tinged with

the threat of winter and death. All through the poem the wind is
blowing seaward; and, if the first two stanzas come to rest with
the butterfly 'content on my shoe', the second two focus on its
readiness to leave, and suggest its final vanishing into air.
Moreover, the repetition of 'Will you go, Will you go' hints at an
undertone of fear; and when the butterfly is at last identified with
the soul, it is bidden an ominous 'farewell' as one that is 'lost'.

The theme of 'Butterfly' is imminent dissolution, without
promise of resurrection or renewal. Its delicacy is the expression
of a recognition of death as an inevitable, natural phenomenon,
necessarily tinged with fear and regret, but a subject neither for
protest nor transcendence. As such it represents a vital element in
the changed tragic tone of *Last Poems*. But its style is not the
pattern for all the poems in that volume. 'Bavarian Gentians',
for example, is much closer to the incantatory rhetoric of 'Almond Blossom'; and it moves towards an ecstatic climax more
appropriate to the earlier confidence in 'creative crisis'. Its two
long, extended sentences seem to embody a process of self-
hypnosis by which the speaker induces a transformation of
darkness (and, implicitly, death) into a strangely paradoxical
form of light. The gentians are 'big and dark' flowers that darken
the day-time, but they also, via a sequence of chanted repetitions
deliberately directed towards a mythic level of meaning, become
dark blue torches which are

> black lamps from the halls of Dis, burning dark blue,
> giving off darkness, blue darkness, as Demeter's pale lamps
>   give off light.

They are thus combined with the legend of Pluto and Persephone to suggest an identification of death with the goddess'
return to the underworld, in 'the frosted September' which is
also the season of the poem. As in 'Butterfly', there is no specific
mention of renewal, but the myth (which has Persephone return
to earth in the spring) brings with it powerful associations of
rebirth; and the hypnotic swirl of the language, drawing the
reader deeper and deeper down a spiral of passionately apprehended darkness, culminates in a triumphant image of sexual
fulfilment: 'among the splendour of torches of darkness, shed-
ding darkness on the lost bride and her groom'.

In 'Bavarian Gentians' the intensity with which darkness and
death are felt generates an ecstacy which is ultimately creative.

It effects a transvaluation of values like that of Blake's *The Marriage of Heaven and Hell*. But it does not repeat the facile assertion of *Look! We Have Come Through!* The finally creative outcome of the poem derives from its complete commitment to the downward spiral to the point where it becomes an all-absorbing imaginative consummation. That it does not seem to be a mere glorification of the death wish is due to the single-minded concentration of the verbal energies within it. The poem's 'dark-blue daze' is an essentially linguistic creation, and to that extent 'Bavarian Gentians' may be regarded as a thoroughly Modernist work; but it is created in, and creates for the reader, nothing like a self-consciously aesthetic mood. For Lawrence, indeed, such self-consciousness must be sharply distinguished from the committed involvement with the experience of darkness that 'Bavarian Gentians' demands. In poems like 'The Hands of God', 'Abysmal Immortality' and 'Only Man' he presents uncommitted self-consciousness as 'knowledge of the self-apart-from-god', and condemns it as the ultimate damnation – a fall which is not the downward movement of the torch-guided descent into darkness, but an 'unfinished plunge / of self-awareness' that is exhaustingly incapable of consummation:

> fathomless, fathomless, self-consciousness wriggling
> writhing deeper and deeper in all the minutiae of
>   self-knowledge, downwards, exhaustive,
> yet never, never coming to the bottom, for there
>   is no bottom;
> zigzagging down like the fizzle from a finished rocket
> the frizzling falling fire that cannot go out,
>   dropping wearily,
> neither can it reach the depth
> for the depth is bottomless,
> so it wriggles its way even further down, further down
> at last in sheer horror of not being able to leave off
> knowing itself, knowing itself apart from God, falling.
>   ('Only Man')

'Bavarian Gentians', on the other hand, is vital in its downward path, because it is urgently focussed on its dark goal. Its rhetorical self-elaboration is not self-centred, but a verbal aura thrown off by the intensity of its committed energy.

It is in 'The Ship of Death', however, that Lawrence reaches his most satisfactory expression of tragedy as 'creative crisis'. It is a complete poem in itself, but has other poems associated with it ('Difficult Death', 'All Souls' Day', 'The Houseless Dead', 'Beware the Unhappy Dead!', 'After All Saints' Day', 'Song of Death', 'The End, The Beginning', 'Shadows' and 'Phoenix') which may be regarded as satellites of the central poem. Through the subsidiary poems Lawrence explores aspects of the major theme of death which may be less fully developed in 'The Ship of Death' itself, and consequently they provide a useful interpretative context for the central poem. 'Song of Death', for example, though a short lyric of only thirteen lines, gives more explicit expression to the conception of death as complementary to life; and it overlaps with 'The End, The Beginning' in affirming that the oblivion of death provides a womb-like condition of unconsciousness which brings 'inward and lovely peace'. 'All Souls' Day' and 'Beware the Unhappy Dead!' are concerned with the need to propitiate the restless dead who cannot accept the fact of oblivion; and the ritual of the ship of death is called upon as a way of helping them to accept its inevitability. 'Phoenix' and 'Shadows', on the other hand, present death as a disintegration preparatory to a new birth; and 'Shadows', in particular, evokes the 'softness' and 'drowse' of autumn (with a reminiscence of Keats even stronger than that of 'Butterfly') to induce the self to accept its dissolution as a natural part of the organic cycle of the seasons:

And if, as autumn deepens and darkens
I feel the pain of falling leaves, and stems that break in storms
and trouble and dissolution and distress
and then the softness of deep shadows folding, folding
around my soul and spirit, around my lips
so sweet, like a swoon, or more like the drowse of a low, sad song
singing darker than the nightingale, on, on to the solstice
and the silence of short days, the silence of the year, the shadow,
then I shall know that my life is moving still
with the dark earth, and drenched
with the deep oblivion of earth's lapse and renewal.

Each of these elements is present in 'The Ship of Death' as well, but it is only in the longer poem that Lawrence succeeds in building them into an imaginative sequence which corrects their individual inadequacies and lapses in tone and feeling. Above all, in 'The Ship of Death' they find their properly adjusted place in a structure which is both unified as meditation and convincing as a dramatic rendering of the actual process of death.

The opening of 'The Ship of Death' has the quiet authority of an impersonal reality recognised as inevitable. The autumnal setting links it to the traditional tragic awareness of change and decay, but through the image of

> The apples falling like great drops of dew
> to bruise themselves an exit from themselves
>
> (I, 3–4)

mutability becomes incorporated with the more peculiarly Lawrentian theme of the weary consciousness which needs the release from its sterile self that the 'oblivion' of death affords:

> And it is time to go, to bid farewell
> to one's own self, and find an exit
> from the fallen self.
>
> (I, 5–7)

   With the resonant question, 'Have you built your ship of death, O have you?' (II, 8) this authority acquires a more ominous note; and in the next line it turns into a command: 'O build your ship of death, for you will need it.' The emphasis thus falling on the word 'need' suggests not only the state of the weary consciousness, but also the threat of some unspecified crisis from which the soul will have to protect itself. What this crisis is becomes more apparent as the seasonal imagery of the opening lines is taken up again, and developed in terms, not of autumnal fruition, but of the 'grim frost', and (implicitly) tempest, which will tumble the apples 'thick, almost thundrous, on the hardened earth' (II, 10–11). It is death as a corrosive force, 'on the air like a smell of ashes!' and made terrifyingly real as both a physical and spiritual threat:

> And in the bruised body, the frightened soul
> finds itself shrinking, wincing from the cold
> that blows upon it through the orifices.
>
> (II, 14–16)

In these circumstances the desire for escape is even greater, and the thought of suicide is a natural response; but, with an allusion to *Hamlet* (III.i.75–6), Lawrence questions whether suicide can in fact provide an answer:

> And can a man his own quietus make
> with a bare bodkin?
>
> (III, 17–18)

In its legal sense 'quietus' means 'acquittance from a debt', and it is used by Shakespeare as a metaphor for the release afforded by death from the anxieties of life. For Lawrence, however, it is also fused with the word 'quiet', and the anxieties he has in mind are those of approaching death (though Hamlet's 'dread of something after death' is also relevant). Suicide offers only physical death, not the peace that the 'quietness' element in his meaning of 'quietus' implies. By calling this mere physical escape 'a bruise or break of exit for his life' (III, 20) Lawrence also associates it with the apples falling from the trees in the first section of the poem, thus suggesting that it is the answer which the weary consciousness instinctively inclines to. But that cannot provide what the consciousness most needs, 'the deep and lovely quiet / of a strong heart at peace', and the question still remains, 'How can we this, our own quietus, make?' (IV, 25–7).

This is the real question to which the poem has to address itself; but it does so indirectly rather than directly – by shaping the tone and attitude necessary to such 'quietus', and thus making its own form the answer. The poem becomes the enactment of a ritual by which the right response to death is defined, and through which the poet schools himself to its requirements. Thus the injunction to build the ship of death, already uttered in Section II, and now taken up again in Section V, is the beginning of an almost religious process. It has its source in the burial rites of the ancient Etruscans, which Lawrence describes in his account of the tombs he visited in 1927: among 'all the amazing impedimenta of the important dead' is a 'little bronze ship of death' which is intended to carry the dead Lucumo over to the other world.[7] Like the inclusion of the autumnal imagery, this is something which adds a mythic dimension to the poem; it does not depend on its own unaided verbal effect, but also carries the powerful aura of suggestion belonging to ancient religious observances associated with death as a journey to be undertaken by the departed. But the ship which is to be built is also, symbolically, the state of mind that the poem is in the course of creating – a means towards the 'quietus' which is 'a strong heart at peace'. Here Lawrence's language of repetition makes an indispensable contribution as well. It takes the phrases already used to express natural and human decay, and – even while it echoes the fearful lamentation over the corruptive and disintegrative force of death – converts them into an iterative incantation which controls and directs the experience, and gives it the new context of 'the long and painful death / that lies between the old self and the new' (V, 30–1).

Throughout Sections V, VI and the first six lines of VII the decaying of the human body is elaborated in cruel and painful detail: 'our bodies', like the earlier apples, 'are fallen, bruised, badly bruised' (32), the dark sea 'is washing in through the breaches of our wounds' (36), and the repeated 'We are dying, we are dying' reaches its climax in disintegration and terror:

> We are dying, we are dying, piecemeal our bodies are dying
> and our strength leaves us,
> and our soul cowers naked in the dark rain over the flood,
> cowering in the last branches of the tree of our life.
>
> (VI, 46–9)

But this process is also alternated with the repeated exhortation to build the ship for 'the longest journey', and provision it 'with food, with little cakes, and wine' (V, 39) –

> A little ship, with oars and food
> and little dishes, and all accoutrements
> fitting and ready for the departing soul.
>
> (VII, 53–5)

The sense of destruction is thus balanced by a sense of creation – though not one that is rhetorically assertive (the rhetoric of repetition and parallel constructions belongs primarily to the death process), but attached to unpretentious, familiar domestic details. When the command comes to launch 'the small ship', therefore, its ability to ride the final death flood is not dependent on the old heroics of apocalyptic defiance, but rather on its already established connection with ordinary life. Like *Birds, Beasts and Flowers*, it draws on experience from the world of commonplace reality, and is the more firmly reassuring for that.

The keynote of the ship, however, is fragility. It is prepared for its ritual launching, and its symbolic condition as an achieved state of mind is now explicitly recognised by its being dubbed the 'ship of courage, the ark of faith'; but it is none the less 'the *fragile* ship of courage' and its passenger is 'the fragile soul' (VII, 57–8). The journey it undertakes is a journey into the terrifying unknown, where the soul risks its own complete annihilation, the extinction of consciousness. And if the ritual has provided a supporting context and a sense of direction and control, that, too, must be recognised as vulnerable, for in this journey 'There is no port, there is nowhere to go' (VII, 65). In the most brilliant of all his imaginings of the dissolving death-process – more persuasive even than the ecstatic downward spiral of 'Bavarian Gentians' – Lawrence evokes the complete reductiveness and defeat of all sense of purpose and orientation which overwhelms the fragile individual consciousness in death:

> There is no port, there is nowhere to go
> only the deepening blackness darkening still
> blacker upon the soundless, ungurgling flood
> darkness at one with darkness, up and down
> and sideways utterly dark, so there is no direction any more.
> and the little ship is there; yet she is gone.
> She is not seen, for there is nothing to see her by.
> She is gone! gone! and yet
> somewhere she is there.
> Nowhere!

(VII, 65–74)

The poem, it may be said, is about Lawrence's own death; and it involves the reader so that he, too, is sympathetically identified with the soul's journey into annihilation. But there has been a slight shift of point of view from the beginning of Section VII, where Lawrence includes himself and his reader in the joint 'We' who must be willing to die and build the ship of death, to the launching of the ship and the subsequent voyage. This is presented as seen – in so far as such an experience of the psyche can be 'seen' – by an observer, straining his eyes to catch the last glimpse of the little ship before it finally vanishes into the absorbing darkness. It is curiously both an enactment in which the reader is caught up, and a process of which he is conscious, because he himself is not undergoing it, but only imaginatively sharing it. In Section VIII it is briefly recapitulated, but at a slightly more removed, and generalising, distance, which brings about the final statement: 'It is the end, it is oblivion.' In other words, it is now not only sympathetically enacted, but also judged as a complete and perfected consummation – the creative 'oblivion' more explicitly defined in 'Song of Death' and 'The End, The Beginning'. It is a demonstrated and inwardly felt realisation of the desired attitude towards death that constitutes true 'quietus'.

Nevertheless, the poem itself is not yet complete. There remain two more sections that would seem to correspond to the traditional rebirth and renewal that we have seen in pastoral elegy from Vergil to Shelley. In these sections Lawrence uses the natural analogies of dawn gradually emerging from darkness, and of waters receding after flood, to suggest a delicate coming back to life. The strengthening of light and colour – from the first, faint pallor, through 'ashy grey', to yellow, and then, at last, 'a flush of rose' (IX, 85–95) – is conveyed with exquisite simplicity and sensitivity; and the changing of rhythm, from hesitancy to the final confidence of

> Swings the heart renewed with peace
> even of oblivion,

communicates the 'faltering and lapsing' of the ship, and the return of 'the frail soul', with beautiful persuasiveness. But Lawrence's renewal does not suppose a transcendence of mortality. It is a mirror-image of the process of corruption and decay. Rhetorically, it stands in its relation to what has gone before like the second half of an antimetabole, repeating in inverse order the sequence preceding it (abc/cba). Emotionally, too, the reader's sympathetic involvement with the voyage into

darkness makes possible the conception of a reversed movement
out of it, from annihilation to light and new life: 'A flush of rose,
and the whole thing starts again' (IX, 96). Logic, of course, is
defied in this. There is not even the logic of the Christian faith,
which supersedes the temporal by the eternal. It has only the
inner coherence of a shaped emotional response to support it.
The image of renewal (for that is what it is, rather than the
promise of actual resurrection in the flesh) is a projection of the
achieved 'quietus', reflecting the creative element in its response
to death, and revealing it as an essential form of life.

The Lawrence of 'The Ship of Death' is thus consistent with the
Lawrence who wrote in the Preface to *Touch and Go* that the
essence of tragedy is 'creative crisis', and who in *Look! We Have
Come Through!* proclaimed that from annihilation he was 'risen,
accomplishing a resurrection'. The difference, however, is that
the tragic imperative that 'a man should go through with his
fate' is now interpreted in a much convincingly tragic manner.
The impatient heroism of kicking at misery is replaced by a
greater honesty in the face of the terror of death, and the
imagined renewal is not willed, but emerges as a plausible
extension of the perfected 'quietus' which the poetry cultivates.
Above all, there is a new humility implicit in the tone with which
the building of the ship of death is urged. The final words of the
poem are not a statement that it has been accomplished, but a
return to the exhortation that it should be attempted:

>   Oh build your ship of death, oh build it!
>   for you will need it.
>   For the voyage of oblivion awaits you.

The poem has suggested how a ship of death may be built, but,
in a very real sense, the work still remains to be done by each
individual, and even by Lawrence himself. It is only an imaginative construction – though one undertaken, we need not doubt,
with as much seriousness and sincerity as Lawrence is capable
of. Its justification is not that it offers a definitive answer to the
question it poses, 'How can we this, our own quietus, make?';

but that it makes its own attempt at providing an answer in terms which recognise the common experience of anxiety and suffering. In short, 'The Ship of Death' is Lawrence speaking with his most human voice.

8 Wilfred Owen: Distance and Immediacy

As one moves from Edward Thomas – writing during wartime, and from 1915 himself a soldier, but one who had not yet been posted to France – to the front-line poets, one is immediately struck by a change to horrific immediacy in the treatment of death:

> Savage, he kicked a soft, unanswering heap,
> And flashed his beam across the livid face
> Terribly glaring up, whose eyes yet wore
> Agony dying hard ten days before;
> And fists of fingers clutched a blackening wound.
> > (Siegfried Sassoon: 'The Rear-Guard')

> A man's brains splattered on
> A stretcher-bearer's face;
> His shook shoulders slipped their load,
> But when they bent to look again
> The drowning soul was sunk too deep
> For human tenderness.
> > (Isaac Rosenberg: 'Dead Man's Dump')

> If you could hear, at every jolt, the blood
> Come gargling from the froth-corrupted lungs,
> Obscene as cancer, bitter as the cud
> Of vile, incurable sores on innocent tongues, –
> My friend, you would not tell with such high zest
> To children ardent for some desperate glory,
> The old Lie: Dulce et decorum est
> Pro patria mori.
> > (Wilfred Owen: 'Dulce Et Decorum Est')

162

These poems are realistic records of the most disgusting side of war, which were meant to be, and even today still succeed in being, deeply disturbing to the reader. They are also, of course, one-sided, but one-sided as, for example, Swift's satire is, in that they present a limited facet of war in intensive close-up, with the purpose of shocking the reader out of any possible complacency of mind with regard to what death means in the conditions of modern warfare. Their justification lies in the sincerity of the moral indignation which is their driving force; and in the fact that experiences of this order (their more recent equivalents would perhaps be atrocities committed by the Nazis against the Jews, or the appalling effects of the atom bomb) temporarily obliterate all other kinds of awareness, making the criticism that they are one-sided seem, at least for a while, irrelevant.

Owen seems to have taken this view himself, for in the intended Preface to his poems he declares:

> Above all I am not concerned with Poetry.
> My subject is War, and the pity of War.
> The Poetry is in the pity.
> Yet these elegies are to this generation in no sense consolatory. They may be to the next. All a poet can do today is warn. That is why the true Poets must be truthful.[1]

The urgency of the subject is placed before the means by which it is expressed, as if there could be a simple division between style and matter – a view which might be dismissed as critically naive. But there are some fruitful contradictions in what Owen says. He declares that he is 'not concerned with Poetry', though he chooses to write in verse, and use many of the traditional devices of poetry, as well as some interestingly original ones such as half-rhyme and pararhyme. He then asserts that 'The Poetry is in the pity'. Poetry is thus reinstated, but as a means to arousing a certain kind of emotional response, not as an end in itself. This may be no more than a way of recognising a greater seriousness and maturity in his own later poetry as compared with the earlier; but it also suggests that, like the Keats of the revised *Hyperion*, Owen has found a deeper imaginative compulsion in themes which arouse feelings of compassion, and which stimulate him to move compassion in others. If so, this is close to recognising that his own bent is towards lyric tragedy, and leads,

understandably, in the next line to the description of his poems
as 'these elegies'. Owen shifts again, however; for, having selected 'elegies', he immediately seeks to cancel out the traditional
association of elegy with consolation, at least 'to this generation'.
As far as his contemporaries are concerned, his role will be to
break through poeticism, and shock them into realisation of the
horror and suffering which they unthinkingly condone; this is
what, for the time being, it means to be 'truthful'. Yet there is
also the concession that his 'elegies' might be 'consolatory' to the
next generation – a further recognition perhaps that they do,
after all, contain elements which properly arouse feelings of grief
and lament, and satisfy a permanent human need, rather than
merely serve to 'warn'.

Dominic Hibberd notes the use of the word 'elegies' in Owen's
Preface, and relates it to what he sees as a development away
from Sassoon-like shock tactics to a more resonant language of
grief: 'Satire aims to stimulate social action, elegy to arouse
memory and grief. It did not take Owen long to perceive that his
talent was more elegiac than satirical.' And he adds that in
December 1917 Owen read a translation of Bion and Moschus,
and in 1918 'considered entitling a volume of his poems *With
Lightning and with Music*, a phrase from Shelley's great elegy, or
English Elegies'.[2] This lends further support to the hint which the
Preface itself contains that Owen was conscious of his place in
the elegiac tradition, but wished to adapt it to the truth about
modern war which he also felt a compulsion to express. It
suggests that his aim was a kind of poetry which would be both
immediate – a tract for the times – and in touch with the
permanent realities of tragedy. If this is so, however, it does not
mean that all his poems were meant to serve both these purposes
– much less that they all succeed in doing so. There is considerable variety in his work, and much variation in individual
poems, ranging over indignation, satire, horrific realism, visionary imagination, pathos, and at times sentimentality; but the
distinguishing quality of his work at its best is just this combination
of immediacy and distance. He is most himself when, without
blurring or generalising vagueness, he is compassionately involved with his subject, but also sufficiently detached to reach
the Vergilian 'lacrimae rerum'[3] – the permanent substratum of
grief that is tapped by tragedy. It is the denial of this level of human

awareness that he most severely condemns in the stay-at-home civilians whom he attacks in the last stanza of 'Insensibility':

> But cursed are dullards whom no cannon stuns,
> That they should be as stones.
> Wretched are they, and mean
> With paucity that never was simplicity.
> By choice they made themselves immune
> To pity and whatever mourns in man
> Before the last sea and the hapless stars;
> Whatever mourns when many leave these shores;
> Whatever shares
> The eternal reciprocity of tears.

In the foregoing stanzas of this poem the blunted state of feeling of the troops is seen as a blessing for them; their 'insensibility' is necessary self-protection – though in the process of explaining why Owen also exemplifies the poetry of 'pity' and 'truth', and makes them real as 'troops who fade, not flowers, / For poets' tearful fooling'. But the civilians who wilfully insulate themselves from this truth not only fail in their duty to their contemporaries, but wither their own humanity. Recognising the one is an essential condition of the other.

Some of Owen's poems are directly about front-line experience; others focus on soldiers crippled and wasted by war, and have their setting behind the lines, or in hospital; still others are set at home, and deal with the civilians' response to the soldiers. It would be much too drastic a simplification to say that the further Owen retreats from the actual front line, the more he achieves tragic distancing of his material; but the conditions for that achievement do often seem to be more readily available when he is not directly evoking the horrors of battle. This is not a question of where Owen himself was at the time of writing any particular poem, but of the quality of his imaginative involvement. 'Dulce et Decorum Est', for example, was written when he was a shellshock patient at Craiglockhart hospital, near Edinburgh (where he first met Siegfried Sassoon), and its dramatic involvement may well have been the consequence of what Jon Stallworthy calls 'nightmare memories'.[4] D. S. R. Welland, on the other hand, attributes it to 'the white-hot indignation to which [Owen] had been brought (as one manuscript reveals) by the patriotic lines of Miss Jessie Pope'.[5] It is highly successful in its purpose of jolting the complacent out of their complacency; and it is especially vivid and precise in its rendering of the sudden change from weary marching to the soldiers' frantic reaction to the gas attack. But its most remarkable lines are those which describe the struggles of the man who fails to get his mask on in time:

> But someone still was yelling out and stumbling,
> And flound'ring like a man in fire or lime. . . .
> Dim, through the misty panes and thick green light,
> As under a green sea, I saw him drowning.

The man and the first-person narrator are both vividly before us, but the suffering of the one, seen by the other through the clouded eyepiece of his own mask, which he has managed to put on, is transformed by perspective. Without it needing to be said, this points the isolation of the 'drowning' man. Momentarily, he becomes a tragic Philoctetes, abandoned, though in this case unwillingly, by his comrades. By comparison the body flung in the wagon is not so much a tragic figure as an emotionally loaded image directed, as its syntactic containment within the double 'If' clause indicates, at the ironic 'friend' who deludes children with his ignorant glorification of war, summed up in the words of a dead poet, in a dead language, which Owen presents as culpably remote from the 'truth' exemplified in the poem.

The colloquial satires which Owen wrote under Sassoon's influence – poems like 'The Dead-Beat', 'The Letter', 'The Chances', 'S.I.W.' and 'The Inspection' – are sardonic rather than tragic. The dialogue is realistic (though still an edited version of the language actually used by soldiers) and perhaps too deliberately prosaic, but, as intended, it is an effective antidote to romantic 'Poetry' of the kind Owen declares himself not to be concerned with; and the abrupt endings, especially of 'The Dead-Beat' and 'The Chances', leave a decidedly caustic impression:

'E's wounded, killed, and pris'ner, all the lot,
The bloody lot all rolled in one. Jim's mad.

In some respects these are the poems most obviously in accord
with the Preface's denial of elegiac consolation; in them the
poetry has to be in the pity because anything more evidently
'poetic' has been cut out. Nevertheless, this anti-poetic style
plays an important part in achieving a certain kind of poetic
effect; and in the more ambitious of these poems structures are
employed which, despite the verbal astringency, add resonance
and depth. Thus, 'S.I.W.' has an opening epigraph from Yeats,
referring to the superficially similar death of one who 'has set his
teeth to die' and cannot therefore be mourned, only to intensify
the real cause for mourning exemplified in this poem; and its
division into sections, each with its own title (I. THE PROLOGUE;
II. THE ACTION; III. THE POEM; IV. THE EPILOGUE), turns it into
a kind of tragic drama. And in 'The Inspection' (strictly speaking, not a front-line poem, but set in the rear) the smear of blood
for which the soldier has to be rebuked prompts a gibe at the
washing out of stains which deepens into a protest against
militarism as such, which sacrifices the blood of youth on the
altar of its own deified system.

In poems like 'Disabled', 'Conscious', 'Mental Cases' and
'Smile, smile, smile', which are more removed from the immediacy of battle, pity takes on a tenderer form, though still stiffened
with the sardonic quality of the front line pieces. Newspapers
argue disingenuously for vast war indemnities on behalf of the
national integrity which the dead and wounded are said to have
preserved; but sufficient comment is made through the under-
stated lines:

> Nation? – The half-limbed readers did not chafe
> But smiled at one another curiously
> Like secret men who know their secret safe.
> ('Smile, smile, smile')[6]

A cripple sits in his wheelchair 'waiting for dark', and, as the
poem slides between his present and his past, and the 'few sick
years' which are now his future, it creates a context of both irony
and pathos for the inappropriately heroic diction of

> He's lost his colour very far from here,
> Poured it down shell-holes till the veins ran dry,
> And half his lifetime lapsed in the hot race
> And leap of purple spurted from his thigh.
>
> ('Disabled')

The hectic language of 'Dulce Et Decorum Est' is echoed:

> Batter of guns and shatter of flying muscles,
> Carnage incomparable
>
> ('Mental Cases')

but this is the nightmare world inhabited by the 'purgatorial shadows' of the insane, whose condition is made imaginatively compelling, not merely to horrify, but to arouse a sense of guilt in us who are responsible for it:

> Snatching after us who smote them, brother,
> Pawing us who dealt them war and madness.
>
> ('Mental Cases')

Further still from the front – at home, in fact – 'The Send-Off' also has our guilt as its theme. Here the sardonic note of 'The Inspection' is present in a muted form. A kind of ironic 'Poetry' is suggested by the flowers given to the departing troops, whose 'breasts were stuck all white with wreath and spray'. Though perhaps meant as tributes to their courage, these flowers seem more like anticipatory funeral offerings for their predestined corpses – as the short, flat succeeding line, 'As men's are, dead', implies. Their send-off is already a thing of the past: their present entraining is watched only by 'Dull porters' and 'a casual tramp' whose sorrow probably has more to do with the scraps he cadged from them at 'the upland camp' than with compassion. The absence of feeling makes itself felt in a complex way in the lines:

> Then, unmoved, signals nodded, and a lamp
> Winked to the guard.

Life is ironically attributed to the signals and lamp, but in a form that suggests they are in complicity with the guard; and 'unmoved' gives them a weird mechanical independence, but also suggests total lack of feeling. All this is an indirect comment on the indifference of society; and yet there is also a sense that society is guiltily uneasy. The giving of flowers becomes almost a propitiation of those who are being treated as scapegoats; the men are banished like secret crimes which 'we' prefer to disown and forget:

> So secretly, like wrongs hushed-up, they went.
> They were not ours:
> We never heard to which front these were sent.
>
> Nor there if they yet mock what women meant
> Who gave them flowers.

Accordingly, the few who may return will 'creep back', not to the accompaniment of 'beatings of great bells', but furtively, 'to still village wells / Up half-known roads'. As Gertrude White remarks, 'we are left to wonder whether their village roads are only half-remembered by them because of the length of their absence or the intensity and terror of the events in which they have taken part'.[7] The unmentioned, and unmentionable, nature of their deaths is even more distanced than the crippling of the soldier in 'Disabled', and yet supplied with a context of before and after which endows it with the biting pathos of tragic irony.

Both battle front and home front come together in 'Anthem for Doomed Youth'. Its form is that of the Shakespearean sonnet, but modified in the third quatrain to rhyme EFFE instead of EFEF, and divided in the Petrarchan fashion between octave and sestet. The octave deals with the weapons of modern warfare, and the sestet with grief at home for the dead; but an elegiac tone is spread over the whole sonnet, unifying its two halves, and the religious mourning at home infiltrates the octave in a series of ironic substitutions of battlefield noises for such things as passing-bells, prayers and choirs. Instead of satire, however, this produces a mingled Shakespearean and Keatsian music of mourning (there are specific reminiscences of 'the surly sullen bell' and the 'Bare ruin'd choirs' of Sonnets 71 and 73 and the 'wailful choir' of 'To Autumn'), which aptly justifies the word 'Anthem' in the title.[8] A sense of indignation and outrage still makes itself felt, but it is blended into the double metaphor that creates 'passing-bells' for the slain ('who die as cattle') out of guns which express 'monstrous anger', and turns the onomatopoeic 'stuttering rifles' rapid rattle' into the padre's hastily mumbled prayers for the dead. In the second quatrain this voice of protest is more muted still as 'mockeries' soften into 'mourning' – high-pitched in 'The shrill, demented choirs of wailing shells', but receding funereally in the dying fall of 'bugles calling for them from sad shires'.

In the sestet the religious theme continues with a farewell ritual which, as Hibberd points out, refers to the custom of 'a household in mourning';[9] but warfare is left behind. The result, it must be admitted, is a little disappointing. An imaginative tension goes out of the verse, and the elegiac music comes perilously near to sentimentality as the ironic substitutions of the octave are replaced by alternatives to conventional grief which are themselves almost as conventional. Even the serious wit of 'The pallor of girls' brows shall be their pall' cannot disguise the rather trite nature of the image; and the last couplet, though a beautifully sounding verbal coda to the 'anthem', does no more than suggest a sadness which might be appropriate to any bereavement. It has lost touch with the youth doomed by modern war.

'Anthem for Doomed Youth' is thus a very fine experiment in combining the realities of war with more traditional elegiac mourning, but it is difficult to accept Gertrude White's judgement that it is a 'wholly successful poem' and 'perhaps the best that Owen wrote'.[10] It does much to satisfy the requirements of melancholy eloquence that Hume discusses in his essay on tragedy, and it has clearly learnt from Keats in this respect; but it is defective, at least in the sestet, in the Keatsian requirement of a 'wakeful anguish' that sharpens and deepens melancholy into tragedy.

It is in another sonnet, 'Futility', that one can see a better and more consistent balance between distance and immediacy. There is no direct mention, it is true, of the horrors of war, and even the fact that it is about a soldier who has just died is not made absolutely explicit. But the reference to France is sufficiently evocative; and the presence of a young war casualty paralysed in a wheel-chair, or hospital bed, and now beyond recovery, is strongly enough felt for him to be realised in the reader's imagination as both a particular and a general, representative case of tragic waste. Moreover, that it is a sonnet is not immediately apparent. It uses six-syllabled and eight- (or sometimes nine-) syllabled lines instead of the usual ten, and it breaks the fourteen lines into two seven-lined stanzas, each of which has a strangely haunting pattern of rhyme: ABAB (in half-rhyme or pararhyme); C [C] C (full rhyme, with pararhyme between).[11] The result is a muted music rising to a broken climax which, even with its final full rhyme, interrupted as it is by the pararhyme in the penultimate line, never quite fulfils its promise.

This sense of unfulfilled promise is also the theme of the poem, worked out in the contrast between the two stanzaic halves which replace the usual division between octave and sestet. The first half presents the sun as a gently reviving power, 'whispering of fields unsown' – 'unsown', but none the less suggesting the sowing of seed, as 'awoke' and 'woke' (in 'Gently its touch awoke him once' and 'Always it woke him', lines 2 and 4) suggest its life-giving and restorative agency. The soldier, moreover, is felt to have always enjoyed a particularly strong relationship with the sun, both 'At home' and 'even in France' – with all that 'France' summons up in the way of destructive antipathy to life. However, 'Until this morning and this snow' hints that something especially ominous has happened to that relationship, intorducing a coldness discordant with the warmth, tenderness and fertility which have so far been the keynote of the poem. The completion of the first half with

> If anything might rouse him now
> The kind old sun will know

counteracts that impression with a suggestion of continuing intimacy between soldier and sun that can still be relied on; yet the rhyming of 'know' with 'snow', the more hesitant 'If anything might' and the slightly more desperate quality of 'rouse', compared with 'woke', and the patronising element in 'The kind old sun', all point to a faltering confidence.

The second half seems to regain the lost, or fading, impetus with the urgent

> Think how it wakes the seeds, –
> Woke, once, the clays of a cold star.

The use of 'wakes' and 'Woke' more than echo their use in
previous lines; they evoke the sun as a universal mover of what
seems impossible, a bringer of life out of lifeless sterility. ('Cold',
in particular, recalls the 'snow' that seemed to impede its power
in the first half only to sweep the impediment away; though the
awkwardly interruptive 'once' also recalls the 'once' of line 2,
with the suggestion that such power might no longer exist in the
present.) It should have little difficulty, therefore, in reviving a
human body with all the complexity of achievement it represents, and 'still warm', not only with the heat of physical life, but
with the conscious love it arouses. But the last five lines are
question, not statement. The earlier, incipient doubt is now
much more evident; and it reaches out not only to the sun's
power to revive the soldier, but also to the purpose of human life,
linked to the long, but now seemingly futile, evolutionary process
via the echo in 'Was it for this the clay grew tall?' of its beginning
with 'the clays of a cold star'. And the final despairing question:

> – O what made fatuous sunbeams toil
> To break earth's sleep at all?

tinged, as it so often is in Hardy, with a sense of fundamental
absurdity, completes the distancing of individual suffering to a
universal tragic vision, while still leaving the pain of the particular situation uppermost.

'Futility' is as near as Owen came to achieving the right
balance between distance and immediacy. It is all the answer
that is needed to Yeats' notorious misjudgement in excluding
him from the 1936 *Oxford Book of English Verse* on the excuse that
'passive suffering is not a proper subject for poetry'. There are,
however, three front-line poems – 'Exposure', 'Spring Offensive'
and 'Strange Meeting' – which demand modification of the
argument that he gains more tragic effect as he deals with
subjects which are at more of a distance from actual conflict. The
first of these, 'Exposure', is descriptive verse, brilliantly onomatopoeic and almost luscious in its assonance and alliteration –
surprising it would seem, only in that it applies this style to such
distinctly untraditional poetic material as barbed wire, artillery

and machine guns. But its recourse to a traditional style is by no means reassuring. It is modified by Owen's own use of para-rhyme, with its sinister disappointment of expected rhyme; and its more usual association with the lavish and benevolent Nature of Romantic poetry serves as an ironic contrast in this Winter context, where natural forces are as inimical to the men in the trenches as the weapons of destruction used against them. Exposure to the elements becomes an extension of the suffering they endure in modern war, as Owen suggests by fusing the rigours of a cold, wet dawn with the grey military uniforms worn by the German soldiers:

> The poignant misery of dawn begins to grow. . . .
> We only know war lasts, rain soaks, and clouds sag stormy.
> Dawn massing in the east her melancholy army
> Attacks once more in ranks on shivering ranks of gray,
>   But nothing happens.

The perversion of Nature becomes something like a perversion of natural feeling. For example, in the description of the snow, 'Pale flakes with fingering stealth come feeling for our faces', the language suggests that what is normally soft and caressing has taken on the groping menace of an assassin. Instinctively the men try to escape by retreating mentally 'back on forgotten dreams' of a kindlier and more 'Poetic' natural world:

>   So we drowse, sun-dozed,
> Littered with blossoms trickling where the blackbird fusses

and to homes where 'crickets jingle' and 'the innocent mice rejoice'; but this is a sentimental illusion from which they are cut off by the unchanging reality of war. They believe, or have been persuaded to believe (Owen here perhaps betrays some of the confusion which made him a 'conscientious objector with a very seared conscience'[12]), that the restoration of this illusion depends on the misery they endure – that somehow their perverted nature will bring the old idea of Nature back: 'For God's invincible spring our love is made afraid.' But the stanza ends with the suggestion that 'love of God seems dying'; and the next, and final, stanza returns to the soldiers' immediate misery, which – depending on whether one reads 'this frost' or 'His frost'[13] – may even be envisaged as the direct infliction of a God of Nature who is anything but benevolent. Their suffering is precisely rendered – the frost 'Shrivelling many hands, puckering foreheads crisp'; but, as in 'Futility', the individual's condition represents a tragic human condition: the wasteful reduction of life and energy to frozen immobility, symbolised in the corpses only half-recognised by the burying-party ('All their eyes are ice') and the repeated refrain which forms the last words of the poem: 'But nothing happens'.

'Spring Offensive' and 'Strange Meeting' are both unfinished, or at least not finally revised, and to that extent comment on them can only be provisional. But they seem to be front line poems which have deeply absorbed the tragically distancing process. It is perhaps significant that 'Spring Offensive', though written in September 1918, refers back to Owen's experience at Fayet in the offensive of 1917; and that 'Strange Meeting', written apparently a month earlier than 'Spring Offensive', is in the form of a semi-mythical encounter with an enemy-friend in an underworld which is both the world of the trenches and something like Dante's Inferno.

Like 'Exposure', 'Spring Offensive' is rich in natural description, and as Keatsian as 'Anthem for Doomed Youth';[14] and with both it also shares elements of religious language. The attack becomes a leap into hell; and, though less obviously, there are hints of the Mass in 'the buttercup / Had blessed with gold their slow boots coming up' and 'earth set sudden cups / In thousands for their blood'. As Hibberd notes: 'Having refused the offered blessing of communion with the natural order, the men have become victims sacrificed to an outraged Nature.'[15] This use of religious language is continued in 'Strange Meeting', where the 'sullen hall' in which the narrator finds himself is 'Hell'; and the enemy-friend, 'Lifting distressful hands, as if to bless', and with his face marked with 'a thousand pains', is clearly a Christ-like figure, willing to give his blood in a purifying protest against the merely destructive bloodshed of war:

Then, when much blood had clogged their chariot-wheels,
I would go up and wash them from sweet wells,
Even with truths that lie too deep for taint.
I would have poured my spirit without stint
But not through wounds; not on the cess of war.
Foreheads of men have bled where no wounds were.

The biblical diction here, and the echo of Wordsworth's 'Thoughts that do often lie too deep for tears' ('Immortality Ode', 204), like some of the phrasing in 'Spring Offensive', suggest a still imperfectly controlled desire to write 'Poetry'; but the mythical and religious distancing do not produce a romanticised view of war. The consolation of courage in the face of death and the comfort of Christian redemption are hinted at only to be rejected. In 'Spring Offensive' when the word of attack is given it is received with 'No alarms / Of bugles, no high flags, no clamorous haste'; and it is with an almost sardonic detachment that Owen reports the religious view that those who die in a just war are instantly redeemed:

> Of them who running on that last high place
> Leapt to swift unseen bullets. . . .
> ....
> Some say God caught them even before they fell.

The survivors themselves react very differently. Having been immersed in the extremely ambiguous heroism of fiendish battle, with its 'superhuman inhumanities' and 'immemorial shames', they only crawl 'slowly back' and by degrees regain 'cool peaceful air in wonder'; and it is left to the reader to answer the question, 'Why speak not they of comrades that went under?' And even the aspirations of the new idealist who, in 'Strange Meeting', seems to have been reborn out of the horrors of war to preach the gospel, not of death, but of 'The pity of war, the pity of war distilled', are abandoned at the end, in lines which are the more quietly moving for coming after the morally exalted (but also obscure) ecstasies which precede them:

> I am the enemy you killed, my friend.
> I knew you in this dark: for so you frowned
> Yesterday through me as you jabbed and killed.
> I parried; but my hands were loath and cold.
> Let us sleep now . . . .

The unemphatic quality of these closing lines is something different from what is to be found in either the elegiac music of 'Anthem for Doomed Youth', or the anguished final question of 'Futility'. Its nearest equivalent is the muted conclusion of 'The Send-Off':

A few, a few, too few for drums and yells,

May creep back, silent, to still village wells
Up half-known roads.

But 'The Send-Off' does not have its own ecstasies as a contrast
to the quietness of these lines; and it cannot, therefore, give the
same impression of withdrawal even from the strenuous business
of preaching a new moral heroism free from the taint of aggressive militarism. The broken last line, 'Let us sleep now', may, of
course, be simply the result of the unfinished condition of the
poem; but, if so, it seems peculiarly appropriate to what is being
said, and the mood that is being evoked. By means of it the poem
seems to turn its back on its own visionary prospects; and, like
the prosaic, but deeply moving, lines spoken by Edgar at the end
of *King Lear*, it gives the sense of obeying the weight of a sad time,
and speaking what is felt, not what ought to be said. But there is
also the particular sense in 'Strange Meeting' of a quiet revulsion
which is ambiguously at once the result of weariness with
continuing bloodshed; the expression of a common humanity
now recognised as beyond and above the temporary condition of
hostility generated by war; and a turning from life to the inevitability of death. The old aggressiveness is there in association
with the narrator of the poem, the first 'I', who 'jabbed and
killed' the second speaker, who is the 'I' of the rest of the poem,
from line 15 to the end. But these two 'I's' are, essentially, both
aspects of the poet himself – a self and anti-self suggestive of the
two selves in Thomas' 'The Other', but reconciled and brought
to an understanding of each other. 'Yesterday' they met and
fought on the field of battle, where the second 'I', already
reluctant, only 'parried'. Here the first 'I' addresses his alter ego
as 'Strange friend', and the second declares his paradoxical
identity as 'the enemy you killed, my friend', and adds his
recognition: 'I knew you in this dark' – echoing the earlier lines
in which he had sprung to meet his opposite 'With piteous
recognition in fixed eyes'. The two are finally joined together in
the last words of the poem, where 'us' is used for the first time;
but what joins them is 'sleep', which in this context is death.

It is difficult to say whether 'Strange Meeting' is tragic or not.
As the two selves speak, both possibilities are suggested:

'Strange friend,' I said, 'here is no cause to mourn.'
'None,' said that other, 'save the undone years,
The hopelessness.

It is tragic in its realisation of the waste and futility of war, and yet it seems to transcend tragedy in its acceptance of death as the ultimate remover of false barriers. In the long speech of the enemy-friend it becomes prophetic rather than tragic, but the impression given by the speaker's final words, of a disillusioned weariness with man's innate aggressiveness, is once more tragic. One must conclude that there is something unresolved in the poem's underlying purpose – that its mixture of earnest moral vision and resignation, like its uncertainty of tone and style, is a sign of its imperfectly finished state. But it remains in some respects uniquely moving. Less finely achieved than 'The Send-Off' or 'Futility', it nevertheless seems Owen's most deeply introspective poem – the poem in which Owen is most profoundly engaged in the creative struggle to understand his own attitude to war and its tragic significance. It is his most ambitious attempt to reconcile distance and immediacy.

9 Sylvia Plath: Death and the Self

The concentration of so much criticism on the schizophrenic condition of Sylvia Plath, and the suicide to which it led, has had the effect of making her tragedy seem a merely private one. Joyce Carol Oates, however, rejects such an approach. In her view tragedy should rise to an impersonal level: 'Tragedy is not a woman, however gifted, dragging her shadow around in a circle, or analyzing with dazzling scrupulosity the stale, boring inertia of the circle; tragedy is cultural, mysteriously enlarging the individual.'[1] What matters is the tragedy, achieved or not achieved, in Sylvia Plath's work. As a critical position this is admirable. Biographers are necessarily concerned with the personal circumstances which caused Plath to try to kill herself at the age of twenty, and then, unfortunately, to succeed in doing so at thirty; and, given the 'confessional' nature of her late poems especially, they, and we, are bound to be interested in the close relation between her life and work. But if the work is valuable in a literary sense, and not simply as personal documentation, it must be for the experience it re-creates. The meaning must arise from the interaction of the words and forms that continue to exist for us on the printed page. Those critics who see her as a kind of Modernist martyr, sacrificing her life to the dangerous depths within her self for the sake of extending the range of human consciousness, run the risk of demoting her poetry to the status of a clinical file, which happens to have the added merit of being an unusually clairvoyant and eloquent one.

However, Oates' own approach to Plath's work also has its dangers. She avoids the mistake of seeing it as a mere record of personal neurosis, but the particular kind of cultural context in which she places it has an equally reductive effect. It belongs, she suggests, to the poetry of late Romanticism, which turns for inspiration to the private anguish of the poet's own soul, and, as a result, risks being confined within a narrow and disabling subjectivity. The poet celebrates his own inner world, rather than the external world, and, though this gives an initially thrilling impetus to his work, eventually it starves him of the material necessary to ensure the continuity of the creative process. 'How can the poet', Oates asks, 'make himself sacred. Once he has exposed himself, revealed himself, dramatized his fantasies and terrors, what can he do next?'[2]

Such a view of the limitations of subjectivity becomes virtually an attack on lyric poetry itself; and Oates does, in fact, reach the point where she suggests that 'Perhaps it is not just Plath's position at the end of her own unhappy life that doomed her and her poetry to premature dissolution, but something in the very nature of lyric poetry itself.'[3] But this at once underestimates the richness of the interior world that the lyric can explore and ignores the long tradition of engagement with the external world that the English lyric in particular exemplifies. It also implies much too exclusivist a view of the form, which in practice is often a hybrid, making generous use of the advantages of drama and narrative, and even at times of the novel. Certain poems by Sylvia Plath may indeed belong to a vein of Romanticism which cultivates its own solipsistic inner world, and the love of 'easeful death' which never lies far below the surface of such poetry is drastically emphasised in her contributions to the kind. To suggest, however, that this is typical of all her verse is wilfully to shut one's eyes to its variety, and to neglect the shifts of tone and stance which are evidence of her dissatisfaction with precisely the romantic manner that Oates deplores. Her contribution to lyric tragedy can be defined neither in terms of 'dragging her shadow around in a circle', nor in terms of a culture which is stigmatised as self-indulgent Romanticism. It is to be seen, rather, in terms of her struggle against the temptation of self-indulgence, and of her experiment with forms and tones which allow greater emotional resilience and contact with something beyond the inner world of 'fantasies and terrors' – even though this world remains the primary subject. It is through such struggle and experiment that her poetry acquires the sense of energetic resistance to destructive forces which is essential to tragedy, and achieves whatever lasting value it has.

Plath is well aware of the extent to which she fishes in her own self for the material of her poetry; but she also strives to see that material as part of the general human inheritance. Through the Jungian dream of the disturbed narrator of her short story, *Johnny Panic and the Bible of Dreams*, she offers what is virtually a parable of her artistic relation to her self:

> I've a dream of my own. My one dream. A dream of dreams.
> In this dream there's a great half-transparent lake stretching away in every direction, too big for me to see the shores of it, if there are any shores, and I'm hanging over it, looking down from the glass belly of some helicopter. At the bottom of the lake – so deep I can only guess at the dark masses moving and heaving – are the real dragons. The ones that were around before men started living in caves and cooking meat over fires and figuring out the wheel and the alphabet. . . .
> It's into this lake people's minds run at night, brooks and gutter-trickles to one borderless common reservoir.[4]

As this parable suggests, the lake, with its disturbingly sinister contents, is both a private fantasy of the narrator's and a common reservoir for all people's minds; and to express it he uses both the contemporary image of the helicopter and the ancient myth of the dragon. Plath's poetry is similarly the product of a fascinating compulsion to explore the dark world of death lurking at the bottom of her own psyche, and to generalise what she finds through both modern and traditional means. In her early poetry she makes use of mainly traditional resources, relying on imitation and a deliberate cultivation of formal elegance that often draws attention away from the subject to its own accomplishment. Later the imitation is better disguised; and in the poems of her last year and a half it seems at first glance as if she has thrown traditional props aside and is relying exclusively on contemporary reference and verse forms of almost unrestricted freedom. In reality, however, the search for a stabilising medium through which to express her destructive material continues; and though death is more evidently her theme than ever before, she still struggles to make it more than a private obsession.

'Pursuit' is a representative example of the early poetry (though in so short a working life 'early' and 'late' are only relative terms: Ted Hughes – Sylvia Plath's husband and the editor of her

Collected Poems – assigns this particular poem to 1956, only seven
years before her death in 1963).[5] Its debt to Blake's 'Tiger' is
obvious, but in its stanzaic structure, and in the relationship to
the demonic energies which the panther, like Blake's tiger,
represents, it is a quite different poem.[6] Blake's unified, incantatory celebration of dangerous creative power becomes in Plath's
poem a less concentrated, and tonally more uncertain, expression of fascination and compulsion. The opening lines:

> There is a panther stalks me down:
> One day I'll have my death of him

is an attempt to distance the emotion with Websterian wit ('I
have caught / An everlasting cold. I have lost my voice / Most
irrecoverably'[7]). The next lines more directly evoke the energy of
the panther, but again slip into the seventeenth-century manner
with an echo of Marvell's 'To His Coy Mistress' in

> Most soft, most suavely glides that step,
> Advancing always at my back.

With 'hemlock' and rooks that 'croak havoc' the atmosphere
becomes Gothic, and then the image of the hunt brings the 'I' of
the poem into prominence as a romantically persecuted victim.
The same uneasy mixture continues through the over-extended
length of the remaining three stanzas, with the addition of
occasional attempts to give the garish metaphor a somewhat
confused allegorical significance, as in the lines at the beginning
of stanza 2 (reminiscent of T. S. Eliot[8]), which mingle suggestions of the Grail legends' waste land, the Christian doctrine of
original sin, and the Freudian concept of repression:

> Insatiate, he ransacks the land
> Condemned by our ancestral fault,
> Crying: blood, let blood be spilt;

and the lines towards the end of stanza 4 which similarly combine
modern psychology and the ancient symbol of the tower:

> Entering the tower of my fears,
> I shut my doors on that dark guilt,
> I bolt the door, each door I bolt.

The final pair of isolated lines replaces the ABBA rhyme-scheme (but with frequently imperfect rhymes) of the preceding stanzas by a couplet that repeats the same word:

> The panther's tread is on the stairs,
> Coming up and up the stairs.

The intention, presumably, is to end the poem with a dramatic climax; but in some ways the effect is an absurd anticlimax. The stairs suddenly become the steps up to the nursery, and the 'I' a child in bed having a nightmare. This, too, can be justified in psychological terms – the primitive is what is experienced in childhood terrors; but it is not sufficiently a part of what has been evoked in the previous stanzas, and the would-be daring relapse into simple, childlike language, 'Coming up and up the stairs', is reductive rather than climactic. (It is a hint, however, of the strategy later to be employed, more effectively, in 'Daddy'.)

In 'Lorelei', a poem written two years later in 1958, there is a narrowing of range by comparison with what was over-ambitiously attempted in 'Pursuit'; but a narrowing which also brings with it a greater unity of tone. The theme of the suicidal death-wish is more directly personal, but it is given a more convincingly impersonal power of suggestion through its use of the Rhine and the seductive enchantment of the mythical *lorelei*. The voice is still first-person, but sparingly used: the nominative form, 'I', appears only once (in the penultimate stanza), and 'me' twice ('Up toward me', stanza 4, and 'ferry me down there', in the final stanza) – against which there are six uses of the second person, in connection with the *lorelei*. Hence, although it is a highly subjective mood that the poem is evoking, the image of the *lorelei* has a persuasively real presence. There is a gradual build-up, from the beginning, through scene-painting of a hazy, but suitably Wagnerian–operatic quality, to the point where the at first vague and unspecified 'these shapes' take on

> limbs ponderous

> With richness, hair heavier
> Than sculpted marble
> (12–14)

and finally sing, and are addressed as 'Sisters' (16). It is only when this realisation of the seductive quality of the as yet unidentified death-wish has been accomplished in the *lorelei* that Plath makes an explicit contrast between its subtly undermining power and the ordered world of normal consciousness:

> Sisters, your song
> Bears a burden to weighty
> For the whorled ear's listening
>
> Here, in a well-steered country,
> Under a balanced ruler.
> Deranging by harmony
>
> Beyond the mundane order,
> Your voices lay siege.
>   (16–23)

The *lorelei* are now lodged 'On the pitched reefs of nightmare' which belie their promise of 'sure harborage'. But the most sinister aspect of their power has yet to come: this is their 'silence', worse even than their 'maddening / Song' – a cold, inhuman menace that is none the less deeply intoxicating:

> At the source
>
> Of your ice-hearted calling –
> Drunkenness of the great depths.
>   (30–2)

finally, the nominative 'I' is introduced, drugged by the spell that has been created, and ready, it seems, to succumb to the death-wish:

> O river, I see drifting
>
> Deep in your flux of silver
> Those great goddesses of peace.
> Stone, stone, ferry me down there.

In this poem form and meaning work effectively together. The seven-syllabled line generates a heavily dragging undertow (as Pamela Smith expresses it, 'each breath wants to be a last gasp'[9]), and the *terza rima*, with its ABA BCB progression of rhymes, blunted and muted in Plath's typical fashion, interlocks each stanza – as do the enjambment and run-on from stanza to stanza. The result is a sinuous movement gliding seductively from unit to unit, as a harmonious counterpart of the song of the *lorelei*.

As the creation of a mood 'Lorelei' is thus a successful poem; but its narrowed range deprives it of tragic significance. There is too little resistance to its 'Drunkenness of the great depths' (a phrase which, Ted Hughes notes, is taken from a book by Cousteau: 'It describes the euphoric visionary state of acute oxygen shortage in which divers blissfully forget all precautions and danger[10]). The 'well-steered country' exists as a possible alternative, but it makes no struggle, creates virtually no tension, and serves only to define the alienness of the *lorelei* world by contrast. In the curiously evasive syntax of this part of the poem it is the voices of the Sisters which are passively active. What they 'derange', and to what they 'lay siege', is left unspecified. It may be the country and its ruler, but the absence of a grammatical object deliberately blurs the conflict. The poem celebrates a kind of negativeness. Its climax is in 'silence' and the paradox of a 'stone' ferryman. In sum, the body of the poem is an ironic complement to its first line: 'It is no night to drown in'. What is shown is precisely that it *is* a night to drown in; and, despite what ought to be the danger signal of the quotation from Cousteau, drowning is presented as a consummation of the *lorelei* seductiveness devoutly to be wished.

Another poem written while Plath was reading Cousteau is 'Full Fathom Five'. This, too, is a death-wish poem; but the use of the father-figure – a composite of Plath's own father, Otto Plath, set against the background of the Atlantic coastline familiar to Plath from her childhood, and Father Neptune, a weird and potent old man of the sea – enables her to suggest more effectively than 'Lorelei' an undertow of destruction which is incorporated in the very substance of life. The paradox that death stems from the source of life is reflected in the image of seaweed as the sea-father's strangling hair extended in 'radial sheaves' (with 'sheaves' carrying the overtone of sheaves of corn) and in the carefully manipulated syntax of

> your spread hair, in which wrinkling skeins
> Knotted, caught, survives
>
> The old myth of origins
> Unimaginable

where the three verbs packed into one line convey almost simultaneous impressions of death, stasis and survival. However, it is again death which in the end predominates. Instead of the vital transformation of death by water implied by the allusion to Ariel's song in *The Tempest*, the vast paternal image of Plath's poem leads only to a reversal of normal life and death associations that is sinister:

> Your shelled bed I remember.
> Father, this thick air is murderous.
> I would breathe water.

The real and the mythical father are also fused in 'Man in Black'. This poem, which again works through the familiar Atlantic scenery, creates a dual impression of remoteness and nearness. The tidal movement of the grey sea, with its suggestion of immemorial rhythms, is collocated with the prosaic contemporariness of 'Deer Island prison / With its trim piggeries', and the father-figure who provides the unifying element to the contradictory scene is a symbolic man in black, yet for the poet an immediate 'you'. The poem is also one sentence picking its way through seven *terza rima* stanzas to the ultimate 'riveting stones, air, / All of it, together'. This final assertion of unity is seemingly at odds with the funereal tone of the preceding lines; but it does in itself have tragic implications, for the tense of the verbs connected with the father ('strode' and 'stood') is past, and his 'dead / Black coat, black shoes' and 'Black hair' emphasise his darkness and death. He was once the unifying principle, the 'Fixed vortex', making the scene a vital whole; but his removal allows the chaotic implications of 'vortex' a new, threatening possibility.

Plath explores the daughter–father relationship once more in 'Electra on Azalea Path'. This is a poem which has its immediately personal occasion in a visit which Plath made to her father's grave in March 1959 (Hughes informs us that 'Azalea Path was the name of the cemetery path', and he reproduces an autobiographical account of the visit which is very close to lines 19–21[11]). Much of the detail is prosaically documentary, down to the 'Six feet of yellow gravel' covering the father's body and 'the basket of plastic evergreens they put / At the headstone next to yours'; and Plath deals frankly with the unpleasant physical fact of her father's death:

> It was the gangrene ate you to the bone
> My mother said; you died like any man.

Here Otto Plath is not sea-father or 'Man in Black', but demythologised, ordinary man.

However, the poem also has another, very different dimension, which this deliberate banality throws into sharp relief – the exalted, histrionic world of the almost wilfully childish imagination. This is a timeless dimension, in accord with the opening of the poem where the speaker represents herself as seeking to escape knowledge and guilt by entering

> the lightless hibernaculum
> Where bees, striped black and gold, sleep out the blizzard
> Like hieratic stones.

There she could think of herself as the offspring of a virgin birth, and free from the anxiety associated with consciousness of her real father, create an epic character for him in the innocent theatre of her mind:

> Small as a doll in my dress of innocence
> I lay dreaming your epic, image by image.
> Nobody died or withered on that stage.

Though not directly stated, the similarity of the 'hibernaculum' to the method chosen by Plath for her first attempt at killing herself, and the allusions to 'twenty years' and, later, to 'an infamous suicide', also seem to suggest that this is the world she sought to re-enter by suicide.

'Nobody died or withered on that stage' belongs to the child's fantasy; but it points forward, by contrast, to the use of a dramatic myth in this poem which is not escapist:

> *The day your slack sail drank my sister's breath*
> *The flat sea purpled like that evil cloth*
> *My mother unrolled at your last homecoming.*

The influence of the early T. S. Eliot, particularly of 'Sweeney Among the Nightingales', is evident here; but Plath is attempting something more ambitious than the satirical juxtapositions of Eliot. Her leap from the 'artificial red sage', which leaks its ersatz dye on the neighbouring headstone, to 'Another kind of redness bothers me', is serious, not ironic. It would seem to be a means of connecting her private sense of guilt for her father's death with the blood theme of the Agamemnon story. Yet the parallels do not quite fit. The 'I' of the poem blames herself: 'It was my love that did us both to death'. The mother is also intermittently blamed, which provides some sort of Clytemnestra–Electra parallel, but why is not clear; nor is the daughter convinced that the mother *should* be blamed. She half-believes that her own immaturity is the root of the trouble, causing her to surround the father-figure with a falsifying emotional aura, when, in fact, he 'died like any man'. She cannot, however, see herself outgrowing this confusion ('How shall I age into that state of mind?'), and so she remains a desperately posturing adolescent, 'the ghost of an infamous suicide'.

Self-destruction is thus presented as both a means of entering a lost, timeless world in which the presiding deity is an inflated father-figure, and as self-punishment for a neurotically misrepresented crime. The Agamemnon associations enhance each of these, but also import a degree of confusion, particularly into the private world (i.e. as it is reflected in the poem) of which the 'I' is aware. The result is a strutting awkwardness of tone which can be deeply moving at one moment and embarrassingly over-done at another – though Plath is self-critically aware of this, too. After her italicised re-enactment of Agamemnon's situation she states quite baldly: 'I borrow the stilts of an old tragedy'; and in a line that has its context both in that ancient myth and in the actual graveyard where the real father's corpse lies, 'The stony actors poise and pause for breath', she seems to see her own

creations as figures frozen in statuesque postures. It is under-
standable, therefore, that she rejected the poem for book publication on the ground that it was 'too forced and rhetorical';[12]
but, despite its shortcomings, it is a poignant comment on her
struggle with her self, and an interesting attempt to find a means
of universalising it.

The initial reference in 'Electra on Azalea Path' to beekeeping is
a reminder of an interest which Plath shared with her father, and
which gave rise to a remarkable group of poems written near the
end of her life: 'The Beekeeper's Daughter' (1959); and 'The Bee
Meeting', 'The Arrival of the Bee Box', 'Stings', 'The Swarm'
and 'Wintering' (all 1962).

Strictly speaking, these are not tragic poems. They are
founded on the beekeeping cycle which involves death, but as
part of a process of renewal; and though it has been suggested
that Plath's own suicide attempts were part of a delusion that
her own death would be followed by renewal, her beekeeping
poems are not based on that kind of self-deception. They are
among the sanest and most clear-sighted of her work – the one
dubious element, perhaps, being her attempt, in 'The Swarm', to
connect the swarming of the bees with Napoleon's grandiose
military exploits (on the pretext of Napoleon's adoption of the
bee-symbol as his personal crest). Her treatment of the bees is
sufficient in itself to achieve a larger, universal significance
without the need for a somewhat factitious parallel of this kind.

The poems stand as separate, individual poems, but all of
them (with the exception of 'The Beekeeper's Daughter') were
written closely together and share a common world. A normal
country activity provides the unifying foundation, on which the
superstructure of the poet's abnormal consciousness is built; the
poet none the less also being a participant in the ordinary
beekeeping business (as Sylvia Plath herself in reality was). This
combination of involvement and detachment is more apparent in
'The Bee Meeting', where the commonplaceness of the beekeeping gathering, with its representative figures from ordinary
village life, 'The rector, the midwife, the sexton, the agent for
bees', are defamiliarised by their protective clothing, till they
become, in the eyes of the gawky, apprehensive speaker of the

poem, slightly comic, Quixote-like figures of romance, and yet sinisterly transformed:

> Which is the rector now, is it that man in black?
> Which is the midwife, is that her blue coat?
> Everybody is nodding a square black head, they are
>   knights in visors,
> Breastplates of cheesecloth knotted under the armpits.
> Their smiles and their voices are changing.

As the poet is drawn into their activity, it acquires the aura of a menacing ritual performed in 'the shorn grove, the circle of hives'. The placing of these two phrases in apposition to each other – one evocatively ominous, the other more neutrally descriptive – indicates the co-presence of two distinct levels of consciousness within the speaker; but as the poem develops, it is the anxiety betrayed by the first which increasingly takes over. She becomes hysterical, and projects her hysteria on the bees as they are smoked out from the hive: 'Here they come, the outriders, on their hysterical elastics.' She is potentially their victim, though trying to believe that if she stands still 'they will think I am cow-parsley'; but she also identifies herself with the queenbee, who feels threatened by the virgins even though on this occasion 'there will be no killing'. She ends 'exhausted', and while the villagers untie their disguises and shake hands she wonders: 'Whose is that long white box in the grove, what have they accomplished, why am I cold.'

Normality and renewal are thus set against the speaker's sense of death, as if to underline how needless it is; she returns once more to recognising herself as a frightened adolescent who needs to grow up – a meaning effectively embodied in the repetition and egotistical exaggeration of the penultimate lines:

> I am exhausted, I am exhausted –
> Pillar of white in a blackout of knives.
> I am the magician's girl who does not flinch.

Nevertheless, the death-threat glimpsed by the girl in her hysteria does have some basis in reality. The queen-bee is 'clever' enough to know that 'she must live another year', but the future belongs to the other females:

While in their fingerjoint cells the new virgins

Dream of a duel they will win inevitably,
A curtain of wax dividing them from the bride flight,
The upflight of the murderess into a heaven that loves her.

The speaker's hysteria has some justification, therefore; it has at least brought a degree of true insight into the tragic element involved in renewal. What she perceives is both invalid and valid.

In the earlier poem, 'The Beekeeper's Daughter', the flowers that await fertilisation by the bees are drenched in an over-poweringly Keatsian sensuousness and sexuality, but the fruit-fulness this suggests is undermined by awareness of doom: 'A fruit that's death to taste: dark flesh, dark parings.' However, none of the later poems in the group indulges in such lusciousness. The alliterative and assonantal rhetoric is pushed aside, and something starker and more radically disturbing is revealed. Although beekeeping remains a familiar creative pursuit, the taste of death which it carries for the poet – an echo of the Miltonic fruit, 'whose mortal taste / Brought death into the world, and all our woe'[13] – is conveyed more economically, and in a new way that is charged with a current of bitter wit. Thus in 'The Arrival of the Bee Box' the imprisoned bees can take on a terribly ominous quality without the need for a wealth of description:

> I put my eye to the grid.
> It is dark, dark
> With the swarmy feeling of African hands
> Minute and shrunk for export,
> Black on black, angrily clambering.

The conjunction of 'swarmy' and 'African hands' is enough to suggest the close-packed furriness of the bees, while the sudden shift to macabre dark comedy in the next line registers the nervous horror of the poet's response as what she sees becomes a vehicle for her dim consciousness of the obscenity lurking in her own mind. As in 'The Bee Meeting', she hopes to escape the anger of the bees by turning into a tree – the Daphne strategy of passivity; but this is again mocked by the macabre humour of an image that turns her beekeeping clothes into the outlandish garb of an astronaut:

> They might ignore me immediately
> In my moon suit and funeral veil.

A touch of self-mockery comes next:

> I am no source of honey
> So why should they turn on me?

And this is followed, in another quick shift of tone, by an ironic presentation of herself as one who is completely in command of the situation:

> Tomorrow I will be sweet God, I will set them free.

> The box is only temporary.

The spacing that leaves the last line standing on its own allows it to be read either as an amplification of the preceding line, or as a comment on the whole poem. Either way, it tacitly marks the fragility of attempts to evade responsibility for the box. It was ordered by the speaker and has arrived. Its contents have to be reckoned with.

'Stings', as its title suggests, is a more abrupt and aggressive poem. It seems to express a resentfully militant feminism. The argument runs as follows: the speaker has identified with the domestic principle embodied in the hive, which, with 'excessive love', she has decorated with pink flowers, 'Thinking "Sweetness, sweetness" '.[14] As a consequence, however, the queen-bee (later explicitly equated with her self: 'I / Have a self to recover, a queen') has become a ragged thing, 'Poor and bare and unqueenly and even shameful', and the speaker has been reduced to one of the 'winged, unmiraculous women, / Honeydrudgers'. Nevertheless, she insists that she is not a mere drudge, and, even at the risk of offending conventional feminine notions, she will recover her lost queen and fly in red-bodied vengeance above the beehive doll's house which has become 'The mausoleum, the wax house'.

There is also a male intruder, who was 'sweet' in the superficial colloquial sense (the speaker was also at one time 'sweet' on him), but 'the bees found him out' and drove him away with their stings, though paying the price for stinging with their own

deaths. This apparently has its origin in an incident when Ted
Hughes, who was not wearing protective clothing, was attacked
by bees as Plath was moving a queen-bee. The poem, according
to Jon Rosenblatt, is 'a veiled reference to Plath's own feeling of
revenge against her husband and is a metaphor for personal
violence'.[15] It is probably a mistake, however, to give this epi-
sode of the 'third person' such central prominence. Though
vividly recorded, in terms of the poem's development it is
something of a digression – a warning of the temptation into
which extreme feminism may fall. This, at any rate, seems to be
implied by the comment which immediately follows the attack:

> They [the bees] thought death was worth it, but I
> Have a self to recover, a queen.

It is the emergence of the self from all-pervasive sweetness (the
words 'sweet', 'queen' plus related phonograms recur throughout the poem[16]) which is the real focus. Anything else is a
distraction – even the justified attack on the male domination
that imposes this false queenly 'sweetness' on women. Far from
being the poem's main theme, the attack, and its consequence
for the bees, is a warning against the danger of destroying the self
by allowing this secondary issue to take precedence.

The true climax of the poem is the flight of the finally liberated
queen:

> Where has she been,
> With her lion-red body, her wings of glass?
>
> Now she is flying
> More terrible than she ever was, red
> Scar in the sky, red comet
> Over the engine that killed her –
> The mausoleum, the wax house.

According to Mary L. Broe, this is a triumphal flight, but one in
which the complexity of the language allows for weakness:
'Imagery of transcendence commingles with hints of illness,
vulnerability ("red scar," "her wings of glass") with ferocity
("lion-red body," "red comet"), to fashion a surprisingly resili-
ent and vital queen. She both conquers and recognizes limi-

tations.'[17] However, there is a suggestion of brittleness in these lines which makes such an interpretation questionable. It is there, for example, in the crackling sound of 'Scar in the sky, red comet'; and, though the thrice-repeated 'red' is, no doubt, symbolic of a new-found vitality, in contrast to the yellow, pink and cream associated with the hive and honey-making earlier, it is too blatantly assertive to carry complete conviction. Similarly, the violent enjambment of 'red / Scar' (which Broe misleadingly quotes as 'red scar') instead of suggesting wounds that are now healed, flaunts its gash of blood in the sky like a warrior's arrogantly displayed sign of combat-experience. The emergence of the self must therefore be treated with some reservation. It is willed, but that is not to say that it is achieved. What does emerge, however, is the anger (another, and rather more persuasive, connotation of 'red') that was before smothered under the pervasive sweetness; and the release of this can be seen as potentially either therapeutic or tragic. Certainly, the queen at the end seems intent on destruction rather than creation; the self has not altogether escaped the peril of which it has been warned.

In 'The Swarm' anger becomes a 'black ball' of bees, 'A flying hedgehog, all prickles', and its defeat by the mere 'Pom! Pom!' popgun effect of the man's shooting, which reduces the swarm to a 'red tatter' (in contrast to the brilliant red associated with the queen in 'Stings'), is a cynical reflection of the futility of rebellion. At the end the bees obediently walk the plank into 'a new mausoleum' (a phrase again reminiscent of 'Stings'). Their relationship to Napoleon is, however, a confusing one. They may, as Broe suggests, be mock-heroically equated with Napoleon's conquests,[18] but the 'man of business' who shoots to bring them down from their grandiose heights seems himself to be Napoleon. Napoleon would thus appear to be self-defeating – which perhaps he was, in the sense that he overreached himself; but it is unsatisfactory as far as this poem is concerned, since the deluded submission of the bees is what is being mocked, rather than the final collapse of the man's strategy. Again, in the lines:

> It is you the knives are out for
> At Waterloo, Waterloo, Napoleon

the 'knives' are apparently the stings of the bees. If so, this is further confusing, for though the bees may sting their Napoleon (as suggested in the last stanza), it is *they* who meet their Waterloo, not he, in that their female anger is finally subdued to his male purpose, which is to make them enter the hive designed for them, and produce his 'ton of honey'. It may be that Plath intends this to be seen as a Pyrrhic victory – to frustrate the anger of the bees is to end up with a spurious sweetness and domesticity. But, again, the mock-heroic device seems an unhelpful way of expressing such meaning. It imports an ambitious historical analogy which, instead of illuminating and universalising the theme of female anger, merely dissipates the tragic potentiality of its 'Stings'.

The last poem of the group, 'Wintering', has been interpreted as an expression of hope. In accordance with his view that Plath's poetry is concerned with initiation rituals involving death and renewal, Rosenblatt sees it as a black moment before rebirth:

> The blackness of the bees in the dead of winter symbolizes for Plath the organic zero point from which new life will emerge. From this center where the poet feels possessed by the bees ('It is they who own me'), she sees an exit. The bees represent a feminine force that will come out from the long white winter and be reborn: 'The bees are flying. They taste the spring.'[19]

That last line is certainly on an optimistic note; but the main body of the poem gives less cause for hope. It celebrates an 'easy time' – a time for resting on accomplishment after the honey has been extracted and ranged in the cellar in its storage jars. But any sense that this might be a serene, quiescent hibernation period is undermined by the depressingly jaundiced quality of the context in which the honey and the bees are placed. The jars winter 'in a dark without window', neighboured by nastiness and falsity:

> Next to the last tenant's rancid jam
> And the bottles of empty glitters –
> Sir So-and-so's gin.

The bees live on Tate & Lyle substitute. The occasional 'warm days' only enliven them enough for them to carry out their dead; and though they have got rid of the drones (normal enough in bees, but Plath bitterly emphasises the human analogy: 'They have got rid of the men, / The blunt, clumsy stumblers, the boors'), the female sexual isolation is symbolised in terms of empty activity and a mockery of fertility:

> The woman, still at her knitting,
> At the cradle of Spanish walnut,
> Her body a bulb in the cold and too dumb to think.

Essentially, the poem is a powerful expression of female deprivation, the 'sweetness, sweetness' having gone sour, and a slow resentful anger taking over. Its setting within the cycle of bee-keeping and honey-production limits the extent of this despair, and provides some justification for the note of hope at the end; but the poem is not structured to enable this final stanza to effect a restrospective transformation. Its questions express the pathos of uncertain longing rather than the confidence of renewal:

> Will the hive survive, will the gladiolas
> Succeed in banking their fires
> To enter another year?
> What will they taste of, the Christmas roses?

Only the laconic affirmations of the final line are assured; and they are not enough to cancel out all that has gone before.

The strength of the beekeeping group of poems is that they support each other. As they accumulate their images of darkness, anger and female deprivation, the whole becomes larger than the parts. The bees become original symbols, and the beekeeping processes provide them with the resonance of a familiar, yet mysterious, cult. Above all, it is their recurrent theme of abused and perverted 'sweetness' which gives them their tragic – if, at times, uncertainly tragic – tone. The containing structure is one of destruction followed by renewal, but their poetic intensity derives essentially from the destructive phase.

This intensity is a frequent element in other poems written during the astonishingly productive last few months of Plath's life. Perhaps the most remarkable of these are 'Daddy' and

'Lady Lazarus' (both dated October 1962). Both also share with
the beekeeping poems a marked change in style, from the elab-
orate syntax of the earlier verse to an abrupt, staccato manner, in
which sentences are often one short line, and in which the harsh,
insistent repetition exacerbates the often extreme violence of
content. In the beekeeping poems this is mostly an incipient
violence, but in 'Daddy' and 'Lady Lazarus' it breaks out at full
pitch. The nursery-rhyme element in Plath's verse has often
been noted. This is at its most obvious in 'Daddy', where it is
used to magnify the effect of deliberate retreat into infantile
aggression through childishly chanted rhythms and the obsess-
ively shrieking recurrence of the sound 'u:', both as end-rhyme
and internal rhyme, from the opening '*You do* not *do, you do* not *do*'
to the final 'Daddy, daddy, *you* bastard, I'm *through*'. In 'Lady
Lazarus' the freedom of childish speech coupled with an almost
jeering parody of showman's rhetoric makes for a language of
uninhibited exhibitionism. In both poems the speaker lets rip, as
if she no longer cares what people think, or as if unable to
prevent the uninhibited spurt of language, while in fact still
shaping it and moulding it with metre, rhyme and rhetoric.

The extent to which the poet is really in control is nevertheless
questionable. These poems seem to lay claim to a kind of
King-Lear-on-the-heath extravagance in which the blaze of
private grief is universalised by its fusion with awareness of evil
in society at large; but the regal authority that makes Lear 'every
inch a king' is completely lacking, and the crimes committed
against the 'I' of Plath's poems can bear no comparison with
those which make Lear 'a man more sinned against than sin-
ning'. Indeed, the very status of the 'crimes' is doubtful. In
'Daddy' what is it exactly that the father has done to warrant the
daughter's railing against him? They share, we must suppose,
the paradox of love and hate which is endemic in the parent–
child relationship, but neither the love nor the hate is properly
focussed. The daughter's love for the father makes him 'a bag
full of God', a massive Colossus-like figure dominating the
childhood seascape previously used in poems like 'Full Fathom
Five' and 'Man in Black'; while her, admittedly more potent,
hatred makes him a tyrant, a devil, a vampire, and a Nazi
butcher responsible for the persecution of the Jews. But it is
impossible to relate either figure to more than distorted childish
fantasy. Their source seems to be Sylvia Plath's own father; but

the real Otto had nothing to do with the Nazis, and very probably little resemblance to the other attributes of 'Daddy'. It can be argued, of course, (and the beginning of this chapter has already conceded the argument) that biographical material should not be obtruded on the poem; that the 'Daddy' here created is not the father of Sylvia, but an imaginative conflation of the conventionally Germanic master-of-the-house and Nazi war criminal. The poem's 'confessional' mode, however, makes it difficult to ignore the biographical evidence, and quite possibly demands the recognition of its own distortion of both the private and public experience on which it draws. The father-figure of the poem does not represent a transcendent poetic truth created, like Wordsworth's leech-gatherer in 'Resolution and Independence', from disparate materials, but a 'gobbledygoo', nightmare projection of the speaker's mind; and, reluctantly, one is forced back on speculations about the psychological condition of that mind.

For all that, 'Daddy' is a very moving poem. It illustrates how near hysteria can come to being great poetry. It is a suicidal poem in the sense that it is a tremendous gesture demanding sympathetic attention. This exhibitionist element is even more apparent in 'Lady Lazarus'. There the speaker makes an exhibition of her own suicide attempts, turning suicide into a flamboyant circus display, with deliberately shocking effect, and, even more than in 'Daddy', flouting all conventions of emotional reticence:

> Dying
> Is an art, like everything else.
> I do it exceptionally well.
>
> I do it so it feels like hell.
> I do it so it feels real.
> I guess you could say I've a call.
>
> It's easy enough to do it in a cell.
> It's easy enough to do it and stay put.
> It's the theatrical
>
> Comeback in broad day
> To the same place, the same face, the same brute
> Amused shout:

'A miracle!'
That knocks me out.

Yet almost all the cynical, slangy bravado is a contradiction of
itself: the real meaning worms away underneath, asking not for
the theatricality but private compassion; not for brutality (any
more than the histrionic assertion in 'Daddy' that 'Every woman
adores a Fascist' really asks to be taken at face value) but sensitive
understanding. The most tragic element in the poem is the despair
it implies of ever getting such a response.

Again Plath attempts to connect with the wider meaning of
suffering embodied in the Jewish holocaust – and this time with
rather more success than in 'Daddy' (especially in the bleak
image of inhumanity created by the reduction of the Nazis'
victims to

> A cake of soap,
> A wedding ring,
> A gold filling).

And the allusions to Lazarus also imply a wider context –
whether they are taken to refer to the Lazarus of 'John' 11–12,
who was raised from the dead, thus suggesting an ironic resurrection of the suicide; or to the beggar who is contrasted with
Dives, the rich man, in 'Luke' 16, thus emphasising the despised
condition of the 'lady'; or, as may well be the case, they refer to
both. But neither the Nazi echoes nor the biblical allusions have a
profound effect on the meaning of the poem. As in the beekeeping
poems, it is the anger of the abused woman which is the real – and
potentially tragic – subject. Even in the climactic ending:

> Out of the ash
> I rise with my red hair
> And I eat men like air

it is this rather than the claimed analogy with resurrection that
comes across most forcefully. The red hair recalls the red body of
the queen-bee at the end of 'Stings'. The self that suffers has its
counterpart in the hidden self that needs to protest against the
conditions that create its suffering, and it is from this inner being
that the poem draws its energy. Its essential subject is not the

tragic nature of man and his world, but the posturing suicide who is a brilliant manifestation of the confused and tormented self.

As a postscript, a word should be said about the final poems of Sylvia Plath. A dozen of these were written in 1963, during the last six weeks of her life. There is something infinitely sad, but comparatively little tragic, about them; they seem to be written in a mood of cynical exhaustion. The possibility of the self making its protest against self-destruction seems to have vanished, and all that is left is a sterile knowledge:

> There is no terminus, only suitcases
>
> Out of which the same self unfolds like a suit
> Bald and shiny, with pockets of wishes,
>
> Notions and tickets, short circuits and folding mirrors.
>
> ('Totem')

The 'Mannequin' and the 'Gigolo' alike only 'glitter' with their mechanical substitutions for life, and 'Kindness' merely offers a spurious sugar that can 'cure everything' – 'Its crystals a little poultice'. Deadliest of all, the very last poem, 'Edge', offers a sentimentally beautiful image of a mother and her children 'perfected' in suicide:

> The illusion of a Greek necessity
>
> Flows in the scrolls of her toga,
> Her bare
>
> Feet seem to be saying:
> We have come so far, it is over.

This is a false version of tragedy, a perversion of Hamlet's 'the rest is silence'. It is lyric drained of the resistance necessary to the true version of tragedy and relapsing finally into the condition of being in love with 'easeful death'. Its gesture towards Greek tragedy – which the speaker acknowledges as an 'illusion' – is a pathetic comment on that second successful suicide attempt which marked the real Sylvia Plath's failure to find the form that would release the red-bodied counterpart of her self into spontaneous flight.

10   Philip Larkin: 'the bone's truth'

Take the grave's part,
Tell the bone's truth.
(Poem XXIX, *The North Ship*)

Only one ship is seeking us, a black-
Sailed unfamiliar, towing at her back
A huge and birdless silence. In her wake
No waters breed or break.
('Next, Please')

Life is first boredom, then fear.
Whether or not we use it, it goes,
And leaves what something hidden from us chose,
And age, and then the only end of age.
('Dockery and Son')

All know they are going to die.
('The Building')

Most things may never happen: this one will.
('Aubade')

The recurrence of this theme of death in each of the volumes
Larkin has so far published (at almost exactly ten-year inter-
vals),[1] and in the poem published in the *TLS* in 1977, suggests a
remarkable consistency, and an equally remarkable traditional-
ism. 'Timor mortis conturbat me' is one of the oldest cries of the
lyric poet; and the end death puts to all human hopes – the crisis

it supremely creates, not only in the affairs of men, but above all
in the consciousness of the individual – is the most fundamental
preoccupation of lyric tragedy. Most poets, however, find, if not
consolation, at least some way of mitigating it. Larkin is unique
in finding none. He cannot urge the launching of the ship of
death: his 'black- / Sailed unfamiliar' tows silent emptiness
behind it – a motionless sterility which is made all the more
telling by the pert alliteration and brittle rhyme of 'In her wake /
No waters breed or break'. He insistently takes 'the grave's part'
and tells 'the bone's truth', removing the comforts of friend and
priest alike. In 'Nothing To Be Said' the very rhetoric deflates
itself before the fact of death:

> The day spent hunting pig
> Or holding a garden-party,
>
> Hours giving evidence
> Or birth, advance
> On death equally slowly.
> And saying so to some
> Means nothing; others it leaves
> Nothing to be said.

The disparate subjects (their conflicting variety intensified by
the zeugma of 'giving evidence / Or birth') converge mockingly
in 'advance / On death'; and the antimetabole of the last three
lines spells out a virtually equal blankness for both the insensitive, who cannot feel the underlying threat of death, and the
sensitive, whose awareness of it makes them mutes. Death is
sheer, unalterable fact, dealing with attitudes towards it, not by
arguing, but by simply coming into its own non-being.

   The bleakest of all Larkin's poems on this theme is, undoubtedly, the most recent, 'Aubade'. The title is a grim bit of play
with tradition – the tradition of the anti-romantic, as well as the
romantic, dawn-song, ironically setting both against the quite
unromantic, and all-too-realistic, waiting for dawn which this
poem records. The hour or two before dawn that Larkin re-
creates is a time of darkness, in which the absence of light means,
not love, but the removal of distractions, like the work and drink
alluded to in the opening line, which screen the truth of approaching death. The questions of how and where and when

death will come – 'Arid interrogation' – are the obsession of this time, and with a literally remorseless honesty Larkin admits that his horror of death has nothing to do with altruistic purposes unfulfilled, or even with mistakes needing correction. The 'glare' at which the mind 'blanks' is the absence of the living state:

> Not to be here,
> Not to be anywhere,
> And soon; nothing more terrible, nothing more true.

The traditional comforts of religion or philosophy are useless, and the very basis of the tragic resort in such circumstances is contemptuously dismissed with the words:

> Courage is no good:
> It means not scaring others. Being brave
> Lets no one off the grave.
> Death is no different whined at than withstood.

Courage is no good in the sense that being either courageous or cowardly makes no difference to the fact that death is somewhere out there in the future waiting its turn. Nothing can alter that. But, it may be argued, courage to live with that knowledge is certainly 'good' in a different sense, and not simply a matter of hiding fear so that others will not be infected by it. The moral attitude to death, it is true, cannot prevent its inevitability. It is not something that can be 'withstood' as one might withstand the attack of an enemy. But the corrosiveness of the idea of death can be resisted – and if one moves outside this poem, with the particular circumstances and state of mind it expresses, it is apparent that some people have so resisted, and that some poems represent an education of emotional attitudes which help to make such resistance possible. 'Aubade' might, therefore, be condemned as a bad poem by the very standard of honesty which it implicitly sets up for itself. But the condemnation is none the less unwarranted, for the essentially honest speaking of the poem has to include the falsifying bitterness which can thus reduce courage to meaning merely 'not scaring others'. This is an authentic part of the pre-dawn horror of death. Paradoxically, it takes courage to say so. (The poem is tough enough to resist the easier explanation that it is merely a dramatic rendering of a moment of panic, which will pass.) The courage that is based on the altruism of consideration for the effect of one's views on others has its admirable, indeed heroic, dimension, but it is deficient in tragic honesty, which demands facing, not editing, one's deepest fears.

Yet 'Aubade' is also peculiarly modern in the further step it takes, of recognising that being honest is not necessarily helpful. The attitude towards death which it embodies is undeceived, but penetration of deception does not lead to reassurance. Perhaps the most moving lines in the poem are those with which the last stanza begins:

> Slowly light strengthens, and the room takes shape.
> It stands plain as a wardrobe, what we know,
> Have always known, know that we can't escape,
> Yet can't accept.

The light that comes now is not the same as the light at the beginning of the poem which was displaced by the 'soundless dark'. That, by implication, was deception; only in the dark could the poet see 'what's really always there'. As the last stanza completes itself, daylight activity is resumed, and 'all the uncaring / Intricate rented world begins to rouse.' But the recorded horror of the poem's night has put a stamp on the new day which changes it for the reader. The light itself is changed: 'The sky is white as clay, with no sun.' And in the final line 'Postmen', symbol of the day-to-day activity that hides death from us, 'like doctors go from house to house' – doctors, inevitably in this context, being reminders of sickness and death – without much in the way of comfort that they are also agents of healing. The most that can be said is that the changed light is a symbol of the deepened significance which the ordinary world acquires after such a night and dawn. That significance may not be something we welcome – any more than Larkin does – or have learnt to cope with; but it at least has the accent of truth.

The effect of tragedy is that it compels this kind of attention, and so satisfies something in us which demands that we should attend, however painful the consciousness may be. Larkin is unsparing in this respect, and has to be taken seriously precisely because he refuses to silence his discomforting voice. No poem of his better illustrates this than 'The Old Fools'. This is one of the finest tragic lyrics of the twentieth century, on a theme which this century (witness, for example, the work of Samuel Beckett) has made peculiarly its own – senility. Its progress is one of deepening attention, moving from a seemingly detached, jeering stance (expressed in that deliberate vulgarity of language that is easily misunderstood both here and in poems like 'Sunny Prestatyn' and 'This Be The Verse'), to an increasingly sympathetic identification with the subject of senile decay, and reaching final awareness that what we simultaneously mock and pity is our own inevitable future.

To begin with, the voice that speaks in the poem strikes a note of incredulous contempt:

What do they think has happened, the old fools,
To make them like this? Do they somehow suppose
It's more grown-up when your mouth hangs open and drools,
And you keep on pissing yourself, and can't remember
Who called this morning?

This would seem to be the insensitivity of the as-yet-uninvolved young towards the old; but gradually throughout the first stanza the coarse language becomes an expression of horror and appalled dread, a protest against mortality which, it is felt, 'the old fools' themselves ought to be making, and which finally emerges from the long, intricately-rhymed stanza in the short twelfth line: 'Why aren't they screaming?'

In the second stanza 'they' is exchanged for the colloquial 'you' – roughly equivalent to the French *on*, yet retaining a personal application:

At death, you break up: the bits that were you
Start speeding away from each other for ever
With no one to see.

This 'you' includes the reader within the poem (it slides easily in the fourth line into 'We'), and with it the tone becomes more gravely introspective. Death is disintegration: 'It's only oblivion, true', as the pre-natal condition was; but (here the poem bursts into a lyrical language totally different from that of the first stanza):

> then it was going to end,
> And was all the time merging with a unique endeavour
> To bring to bloom the million-petalled flower
> Of being here.

The second 'oblivion', however, is bleak and final, with none of the restorative overtones of Lawrence's use of the word; and what is happening to 'the old fools' is the mark of its approach: 'Their looks show that they're for it'. (The external 'they' returns, and a touch of the language of colloquial dismissiveness, but with a quite other than detached and dismissive effect.) In contrast to the 'million-petalled' uniqueness of potential life, the harshly realised features of this promised extinction – 'Ash hair, toad hands, prune face dried into lines' – become a terrifying anti-lyrical lyricism.

The move towards identification with the old is still more apparent in the third stanza. The nominally detached observer speculates on what it is like to inhabit their world, but in terms once more of 'you', and with a sympathetic awareness of the bewildered nostalgia of senility which breaks again into a lyrical tenderness:

> chairs and a fire burning,
> The blown bush at the window, or the sun's
> Faint friendliness on the wall some lonely
> Rain-ceased midsummer evening.

This is the sentimentalised world of the past, 'where all happened once'. It is there that the old try to continue living, being incapable of adjusting to the present, which none the less cruelly asserts itself in the final stanza, and to which a bridge – unrecognised by the old, but poignantly effective for the reader – is built by the Keatsian run-on from one stanza to the next:

> That is where they live:
> Not here and now, but where all happened once.
> This is why they give

> An air of baffled absence, trying to be there
> Yet being here.

The old are 'they' again because of the necessary distinction between 'there' and 'here', on the contrast between which the stanzas are hinged. Their warm rooms of nostalgia recede, giving way to the present reality of 'Incompetent cold' and the powerfully tragic image of

> them crouching below
> Extinction's alp, the old fools, never perceiving
> How near it is.

This image, which seems to isolate the old in a landscape of pathetic delusion, in fact connects them, and ultimately fuses them, with us. The peak, which we are able to see because of our distance from it, for them is so near that it only appears as 'rising ground'. But the journey to it is the same for both – they are merely further along it. That they are not 'screaming' with horror can only be attributed, by us, to their ignorance: 'This must be what keeps them quiet'. In the last lines of the poem, however, we scream on their behalf in a crescendo of exasperated, desperate questions, which release the horror that the spectacle of 'their' delusions and decrepitude causes to well up within us. Its climax comes in the last line, as we acknowledge that what is 'theirs' is destined to be ours:

> Can they never tell
> What is dragging them back, and how it will end? Not at night?
> Not when the strangers come? Never, throughout
> The whole hideous inverted childhood? Well,
> We shall find out.

In his finest poems Larkin is familiar and commonplace, in a way that clears both words of any taint of disparagement. 'The Old Fools' comes out of everyday readily recognisable experience – the jeering, the sympathy and the unifying, appalled horror speaking directly to the common condition that all share as human beings. What is unique is the shock inflicted on our defences. Likewise his settings are contemporary, though without any sociological or fashionable axe to grind, and the uniqueness is again in the revelations that come from facing what we all know to be there, but would rather not see. We are like the women and children in 'Ambulances' who from the middle of their daily casualness see:

> A wild white face that overtops
> Red stretcher-blankets momently
> As it is carried in and stowed,
>
> And sense the solving emptiness
> That lies just under all we do,
> And for a second get it whole,
> So permanent and blank and true.

Not that Larkin makes a moral point out of this. It is the experience rather than the moral lesson that matters: the sudden, sharp reality of feeling, divested of the protective layers that are necessary to maintain daily life, but can also smother life.

The poetry is flexible enough, however, to respond both to the need to 'get it whole' ('for a second' at least) and the need for defences. Even the 'Arid interrogation' of 'Aubade', while rejecting the futility of religion, concedes something to its efforts in the oxymoron of

> That vast moth-eaten musical brocade
> Created to pretend we never die.

Such lines are emphatic that the consolations of immortality are outmoded; but, like Hardy's 'The Oxen', which rejects fair fancy, but concludes with 'Hoping it might be so', they leave a suggestion of regret. Death and religion remain closely linked, and the link is serious, not trivial. Hence the conclusion of 'Church Going':

> A serious house on serious earth it is,
> In whose blent air all our compulsions meet,
> Are recognised, and robed as destinies.
> And that much never can be obsolete,
> Since someone will forever be surprising
> A hunger in himself to be more serious,
> And gravitating with it to this ground,
> Which, he once heard, was proper to grow wise in,
> If only that so many dead lie round.

The two poems which most delicately, though in quite different ways, acknowledge this associated seriousness of death and religion are 'The Building' and 'The Explosion'. Of these two 'The Building' is more unreservedly contemporary. Its theme is similar to that of 'Ambulances', but it is both longer and more complex. In 'Ambulances' the hospital vehicles are presented mysteriously, and, as the beginning ('Closed like confessionals') suggests, with an aura of religious mystery about them; but they function essentially *as* ambulances, collecting the sick and separating them from the rest of society, and only in this way bringing death to the minds of the onlookers. The high-rise structure from which 'The Building' takes its title is at once more obviously a commonplace feature of the contemporary urban scene and a more disturbing intrusion on it. Eventually, of course, it is recognised as a modern hospital, but, in keeping with the evasiveness that characterises the modern attitude to illness and dying – and also to preserve for it the possibility of a much wider significance – it is never named as such. 'Higher than the handsomest hotel' and, inside, partly resembling 'an airport lounge', it is nevertheless stranger than either. It is a 'lucent comb', surrounded with ordinary, drab city streets, which, however, have a curiously animated, tragic life of their own:

> All round it close-ribbed streets rise and fall
> Like a great sigh out of the last century.

It is familiar and near to home (those who sit in its waiting-room 'Haven't come far'), and yet inside it what is familiar becomes sinisterly transformed, as suggested by the zeugma which rounds off the first stanza:

> and in the hall
> As well as creepers hangs a frightening smell.

Those who have come to this building are subtly set apart from others; they are

> Humans, caught
> On ground curiously neutral, homes and names
> Suddenly in abeyance.

They are 'restless and resigned', and, without evidently being
deprived, they seem to have lost some vital control over their
comings and goings: 'Every few minutes comes a kind of nurse' –
with the disrupting jump from one stanza to the next which
Larkin also employs in 'The Old Fools' – 'To fetch someone
away'. Again, they are a mixture of ages, including both young
and old, but the majority belong to 'that vague age that claims /
The end of choice, the last of hope'. There is a sense that they are
facing a radical crisis, though they do not know what it is, and,
dislocated from ordinariness in familiar, yet defamiliarised, surroundings, they experience an almost guilty unease – an incipiently
tragic recognition, which has, once again, religious associations.
Awaiting the doctor-priest, they are 'all' – with another characteristically disturbing stanzaic jump –

> Here to confess that something has gone wrong.
> It must be error of a serious sort,
> For see how many floors it needs, how tall
> It's grown by now, and how much money goes
> In trying to correct it.

In a hushed, awed silence they are drawn more deeply into the
building, casting apprehensive glances at each other and those
already absorbed, made quiet by the realisation of 'This new
thing held in common'; while the outside world takes on a tender
commonplaceness because now seen for what it is:

> unreal,
> A touching dream to which we all are lulled
> But wake from separately.

The waking reality is the building, with its tacit air of religious
authority, and 'The unseen congregrations' which all will ultimately join:

> All know they are going to die.
> Not yet, perhaps not here, but in the end.
> And somewhere like this.

With this first explicit mention of dying the religious implications already carried by such words as 'confess', 'error' and

'congregations' at last break into full consciousness, and bring the poem to its final statement:

> That is what it means,
> This clean-sliced cliff; a struggle to transcend
> The thought of dying, for unless its powers
> Outbuild cathedrals nothing contravenes
> The coming dark, though crowds each evening try
>
> With wasteful, weak, propitiatory flowers.

In one sense the building means 'a struggle to transcend / The thought of dying' because it represents the whole effort of modern medical science to heal the sick and ward off death – an effort which is nevertheless finally unavailing, for it is the fact of mortality which makes coming here, or 'somewhere like this', inevitable for everybody. The reverence accorded medicine is the modern substitute for religion, and the limit to the building's powers, vainly competing with the confidence in an after-life offered by an age of faith, should logically, perhaps, make it a subject of satire. A faint hint of this may be found in the potentially sardonic pun incorporated in the building's outbidding attempt to 'Outbuild cathedrals'; but, on the other hand, the tone runs counter to such a reading. From the beginning the poem is both ominous and grave; and its alliteratively emphasised conclusion – precipitating a final line that stands uniquely apart from all the previous seven-line stanzas[2] – has the dying fall of elegy rather than the sharp sting of satire, almost of prayer rather than protest. The crowds who come each evening to visit those whom the building has already claimed as its victims are themselves potential inmates, and their gifts of flowers are the means by which they hope to propitiate the powers that work to draw them also into the building.

Yet the poem remains secular and agnostic. There is little hope that the ritual which the visitors feel the need for will, in reality, sustain and protect them. They are united with those whom they come to visit in their affliction with the same basic human sickness – which the building is supposedly there to relieve, but which, on the contrary, it can only make them more reluctantly aware of. Like Margaret in Gerard Manley Hopkins' 'Spring and Fall' they arrive at a consciousness of 'the blight

man was born for'; and though the 'blight' is robbed of its
theological meaning of 'original sin', becoming simply human
mortality, their act of propitiation implies a sense of guilt (akin
to that felt by those who waited earlier in the poem) and the urge
to expiate it in some sort of religious context. Thus, their deepest
needs and fears are stirred, which the poem sympathetically
echoes, while also being compelled to register the futility of their
gropings towards the traditional comfort of religion. These visitors and potential patients belong inescapably to the contemporary world, and the poem honestly recognises their plight as
universally, and tragically, incapable of comfort.

'The Building', though not a church, might well qualify for the
words spoken of the church in 'Church Going':

> A serious house on serious earth it is,
> In whose blent air all out compulsions meet,
> Are recognised, and robed as destinies.

It is the most serious, and profound, and centrally human of Larkin's tragic poems. Other poems, however, can also be seen as
'gravitating' towards 'this ground' – 'Church Going' itself, but
also 'The Whitsun Weddings', in which the documentary poetry
of the train journey converts, via hints of 'a religious wounding', to

> A sense of falling, like an arrow-shower
> Sent out of sight, somewhere becoming rain;

and 'An Arundel Tomb', which survives its own irony at the
expense of 'The stone fidelity' of its lovers 'to prove / Our
almost-instinct almost true'. 'Show Saturday' is another poem,
which, like 'The Whitsun Weddings', moves from documentary
to a more serious rhythm 'That breaks ancestrally each year into /
Regenerate union', and it concludes with what is almost the
benediction of 'Let it always be there'. Each of these poems
suggests a seriousness shared with 'The Building', but also a
more positive, and even consolatory, feeling which must be taken
into account before Larkin can finally be pronounced a bleak
and uncompromisingly tragic poet. The other poem which must

particularly come into this reckoning is 'The Explosion'. This deals with tragic experience and its religious associations in what is for Larkin a most unusual way.

'The Explosion' divides into two sections, the first of fifteen lines, and the second of ten, corresponding to action before and after the pit explosion. The first section concerns miners who were on their way to work when one of them found 'a nest of lark's eggs'; and the second their wives who had a momentary vision in which 'men of the explosion' were seen

> Gold as on a coin, or walking
> Somehow from the sun towards them,
>
> One showing the eggs unbroken.

The second section opens with the simple words of the funeral service:

> *The dead go on before us, they*
> *Are sitting in God's house in comfort,*
> *We shall see them face to face.*

This is a consoling frame in which the wives are able to place their dead husbands, and the gentle Easter symbolism of the eggs gives it confirmation. In the first section the men are felt as warm and living persons, and in the second the vision of the wives is unpatronisingly celebrated.

Yet the whole poem is slightly detached and has a pastoral unreality. The verse has an almost consciously archaic effect, as if Larkin, like Shakespeare in certain parts of his last plays, were trying to create a romance level of meaning beyond that of ordinary life – one that in the words of Paulina in *The Winter's Tale* requires 'You do awake your faith'[3]. In contrast to 'The Building', it is also narrated mostly in the past tense — the exception being the italicised words, which place the dead miners in an eternal present (echoed in the present participles, 'walking' and 'showing', of the wives' vision of them), and which include the one instance of the future tense, embodying a specific expression of belief: *'We shall see them face to face'*. The effect of this is again to remove the action from the ordinary, contemporary world, and permit the transformation of the men, though only 'for a second', into figures 'Larger than in life they managed'. Tragedy is thus converted through the lens of religion, and the faith of the wives, into a glory like that of *Lycidas*. The Christianised pastoral elegy, which looks beyond suffering to the resurrection and the exaltation of the dead, is given a new and strangely beautiful variation.

'The Explosion' is the last poem in the volume, *High Windows*. Each collection up to now gives the impression of having been carefully arranged, with an eye to a kind of musical effect; and this poem can be seen as a quiet coda after the more disturbingly tragic chords of 'The Old Fools' and 'The Building', which form the volume's centre. Where 'Aubade' might stand in relation to a fifth volume, yet to come, can only be the subject of speculation. Evidence certainly exists that Larkin is a more serene poet than is often supposed; but, as Andrew Motion remarks, 'It would be wrong to say that Larkin's emphasis on the potential and resilience of the human spirit cancelled out his pessimism'[4]. 'Aubade' suggests that his view of the tragedy of the human condition continues to be, or is even increasingly becoming, a singularly unconsoling one. Its position is still likely, therefore, to be central. His recognition of the lonely individual's need for the support of ritual and religion is part of the honesty of his vision, but he remains what, from the first to the last of the published volumes, he has always seemed to be: a traditional poet in much of his form, and some of his attitudes, but also the most contemporary of our contemporaries in his straightforward acceptance that this is the only life we have, and that we cannot escape the tormenting consciousness of its 'only end'. The terrible longing to do so, however, leaves us with the tragic dilemma that makes us, along with the 'crowds' of 'The Building', still attempt to contravene it

With wasteful, weak, propitiatory flowers.

Notes

NOTES TO CHAPTER I: INTRODUCTION

1. Aristotle, *On the Art of Poetry*, in *Classical Literary Criticism*, trans. T. S. Dorsch (London, 1965) p. 40.
2. John Jones, *On Aristotle and Greek Tragedy* (London, 1962) p. 37.
3. *Classical Literary Criticism*, p. 49.
4. A. C. Bradley, *Shakespearean Tragedy* (London, 1904, rpt., 1952) p. 12.
5. Jones, *Aristotle and Greek Tragedy*, p. 33.
6. W. B. Yeats, *Essays and Introductions* (London, 1961) p. 245.
7. W. B. Yeats, *The Variorum Edition of the Plays of W. B. Yeats*, ed. Russell K. Alspach and assisted by Catharine C. Alspach (London, 1966) ll. 469–73. Second quotation, ll. 474–85.
8. Quotations from *The Testament of Cresseid* are taken from *The Poems of Robert Henryson*, ed. Denton Fox (Oxford, 1981) pp. 111–31.
9. Ibid., p. 339.
10. *English and Scottish Popular Ballads*, ed. from the collection of Francis James Child by H. C. Sargent and G. L. Kittredge (London, 1904).
11. Gordon H. Gerould, *The Ballad of Tradition* (Oxford, 1932) p. 3.
12. *Classical Literary Criticism*, p. 50.
13. Wordsworth, *The Borderers*, ll. 1539–44.
14. David Hume, 'Of Tragedy' (1757), in *Essays: Moral, Political and Literary*, ed. T. H. Green and T. H. Grose (London, 1875) p. 260.
15. The various possibilities of interpretation are spelt out by John Barnard in his note on ll. 49–50, *John Keats: The Complete Poems*, ed. John Barnard (London, 1973) p. 652.
16. Ibid., p. 675.
17. See Chapter 2 below, where I discuss the views advanced by Clay Hunt in *'Lycidas' and the Italian Critics* (New Haven, Conn. and London, 1979).
18. T. S. Eliot, *Collected Poems, 1909–1935* (London, 1936). The quotation from *The Love Song of J. Alfred Prufrock* appears on p. 15, and that from *The Waste Land* on p. 77.
19. 'Tragedy', *The Complete Poems of D. H. Lawrence*, ed. V. de S. Pinto and Warren Roberts (London, 1964, rev. edn 1972) p. 508.
20. 'Aspens', *The Collected Poems of Edward Thomas*, ed. R. George Thomas (Oxford, 1978) p. 233.
21. 'Lady Lazarus', *Sylvia Plath: Collected Poems*, ed. Ted Hughes (London, 1981) p. 245.
22. *King Lear*, III. vi. 77–8.

23. 'Preface', *Wilfred Owen: War Poems and Others*, ed. Dominic Hibberd (London, 1973) p. 137.
24. 'The Going', *The Variorum Edition of the Complete Poems of Thomas Hardy*, ed. James Gibson (London, 1979) pp. 339.
25. Introduction, Philip Larkin, *The North Ship* (London, 1945; 2nd edn 1966) p. 10.
26. 'The Triple Foole', *The Poems of John Donne*, ed. Sir Herbert Grierson (Oxford, 1933; rpt. 1964) p. 15.

NOTES TO CHAPTER 2: *LYCIDAS* AND THE PASTORAL ELEGY

1. Samuel Johnson, *The Lives of the Poets*, ed. G. B. Hill (Oxford, 1905) vol. 1, p. 163.
2. See W. W. Greg, *Pastoral Poetry and Pastoral Drama* (London, 1906); the convenient summary of pastoral elegies prior to Milton in *A Variorum Commentary of the Poems of John Milton*, ed. A. S. P. Woodhouse and Douglas Bush (London, 1972) vol. 2, Part 2, pp. 549–65; and E. Z. Lambert, *Placing Sorrow: A Study of the Pastoral Convention from Theocritus to Milton* (Chapel Hill, NC, 1976).
3. Translations of the Eclogues are from *Virgil: The Eclogues and The Georgics*, translated into English verse by R. C. Trevelyan (Cambridge, 1944).
4. The editors of the *Variorum Commentary* cite the *Egloga duarum sanctimonialium* of Radbertus as the first example of a specifically Christian pastoral, and they speak of Christianity as giving 'access to the *Old* Testament' (*Variorum Commentary*, p. 555 – italics mine). Both the Old and the New are clearly relevant to Renaissance pastoralism, but at least in the work of Spenser and Milton the New Testament overtones would seem to be the more important.
5. Quoted by Clay Hunt, *'Lycidas' and the Italian Critics*, p. 9.
6. Ibid., p. 151.
7. Ibid., p. 152.
8. See *Variorum Commentary*, p. 731.
9. J. B. Leishman, *Milton's Minor Poems* (London, 1969) p. 297.
10. See *Variorum Commentary*, p. 662.
11. Ibid., p. 664.
12. Ibid., p. 664. The editors of the *Variorum Commentary* also cite Pyramus/Bottom's 'O Fates! come, come; / Cut thread and thrum' (*A Midsummer Night's Dream*, V.i.277–8) as an example from 'tragedy'. The significant point to be made, of course, is that this example comes not from straight tragedy, but tragic farce; it is part of the antiquated 'high style' and ludicrous ineptitude of *Pyramus and Thisbe* as performed by Bottom and the 'rude mechanicals'.
13. First Epistle of Paul to the Corinthians, 13:12.
14. See *Variorum Commentary*, p. 670. (Quoted from M. Mack.)
15. Ibid., p. 670.
16. Ibid., pp. 686–706.
17. Milton may also have expected his readers to remember that, although

Peter was trusted with the foundation of the Church, his zeal in cutting off the ear of the servant who tried to arrest Jesus was not approved by his master; and that the imperfection of his zeal was likewise shown in his subsequent denial (John, 18).

18. See *Variorum Commentary*, p. 727.
19. Ibid., p. 731.

NOTES TO CHAPTER 3: THE PASTORAL ELEGY AND DOUBT

1. Jean Hall, *The Transforming Image: A Study of Shelley's Major Poetry* (Urbana, Ill., 1980) p. 134.
2. Richard Cronin, *Shelley's Poetic Thoughts* (London, 1981) p. 174.
3. See, for example, the conclusion of stanza XLII, which, as Milton Wilson puts it, introduces 'a somewhat jarring echo of Christianity' – *Shelley's Later Poetry* (New York, 1959) p. 248.
4. Edwin B. Silverman argues for the specific influence of Spenser's *Astrophel*, taken together with 'The Dolefull Lay of Clorinda' – *Poetic Synthesis in Shelley's 'Adonais'* (The Hague, 1972). Cronin (*Shelley's Poetic Thoughts*) stresses the importance of *Lycidas*.
5. *The Letters of Percy Bysshe Shelley*, ed. F. L. Jones (Oxford, 1964) vol. 2, p. 294.
6. T. S. Eliot, 'Ash Wednesday', I.ll. 23–4.
7. *The Complete Works of Percy Bysshe Shelley*, ed. Roger Ingpen and Walter E. Peck (New York, 1965) vol. 2, p. 387.
8. *Shelley's Poetic Thoughts*, p. 179.
9. Robert Henryson, *The Testament of Cresseid*, l. 461.
10. Quoted in *Tennyson: 'In Memoriam'*, ed. Susan Shatto and Marion Shaw (Oxford, 1982), p. 24, n. 2. (All quotations from *In Memoriam* are taken from this edition.)
11. See Alan Sinfield, *The Language of Tennyson's 'In Memoriam'* (Oxford, 1971), and, in particular, Chapter 2, ' "*In Memoriam*": The Linnet and the Artifact'.
12. Robert Pattison, *Tennyson and Tradition* (Cambridge, Mass., 1979) p. 108.
13. *Tennyson: 'In Memoriam'*, p. 24.
14. Ibid., pp. 8–25.
15. Ibid., p. 161.
16. Aubrey de Vere records hearing Tennyson read parts of *In Memoriam* aloud, and he notes both the intoned manner and the musical effect: 'The pathos and grandeur of these poems were to me greatly increased by the voice which rather intoned than recited them, and which, as was obvious, could not possibly have given them utterance in any manner not thus musical.' Quoted *Tennyson: 'In Memoriam'*, p. 16.
17. *The Language of Tennyson's 'In Memoriam'*, p. 140.
18. A. Dwight Culler, *The Poetry of Tennyson* (New Haven, Conn., and London, 1977) p. 150.
19. The identification of the potential friend in Section 85 is not certain, but it may well be Edmund Lushington, to whom the Epilogue is addressed on the occasion of his marriage to Tennyson's sister, Cecilia, on 10 October 1842. See *Tennyson: 'In Memoriam'*, pp. 239 and 292.

20. *'In Memoriam'* (1936) rpt. in *Selected Prose of T. S. Eliot*, ed. Frank Kermode (London, 1975) pp. 243–4 and 245.
21. Letter to J. C. Shairp; quoted by A. Dwight Culler, *Imaginative Reason: The Poetry of Matthew Arnold* (New Haven, Conn., and London, 1966) p. 261.
22. Quoted in *The Poems of Matthew Arnold*, ed. Kenneth Allot, 2nd edn ed. Miriam Allott (London, 1979) p. 357.
23. Ibid., p. 356.
24. Ibid., p. 369.
25. Ibid., p. 369. (Comment of William Beloe, translator of Herodotus.)
26. According to Kenneth Allott this is misleading: 'Clough's social conscience (ll. 46–7) had nothing to do with his leaving Oxford, and his poetry was no more troubled after than before Oct. 1848.' (*Poems*, p. 540).
27. 'The Fall of Hyperion: A Dream', ll. 148–9. See above, Chapter 1, p. 17.

NOTES TO CHAPTER 4: WORDSWORTH: 'THE STILL, SAD MUSIC OF HUMANITY'

1. A note on the Immortality Ode dictated to Isabella Fenwick by Wordsworth. Quoted in *William Wordsworth: The Poems*, ed. John O. Hayden (New Haven, Conn., and London, 1981) vol. 1, p. 978.
2. Ibid., p. 978.
3. See the discussion of the defects of Wordsworth's poetry in *Biographia Literaria*, ch. 22: *The Collected Works of Samuel Taylor Coleridge*, 7, *Biographia Literaria*, ed. James Engell and W. Jackson Bate (Princeton, N. J. and London, 1983) vol. II, pp. 136–8.
4. See above, Chapter 1, pp. 15–16.
5. *Poems*, vol. 2, p. 915.
6. Letter to Sara Hutchinson, 14 June 1802. Quoted *Poems*, vol. 1, p. 986.
7. *King Lear*, III.iv. 34.
8. Quoted by Jonathan Wordsworth, *The Music of Humanity* (London, 1969) p. 70.
9. Ibid., p. 153.
10. Ibid., pp. 151–2.
11. Quotations from 'The Ruined Cottage' are taken from the text printed in *The Music of Humanity*, pp. 33–49.
12. See David B. Pirie, *William Wordsworth: The Poetry of Grandeur and of Tenderness* (London, 1982) pp. 55–6.

NOTES TO CHAPTER 5: HARDY: ILLUSION AND REALITY

1. F. B. Pinion, *A Commentary on the Poems of Thomas Hardy* (London, 1976) p. 222.
2. Wordsworth, 'Ode: Intimations of Immortality', l. 187.
3. *The Variorum Edition of the Complete Poems of Thomas Hardy*, ed. James Gibson (London, 1979) p. 557. All quotations from Hardy's poems are from this edition.

4. Tom Paulin, *Thomas Hardy: The Poetry of Perception* (London, 1975) p. 63.
5. Wordsworth, 'A slumber did my spirit seal', l.8.
6. Note dated 28 September 1877 in Florence Emily Hardy, *The Life of Thomas Hardy* (1928 and 1930; London, 1962) p. 116. Despite the attributed authorship, this is now recognised as Hardy's autobiography.
7. Hardy, *The Dynasts*, Part Third, VI.viii.
8. *A Commentary on the Poems of Thomas Hardy*, p. 7.
9. *The Life of Thomas Hardy*, p. 361.
10. *A Commentary on the Poems of Thomas Hardy*, p. 106.
11. Cf. 'Something that life will not be balked of / Without rude reason till hope is dead' ('At Castle Boterel', ll.13–15) and 'War's annals will cloud into night / Ere their story die' ('In Time of "The Breaking of Nations" ', ll.11–12).
12. Robert Gittings, *The Older Hardy* (London, 1978, rev. edn 1980) p. 207.
13. *The Woodlanders* (The New Wessex Edition, London, 1975), Chapter 1, pp. 39–40.
14. Gittings suggests that the details derive from an account given by Emma of her family and their different houses in Plymouth. See Emma Hardy, *Some Recollections*, ed. Evelyn Hardy and Robert Gittings (Oxford, 1979) pp. 42–3.
15. 'Ironically', because the plough as such destroys in order to make way for new growth, but this ploughing is merely destructive. (Cf. the cancellation of fertility associations with the word 'rain' at the end of 'Proud Songsters', discussed above, pp. 115–16.)

NOTES TO CHAPTER 6: EDWARD THOMAS: THE UNREASONABLE GRIEF

1. All quotations from Thomas' poems are from *The Collected Poems of Edward Thomas*, ed. R. George Thomas (Oxford, 1978).
2. Quoted ibid., p. 402.
3. Ibid., p. 417.
4. Andrew Motion, *The Poetry of Edward Thomas* (London, 1980) p. 39.

NOTES TO CHAPTER 7: D. H. LAWRENCE: TRAGEDY AS CREATIVE CRISIS

1. Letter to A. W. McLeod, 6 October 1912.
2. D. H. Lawrence, *Phoenix II* (London, 1968), pp. 291–3. The Preface was first printed with the text of the play, *Touch and Go* (1920), but, according to Warren Roberts, was written in the summer of 1919. See *A Bibliography of D. H. Lawrence* (London, 1963), p. 42.
3. *The Complete Poems of D. H. Lawrence*, ed. V. de S. Pinto and Warren Roberts (London, 1964, rev. edn 1972) p. 191.
4. For a fuller discussion of Lawrence and 'the poetry of that which is at hand:

the immediate present' see my article, 'Form and Tone in the Poetry of D. H. Lawrence', *English Studies*, XLIX, no. 6 (December 1968) pp. 498–508.

5. 'Fish', ll.32–7; 'The Mosquito', l.39; 'Bat', l.37; 'Tortoise Family Connections', ll.5 and 7; 'Turkey-Cock', ll.12–13.
6. Foreword to *Women in Love, Phoenix II*, p. 276.
7. *Etruscan Places* (1932, rpt. 1950) p. 26.

NOTES TO CHAPTER 8: WILFRED OWEN: DISTANCE AND IMMEDIACY

1. 'Preface', *Wilfred Owen: War Poems and Others*, ed. Dominic Hibberd (London, 1973) p. 137.
2. Ibid., p. 41. 'With lightning and with music' occurs at *Adonais*, 104.
3. *Aeneid*, I.l.462.
4. Jon Stallworthy, *Wilfred Owen* (Oxford and London, 1974) p. 228.
5. D. S. R. Welland, *Wilfred Owen* (London, 1960) p. 60.
6. The title, which also makes its ironic comment, derives from the popular wartime song, 'Pack up your troubles in your old kit bag, / And smile, smile, smile'.
7. Gertrude M. White, *Wilfred Owen* (New York, 1969) p. 77.
8. The title was suggested by Siegfried Sassoon, and is in itself a perceptive piece of literary criticism.
9. *Wilfred Owen: War Poems and Others*, p. 147.
10. Gertrude White, *Wilfred Owen*, p. 70.
11. As Hibberd points out, there is also a link in sound between all the rhyme-words of each stanza. (*Wilfred Owen: War Poems and Others*, pp. 130–1.)
12. Quoted ibid., p. 37.
13. The Blunden and Day Lewis texts read 'His', but the MS seems to read 'this', as given by Hibberd and Stallworthy.
14. Cf. 'By the May breeze, murmurous with wasp and midge' ('Spring Offensive', l.8) and 'The murmurous haunt of flies on summer eves' ('Ode to a Nightingale', l.50); 'For though the summer oozed into their veins' ('Spring Offensive', l.9) and 'Thou watchest the last oozings hours by hours' ('To Autumn', l.22).
15. *Wilfred Owen: War Poems and Others*, p. 135.

NOTES TO CHAPTER 9: SYLVIA PLATH: DEATH AND THE SELF

1. Joyce Carol Oates: 'The Death Throes of Romanticism: the Poetry of Sylvia Plath', in *Sylvia Plath: The Woman and the Work*, ed. Edward Butscher (London, 1979) p. 206.
2. Ibid., p. 218.
3. Ibid.
4. Sylvia Plath, *Johnny Panic and the Bible of Dreams and Other Prose Writings* (London, 1977) p. 25.
5. *Sylvia Plath: Collected Poems*, ed. Ted Hughes (London, 1981) p. 22.

6. The epigraph of the poem is, of course, not from Blake, but Racine: 'Dans le fond des forêts votre image me suit' (*Phèdre*, II.ii.82). As an isolated line this may carry something of the sinister reverberation that would make it seem relevant to 'Pursuit', but in its context in *Phèdre* (Hippolyte's declaration of love to Aricie) it is less appropriate. However, the real reason for its appearance as epigraph may be its association in Plath's mind with other features of Racine's play, notably Hippolyte's horrific killing by Neptune's sea-monster, and Phèdre's sense of irremediable self-contamination by her love for Hippolyte.

7. John Webster, *The White Devil*, V.vi. 268–70.

8. There is a generally pervasive debt to T. S. Eliot as well, especially to 'East Coker', Section IV, where Eliot himself imitates (not very happily) the seventeenth-century manner in a lyric on the Incarnation and 'Adam's curse', which, like Plath's, is obsessed with 'dripping blood' and 'bloody flesh'. Another hint for the 'panther' may well have come from 'Ash Wednesday', Section II.

9. Pamela Smith, 'Architectonics: Sylvia Plath's Colossus', in *Sylvia Plath: The Woman and the Work*, ed. Edward Butscher (London, 1979) p. 119.

10. *Collected Poems*, p. 287.

11. Ibid., p. 289.

12. Ibid., p. 289.

13. Milton, *Paradise Lost*, I. 2–3.

14. This is reminiscent of the Tate & Lyle motto, 'Out of the strong came forth sweetness'; but it is spurious, for, as the reference to Tate & Lyle in 'Wintering' shows, the sugar substitute is what the bees are fed in winter instead of real honey.

15. Jon Rosenblatt, *Sylvia Plath: The Poetry of Initiation* (Chapel Hill, NC, 1979) p. 129.

16. 'Our cheesecloth gauntlets neat and sweet . . . a thousand clean cells between us. . . . Thinking 'Sweetness, sweetness! . . . queen. . . unqueenly. . . . I have eaten dust. . . . And seen my strangeness . . . my honey-machine . . . the creaming crests . . . sea . . . with the bee-seller or with me. . . . He was sweet [plus, as a half-echo, 'The sweat']. . . . The bees . . . his features . . . a queen . . . sleeping. . . . Where has she been. . . . The mausoleum.' Such a sequence, perhaps only partly conscious, underlines the central concept of bees as producers of sweetness, and also the fact that they are female workers, representatively summed up in their queen.

17. Mary L. Broe, *Protean Poetic: The Poetry of Sylvia Plath* (Columbia, NY, and London, 1980) p. 152.

18. Ibid., p. 155.

19. *Sylvia Plath: The Poetry of Initiation*, p. 129.

NOTES TO CHAPTER 10: PHILIP LARKIN: 'THE BONE'S TRUTH'

1. *The North Ship* (1945); *The Less Deceived* (1955) – includes 'Next, Please'; *The Whitsun Weddings* (1964) – includes 'Dockery and Son'; *High Windows* (1974) – includes 'The Building'.

2. This final line is, however, tied in with the rest of the poem both syntactically and through the rhyme-scheme, which constantly provides connections between one stanza and the next, and here rhymes 'flowers' with the preceding 'powers'.
3. *The Winter's Tale*, V.iii.94. However, the metre, as Simon Petch points out, recalls the trochaic measure of Longfellow's *Hiawatha* – which still gives an archaic effect. See Simon Petch, *The Art of Philip Larkin* (Sydney, 1981) p. 107.
4. Andrew Motion, *Philip Larkin* (London, 1982) p. 72. A persuasively argued case for a more positive, less pessimistic, Larkin is J. R. Watson's 'The Other Larkin', *Critical Quarterly*, vol. 17, no. 4 (Winter 1975) pp. 347–60.

Bibliography

Aristotle, *On the Art of Poetry*, in *Classical Literary Criticism*, trans. T. S. Dorsch (London, 1965).

Arnold, Matthew, *The Poems of Matthew Arnold*, ed. Kenneth Allott, 2nd edn, ed. Miriam Allott (London, 1979).

Auden, W. H., *Collected Poems, 1927–1957* (London, 1966).

Bergonzi, Bernard, *Heroes' Twilight: A Study of the Literature of the Great War* (London, 1965).

Bradley, A. C., *Shakespearean Tragedy* (London, 1904, rpt. 1952).

Brereton, Geoffrey, *Principles of Tragedy* (Coral Gables, Fla, 1969).

Broe, Mary L., *Protean Poetic: The Poetry of Sylvia Plath* (Columbia, NY, and London, 1980).

Butscher, Edward (ed.), *Sylvia Plath: The Woman and the Work* (London, 1979).

Calarco, Joseph N., *Tragic Being: Apollo and Dionysus in Western Drama* (Minneapolis, Minn., 1968).

Child, Francis James, *English and Scottish Popular Ballads*, ed. H. C. Sargent and G. L. Kittredge (London, 1904).

Corrigan, Robert W. (ed.), *Tragedy, Vision and Form* (San Francisco, Calif., 1965).

Cronin, Richard, *Shelley's Poetic Thoughts* (London, 1981).

Culler, A. Dwight, *Imaginative Reason: The Poetry of Matthew Arnold* (New Haven, Conn., and London, 1966).

———, *The Poetry of Tennyson* (New Haven, Conn., and London, 1977).

Dixon, W. MacNeile, *Tragedy* (London, 1924).

Donne, John, *The Poems of John Donne*, ed. Sir Herbert Grierson (Oxford, 1933, rpt. 1964).

Draper, R. P., *D. H. Lawrence* (New York, 1964).

——— (ed.), *Hardy: The Tragic Novels* (London, 1975).

——— (ed.), *Tragedy: Developments in Criticism* (London, 1980).

——— 'Form and Tone in the Poetry of D. H. Lawrence', *English Studies*, XLIX, no. 6 (December 1968) pp. 498–508.

Eliot, T. S., *Collected Poems, 1909–1935* (London, 1936).

———, *Selected Prose of T. S. Eliot*, ed. Frank Kermode (London, 1975).

Fergusson, Francis, *The Idea of a Theater* (Princeton, NJ, 1949).

Frye, Northrop, *Anatomy of Criticism* (New York, 1967).

Gerould, Gordon H., *The Ballad of Tradition* (Oxford, 1932).

Gittings, Robert, *The Young Thomas Hardy* (London, 1975).

———, *The Older Hardy* (London, 1978).

223

Greg, W. W., *Pastoral Poetry and Pastoral Drama* (London, 1906).

Hall, Jean, *The Transforming Image: A Study of Shelley's Major Poetry* (Urbana, Ill., 1980).

Hardy, Emma, *Some Recollections*, ed. Evelyn Hardy and Robert Gittings (Oxford, 1979).

Hardy, Florence Emily, *The Life of Thomas Hardy* (1928 and 1930; London, 1962).

Hardy, Thomas, *The Variorum Edition of the Complete Poems of Thomas Hardy*, ed. James Gibson (London, 1979).

——— , *The Dynasts*, with an Introduction by John Wain (London, 1965).

——— , *The Woodlanders* (The New Wessex Edition, London, 1975).

Henn, T. R., *The Harvest of Tragedy* (London, 1956).

Henryson, Robert, *The Poems of Robert Henryson*, ed. Denton Fox (Oxford, 1981).

Hume, David, *Essays: Moral, Political and Literary*, ed. T. H. Green and T. H. Grose (London, 1875).

Hunt, Clay, *'Lycidas' and the Italian Critics* (New Haven, Conn., and London, 1979).

Huxley, Aldous, 'Tragedy and the Whole Truth', *Virginia Quarterly Review*, vol. 7 (1931) pp. 176–85.

Hynes, Samuel, *The Pattern of Hardy's Poetry* (Chapel Hill, NC, 1961).

Johnson, Samuel, *The Lives of the Poets*, ed. G. B. Hill (Oxford, 1905).

Jones, John, *On Aristotle and Greek Tragedy* (London, 1962).

Keats, John, *The Complete Poems*, ed. John Barnard (London, 1973).

Krook, Dorothea, *Elements of Tragedy* (New Haven, Conn., and London, 1969).

Krieger, Murray, *The Tragic Vision* (New York, 1960).

Lambert, E. Z., *Placing Sorrow: A Study of the Pastoral Convention from Theocritus to Milton* (Chapel Hill, NC, 1976).

Larkin, Philip, *The North Ship* (London, 1945; 2nd edn 1966).

——— , *The Less Deceived* (Hessle, Yorks, 1955).

——— , *The Whitsun Weddings* (London, 1964).

——— , *High Windows* (London, 1974).

——— , 'Aubade', *TLS*, 23 December 1977, p. 1491.

Lawrence, D. H., *The Complete Poems of D. H. Lawrence*, ed. V. de S. Pinto and Warren Roberts (London 1964; rev. edn 1972).

——— , *Phoenix II* (London, 1968).

——— , *The Letters of D. H. Lawrence, 1901–13*, ed. James T. Boulton (London, 1979).

——— , *The Letters of D. H. Lawrence, 1913–16*, ed. George J. Zytaruck and James T. Boulton (London, 1981).

Leech, Clifford, *Tragedy* (London, 1969).

Leishman, J. B., *Milton's Minor Poems* (London, 1969).

Lenson, David, *Achilles' Choice: Examples of Modern Tragedy* (Princeton, NJ, 1975).

Michel, Laurence, *The Thing Contained: Theory of the Tragic* (Bloomington, Ind., 1970).

——— and Sewall, Richard B. (eds), *Tragedy: Modern Essays in Criticism* (Englewood Cliffs, NJ, 1963).

Milton, John, *The Poetical Works*, ed. Helen Darbishire (Oxford, 1958, rpt. 1963).

———, *The Poems of John Milton*, ed. John Carey and Alistair Fowler (London, 1968).

———, *A Variorum Commentary of the Poems of John Milton*, ed. A. S. P. Woodhouse and Douglas Bush (London, 1972) vol. 2, part 2.

Motion, Andrew, *The Poetry of Edward Thomas* (London, 1980).

———, *Philip Larkin* (London, 1982).

Owen, Wilfred, *The Collected Poems of Wilfred Owen*, ed. C. Day Lewis (London, 1968).

———, *War Poems and Others*, ed. Dominic Hibberd (London, 1973).

Pattison, Robert, *Tennyson and Tradition* (Cambridge, Mass., 1979).

Paulin, Tom, *Thomas Hardy: The Poetry of Perception* (London, 1975).

Petch, Simon, *The Art of Philip Larkin* (Sydney, 1981).

Pinion, F. B., *A Commentary on the Poems of Thomas Hardy* (London, 1976).

Pirie, David B., *William Wordsworth: The Poetry of Grandeur and of Tenderness* (London, 1982).

Plath, Sylvia, *Collected Poems*, ed. Ted Hughes (London, 1981).

———, *Johnny Panic and the Bible of Dreams and Other Prose Writings* (London, 1977).

Ricks, Christopher, *Tennyson* (New York and London, 1972).

Roberts, Warren, *A Bibliography of D. H. Lawrence* (London, 1963, rev. edn 1982).

Rosenblatt, Jon, *Sylvia Plath: The Poetry of Initiation* (Chapel Hill, NC, 1979).

Rutherford, Andrew, *The Literature of War* (London, 1978).

Sewall, Richard B., *The Vision of Tragedy* (New Haven, Conn., 1959).

Shaw, David W., *Tennyson's Style* (Ithaca, NY, and London, 1976).

Shelley, Percy Bysshe, *The Complete Works of Percy Bysshe Shelley*, ed. Roger Ingpen and Walter E. Peck (New York, 1965).

———, *The Letters of Percy Bysshe Shelley*, ed. F. L. Jones (Oxford, 1964).

Silverman, Edwin B., *Poetic Synthesis in Shelley's 'Adonais'* (The Hague, 1972).

Sinfield, Alan, *The Language of Tennyson's 'In Memoriam'* (Oxford, 1971).

Stallworthy, Jon, *Wilfred Owen* (Oxford and London, 1974).

Steiner, George, *The Death of Tragedy* (London, 1961).

Tennyson, Alfred, Lord, *Tennyson: 'In Memoriam'*, ed. Susan Shatto and Marion Shaw (Oxford, 1982).

Tennyson, Hallam (ed.), *Studies in Tennyson* (London, 1981).

Thomas, Edward, *The Collected Poems of Edward Thomas*, ed. R. George Thomas (Oxford, 1978).

Timms, David, *Philip Larkin* (London, 1973).

Vergili, Maronis P., *Opera*, ed. R. A. B. Mynors (Oxford, 1969).

———, *Virgil: The Eclogues and the Georgics*, trans. R. C. Trevelyan (Cambridge, 1944).

Watson, J. R., 'The Other Larkin', *Critical Quarterly*, vol. 17, no. 4 (Winter 1975).

Welland, D. S. R., *Wilfred Owen* (London, 1960).

White, Gertrude M., *Wilfred Owen* (New York, 1969).

Wilson, Milton, *Shelley's Later Poetry* (New York, 1959).

Wordsworth, Jonathan, *The Music of Humanity* (London, 1969).

Wordsworth, William, *The Poems*, ed. John O. Hayden (New Haven, Conn., and London, 1981).

Yeats, W. B., *The Collected Poems of W. B. Yeats* (London, 1950).

——, *Essays and Introductions* (London, 1961).

——, *The Variorum Edition of the Plays of W. B. Yeats*, ed. Russell K. Alspach, assisted by Catharine C. Alspach (London, 1966).

Index